CONTENTS

FOREWORD AND INTRODUCTION 4

1. AVE 13

2. FERNS 17

3. THE GARDEN 43

4. BACKGROUND FOR FATHER 55

5. BACKGROUND FOR MOTHER 75

6. FATHER AND HIS COLLEAGUES 91

7. NEIGHBOURS 107

8. MANCHESTER 127

9. ALDERLEY EDGE LADIES 155

10. SUNDAYS 171

11. EDUCATING A DAUGHTER 185

12. HOLIDAYS 205

13. POLITICS 229

14. A DAUGHTER AT HOME 237

15. YOUNG MEN AND MAIDENS 251

16. VALE 263

    APPENDIX 269

    INDEX 270

FOREWORD

My mother would have been delighted to learn that 'Manchester Made Them' was to be re-published after fifty years, and that the initiative had come from a local publishing house. My only sadness is that my sister, Gillian Goodwin, did not live to see this project come to fruition. Her knowledge of family history was far better than mine and it was her contact with Rosemary Marsh, of the Friends of Whitworth Art Gallery, that brought us into touch with the Silk Press.

When 'Manchester Made Them' was originally published by Faber and Faber it had no illustrations. Why that should be I do not know, but the Silk Press had very different ideas and it has been an enjoyable task, enormously helped by the enthusiasm of my editor, Christine Pemberton, going through the old family photograph albums, in making our selection. Before she died my mother had added captions; without them we would have been stuck and indeed, in some cases, she herself was defeated. So, sadly, there are some gaps.

Like many family clans, the Hopkinson family is quite confusing unless you have been brought up within it, and so we have added a short potted history to aid either the confused or industrious reader.

THE HOPKINSON CLAN

The Hopkinson family starts in the early 19th century with Alice Hopkinson, who had a life-long liaison with John Lomax. They never married and the family tradition has it that his parents so disapproved that they threatened to 'cut him off'. When eventually they died he sought her hand, but being proud, she refused. It is a nice legend but the truth is probably more prosaic - that he had already made an unfortunate marriage in South America. We shall never know. Either way, there is little doubt that Alice was a quite considerable person. She had one son, John, and four daughters, one of whom married H O Wills of the tobacco family. They feature in some of the holiday photographs that we have chosen to include.

John Hopkinson, (1824-1902) was a successful engineer who was active in Manchester civic life, becoming an alderman and then, in 1882, Mayor. He married Alice, of the Yorkshire family of Dewhursts; they were related to the Slingsbys of Carleton, in Craven. Cecil Slingsby was a noted mountaineer and made a number of first ascents and expeditions with John Hopkinson's five sons.

The five sons were John, Alfred, Charles, Edward and Albert; there were also two others who died in infancy. And there were three sisters, two of whom figure in this book: Mary, who remained a spinster, and whom I can just remember as being thin and formidable, and Mabel who married George Anson. Their daughter, Gertrude, was one of my mother's closest friends and she married my father's best man, Richard Graham, so our two families were closely intertwined.

Dr John Hopkinson FRS (1849-1898) was an electrical engineer and scientist of great distinction. He married Evelyn Oldenburg. Two sons, Bertram and Cecil, were not involved in the tragic accident of 1898, but both were killed in the Great War. Bertram was also a scientist of distinction; all his seven children were girls and they form a large part of the family tree - they had twenty-nine children.

Sir Alfred Hopkinson (1853-1939) married Esther Wells. I can remember him coming to lunch before the war - he looked immensely handsome and distinguished, as indeed was his career: academic, the law, parliament and the first Vice-Chancellor of Manchester University. He had seven children. His eldest son went into the church and one of his sons was Tom Hopkinson of *Picture Post*. Another, Stephan, became a charismatic parson who has devoted much time to christening and marrying cousins. Alfred's daughter Margaret married (Sir) Gerald Hurst and their daughter Eve married (Lord) Frederic Seebohm, the banker and humanitarian; the writer Victoria Glendinning is their daughter. Another granddaughter of Alfred is the writer Georgina Battiscombe.

Charles Hopkinson (1855-1920) married Mabel, Minnie Campbell's sister. They had no children, but we used to visit Auntie May during the war. She was an enthusiastic player of an Edwardian game called 'Shovette'; this consisted of flicking counters at your opponent's counters so as to knock them off the board. Charles was also an engineer by profession and contributed to Manchester civic life - I believe he was actively involved with the Royal Infirmary.

Edward Hopkinson (1860-1922) married Minnie Campbell of Belfast. Their two children were Campbell and my mother Katharine. She had three children, of whom I am the middle one. I have continued the Hopkinson mountaineering tradition, being a former President of the Alpine Club and later the Royal Geographical Society; I was also Chairman of the National Trust. Sadly, I have no engineering talents.

Albert Hopkinson (1863-1949) married Olga Cunliffe Owen. He was a physician both professionally and as an academic, first in Manchester and then at Cambridge. They had five children one of whom, Alice, became a mayor of Cambridge and married Sir Laurence Bragg, the physicist. Their daughter Patience married David, the son of Sir George Thomson, so their children have Nobel Prize winners on both sides of the family - a rather daunting inheritance.

Roger Chorley

Minnie and Edward Hopkinson
c1890

Katharine and Campbell c1903

INTRODUCTION

'Manchester Made Them', part memoir, part social commentary, is a warm but acutely observed account of middle class professional life in well-to-do Alderley Edge in its golden Edwardian years. The blurb on the dust jacket when it was published in 1950, remarks rather portentously but accurately, that "the result is a valuable study of a society and period, critical and sympathetic, and with all the intimacy and vitality of personal memories". It is difficult today to appreciate the cataclysm of the 1914 Great War which poignantly brings the book to a close, and which together with the economic mismanagement of the 1920s, followed by World War II, almost brought Manchester to its knees.

For me, the special interest in my mother's book is not, surprisingly, the account of her family, friends and relations. Some of course I knew much later as grown ups. But my particular regret is never to have known my grandfather, Edward, and his four brothers - to have known them as part of the small brotherhood of pioneers of rock-climbing in Britain in the 1880s. Charles must have been a rock-climber of real brilliance. Many years ago, and now well over a hundred years since his first ascent, I repeated one of his climbs on Dow Crag. In those days equipment and technique were primitive, so his lead up this particular piece of virgin cliff was extraordinarily bold. Nor do I forget, and my mother quotes the passage, the tribute of that doyen of Edwardian mountaineers, Geoffrey Winthrop Young: *"I had heard so often from eye-witnesses that the combination of the famous brothers was a model of what teamwork might be made."*

It would have been fascinating to have talked to Edward about the early days of the electrical engineering industry in which he and his eldest brother John had played such a prominent part. He must have been one of the earliest University graduates to have been recruited into industry - in this case by Sir William Mather, a bold and far sighted entrepreneur. Many of Edward's most important papers were written in conjunction with John and, as another brother, Sir Alfred Hopkinson (first Vice-Chancellor of Manchester University) put it, *"But for the work undertaken by them and by others, especially by Edison in the United States, we should not have seen the rapid development of electrical lighting, traction and driving power which marked the close of the last century."* My mother refers to their important and innovative improvements in the design of dynamos. Another illustration of their fertile brains, and a fascinating example of lateral thinking, was their invention of the two-part tariff for charging for electricity. My mother also refers to Edward's design for the first electric traction locomotive, built for the City and South London underground system. I was taken to see this as a child at the Science Museum in London, but I really only appreciated it thirty years later when taking my own children, prompted no doubt by the same motive: parents are often far more interested than the children they are escorting. There is also the story of how my grandfather proved that electric current was safe for the Giant's Causeway Tramway, which was, I believe, the first electric tramway in the country. This vivid account, which I found in a box of family papers and lacking any attribution, has been reproduced as an Appendix.

Mather & Platt, from being a leader in the field at the end of the 19th century, seems thereafter to have lost its way. One is bound to speculate as to what went wrong. Could the tragic alpine accident in 1898, when John Hopkinson and half his family and their guide were killed on an easy peak, have had anything to do with it? Clearly John was a scientist of great brilliance and in 1898 still only in early middle age and with huge potential; but I am not sure he had anything to do with the business side of Mather & Platt. Perhaps it was my grandfather's increasing ill-health from about 1910 onwards - his cutting edge was blunted. Perhaps electric power was not considered a "core business", to use the fashionable management jargon of today.

The impact of John Hopkinson's death on the Hopkinson clan, but also nationally, was enormous. It was the first big Alpine accident since the disaster on the Matterhorn in 1865. By 1898 mountaineering had become a mature sport, ladies had by now climbed the Matterhorn and had indeed made first ascents. And yet here was an experienced mountaineer with a guide getting killed on an easy route, and killed with half his family. We will never know what happened. He was one of Britain's most distinguished scientists. It is hard to put oneself in the shoes of the remaining brothers and their wives and sisters. They were after all from tough northern stock, nevertheless their climbing came to an end. My mother used to say that it was the wives who went on strike. It was said the most gifted climber of the brothers, Charlie, took up golf. (Whoever told me this must have been a rock-climber as there was a hint of scorn in his voice!)

Mountains and hill country were clearly just as much in my mother's blood as they had been in her father's and uncles', so by the early 1920s she was beginning to break away from the inhibiting tragedy of 1898. She met my father in the Lake District and they were married in 1925, honeymooning in Snowdonia. My father was from Kendal and at that stage a young barrister on the northern circuit, although their home was in Hampstead. But in 1930 he moved into academia as Professor of Commercial Law at the London School of Economics. That was his real home; it provided a base which enabled him to found and edit for many years, the Modern Law Review. It also enabled him to give time to conservation organisations such as the National Trust, then in its early stage of development, and founding organisations such as the Council for the Protection of Rural England and the Friends of the Lake District. For a short time he was in politics; having failed to get elected in 1945 by a handful of votes, he was ennobled by Attlee and was a junior minister for a number of years. And, as with his move to the L.S.E. twenty years earlier, the Lords gave him a natural base to develop his wide interests in the social aspects of law and landscape conservation.

In 1929 my parents moved from Hampstead to Stanmore. In those days Stanmore was a village and not part of London. Almost all our family holidays were in the Lake District, and so we would usually break the journey at Alderley Edge, spending the night at Ferns. I was just old enough to remember Ferns and my grandmother, although I must confess that most of my memories depend on the family 16mm. cine film. They show Ferns as a rather heavy and large Victorian house, although my memories are more of the large, to a child huge, garden with its rocky outcrops which we clambered up with midget rucksacks which my parents had bought us on a Norwegian climbing trip.

My grandmother died in 1936 and so our visits came to an end. Ferns was, I believe, considerably reduced in size. Luckily granny's close friends, the Pilkingtons, who lived next door at Firwood, bought a part of the garden which we knew as the Dell. And so during and after the War, when staying at Firwood, we would often visit the Dell. It was an enchanting spot - a sort of gulch about sixty feet wide, bounded by small sandstone cliffs, and perhaps fifty yards long. Much later in the late '60s Margaret and Dorothy Pilkington, who carried on at Firwood after their parents had died, built a lovely modern house at the head of the Dell, which they retired to. So the Dell was preserved.

Between 1925, when she married, and 1986 when she died, my mother led an active life. She produced and reared three children: my sister Gillian, myself and my brother Patrick. She ran a large house and garden (in those pre-war days, it is perhaps more accurate to say that she managed the servants who ran the large house and garden). The "Rookery" was our Ferns. During World War II, when we evacuated to the Lake District, she ran, solo, a servantless household without running drinking water or electricity - and got great satisfaction in doing so. The Rookery had been requisitioned during the War, but we returned to it in

1945 and my mother reorganised it, as so many others had to, to make it work with one gardener and an inside help.

She also found time to be involved in a great many things: being a Vice-President of the Fell & Rock Climbing Club and editor of its journal and later on being a President of the Ladies Alpine Club, a Council Member of Queen's College London, and so on. And she found the time to write.

She wrote four books, each quite different. Her first was *Hills and Highways* in 1928. It is a series of essays on landscapes, on people's reactions over the centuries to landscape, and usually with a mountain theme. The chapter end-pieces have charming woodcuts by her old friend and later the curator and benefactor of the Whitworth Art Gallery, Margaret Pilkington. Next came *Armies and the Art of Revolution*. It was written largely before, but published during the War (1943). Its title is its theme: the crucial role that armies play or can play in revolutions. Many years ago, in 1961 in Lahore of all places, I was told that it was required reading in the Pentagon and commanded a high price in Washington's second-hand book market. The third book was *Manchester Made Them*. And her fourth and last book was a biography of Arthur Hugh Clough, published in 1962, before this poet's importance was generally recognised. Later she worked on the connection between man's literary and visual perceptions of landscapes.

They were a remarkable clan, the Hopkinsons. To me they epitomise all that is best about Victorian England: energetic and enterprising in work and play, they reflect a Manchester at the height of its power and self-confidence. A Manchester which was second only to London, and I suspect most Mancunians felt that it was really rather superior to the capital city. Yet on re-reading *Manchester Made Them* I get no sense of it being a triumphalist society. A society at ease with itself perhaps, certainly a cultivated society. It was also a society capable of questioning its values and it had a strong sense of social responsibility. While my mother rebelled against some aspects of it, as did many of her generation, she came in later years to look back on many of its values with nostalgia. It is this interplay which is captured in *Manchester Made Them*.

Roger Chorley
London, 2001

For
Olive Schill
and
Margaret and Dorothy Pilkington
and
my cousins Margaret and Gerald Hurst

Acknowledgments
The publishers would like to thank the following for their assistance during the preparation of this book:

Lord Chorley for permitting unlimited access to the family archives.

Christine Pemberton for her tireless work in researching photographs and illustrations and in typesetting, laying-out and re-designing the original work

Local historians Basil Jeuda and Chris Makepeace for the loan of early photographs from their respective collections of early Manchester material.

Matthew Hyde for the loan of his own copy of the original edition of 'Manchester Made Them'.

Katharine Chorley 1917

Chapter One
AVE

You gaze into a deep sea pool to pick out the objects which pattern its bed. They lie on the sandy floor, each one distinct and gleaming, but their clarity is made strange by the translucent water through which you look. Every now and then, too, they are distorted by the ripples which break over the surface, or by the shadow of a moving cloud.

So it is, looking down through the years in order to picture the people and the scenes of childhood and youth. The past emerges so clearly when you send your vision back, and yet you wonder whether the view is normal because the intervening years have spread between you and it an atmosphere shot with twisting lights and shadows. Is it true to the facts and would it be recognized by the other actors in the scene of life in which you played yourself only as a child? You cannot eliminate your own experience during the intervening years. It reflects on the picture so that what is truth for you might well not be so true for those adults with whom you were a child contemporary. Indeed, you should not blot out your own experience even if you could. For the past is valuable in so far as it is linked with the present and suggests a form for the coming links which will join the present to the future. Every reconstruction must be interpretative as well as factual.

I am setting out to evoke from the past my home and surroundings, my parents and their friends. And what I write will be a rendering of the swan-song of the English bourgeoisie, the part of it which was sung to me from my cradle in the year of Queen Victoria's Jubilee until I was near the threshold of grown-up life in 1914. I choose my own home for the experiment because I knew it and loved it better than any other; and though in some ways it may not have been altogether typical, yet taken along with the homes which interwove with it, I think it was pretty nearly a microcosm of north-country English bourgeois and professional life in those golden Edwardian days which were the culmination of a century of middle-class endeavour.

The singers did not know that they were performing a swan song. But the three and a half troubled decades between 1914 and 1949 which have hammered me into a maturity so different from theirs have made this clear. My hopes and fears and disillusions derive from and my certainties have been won from living in a world of storm and generous enthusiasms gone sour which they never knew at all, or knew only when they were elderly and already formed by the secure civilization of their youth and prime. Their world came to an end and mine was born at midnight on the 4th August 1914. Thus I can only recapture the notes of their song as if I were hearing them at the further end of a long and winding track of experience. So what I am going to write must appear as an interaction of interpretation and criticism.

There must be the criticism of the vanished society in which I was a child upon its post-war successor and there must be the criticism of that troubled society of the 1920s and the 1930s upon its progenitor. And finally, since one cannot lose the trail of one's own experience, I must write from the viewpoint to which it has led me, and a viewpoint is also an interpretation and a criticism.

In so far as we understand the past in which we have been rooted we shall be better fitted to understand and judge the present which is partly of our own making but partly a legacy which we must accept whether we will or no, and perhaps we shall be more sensitive and sympathetic also to the changes which our children, in their time and circumstance, will impose upon us.

Mother, Campbell and Katharine

Katharine and Mother c1905   Katharine, November 1907

Katharine in her Liberty Bridesmaid's dress at the wedding of
Gerald and Margaret Hurst, c1907.

Ferns in 1906

Tea in the garden - Mother and Katharine c1912

Chapter Two
FERNS

Manchester was sprawling over and dirtying more and more acres and even miles of the flat pasture country on its southern side as the last decades of the nineteenth century swept ever-increasing wealth into the hands of the industrial and merchant North. And manufacturers and merchants were wanting to take themselves and their families into cleaner air and country surroundings. Quick rail transport made the great exodus into Cheshire possible, so when the London and North-Western Railway Company built a station at the foot of Alderley Edge, thus linking it to Manchester fifteen miles away, the cape of wooded hill more than four hundred feet high which juts into the Cheshire plain became an attractive settlement. The houses sprang up on the southern and western and northern slopes of the Edge; behind them an undulating rib of country surfaced with woods and farmland and the tree-studded parks of old Cheshire houses linked the Edge to the harsh moors above Macclesfield. Pheasants whirred out of copses, the crack of guns sounded through the winter, cattle churned to a muddy porridge the good Cheshire soil at the entrance gates of fields.

'The residence of the merchant princes of Manchester' - so an early edition of Baddeley's Guide was said to have described Alderley Edge. It always sounded a rather shaming description, because it seemed pompous and opulent to be classed as a mercantile princeling. Besides, a real prince had ridden the old pack-horse road over the Edge and through the woods on his march from Manchester to Derby in 1745 and princely glamour belonged to him and assuredly not to the business men who took their Sunday afternoon constitutionals over the same track.

Baddeley could not enlarge on his terse description by trying to make it vie with those star-spangled accounts given by his opposite number Baedeker of other residences of merchant princes in Venice or Florence or Genoa, for instance, but at least his Manchester princes had built themselves well-found and roomy houses mostly of the gritty pleasant-hued local sandstone, but sometimes less happily of custard-yellow brick. Almost all had good gardens, set in folds of the hillside or with wide views over the plain.

Ferns was one of these. It had been built soon after the railway came when the best sites with the finest views were still free to be chosen and cleared.

I can see Ferns from a double angle; it was my home for twenty-one years, but I was not born there for we had moved from a village on the plain much nearer to Manchester when I was six and my only brother fourteen. Thus I have the impression of a small child to whom the new place is charged with magic and I have those other impressions of the home one grows up in, vivid and various and entangled, sometimes sharply lit and separate, sometimes fused into an unconscious generalization. I can recall the slightly fearsome delight when we visited Ferns some weeks before moving in and I realized the wide spaces of the garden and its mysterious recesses. And for the rest, the details and the moods and the actions are like a long necklace strung on the thread of those twenty-one years.

The house was built on a square plan, the rusticated sandstone walls rising to finish in well-proportioned gables, two for each of the three sides; the fourth side was complicated by a kitchen yard, outbuildings and a big coach-house yard. Above the front door there was a tower with a battlemented top, but the balance of the house could carry that. The windows were tall and wide with stone sills and made an orderly pattern on the walls.

Windows are important to all houses, but to Ferns they were vital, particularly the drawing-room window which faced west over the plain and which as I picture it reminds me of Belloc's charming homily on windows in *The Path to Rome*. 'To a building, windows are everything', he says; 'they are what eyes are to a man. Out of windows a building takes its views; in windows the outlook of its human inhabitants is framed.' We had afternoon tea near that window, sitting at a slender mahogany table with a border of lovely inlay and a satin surface only half hidden by the cloth which was always of white linen with a firm and deep crochet fringe. And the china, the worn Rockingham blue and gold with rivets to several of the cups and a shortage of plates so that they had to be white, did not change either, any more than the recipe for the scones and the chocolate or ginger cake.

Outside, the lawn curved down in a broad sweep of green and beyond and below there was the village with two spires emerging, those of the Anglican and Wesleyan churches, and beyond that again the receding plain patterned with trees and hedges and toned with a flux of light and shadow like the sea. Sometimes lances of sunshine would flash on the glass of a greenhouse or a big window belonging to some house far out on the plain. Often there seemed more sky than earth to the view. Each evening, the setting sun made its exit in a different mood, and every tea-time at certain months of the year the rooks went home, hundreds of them winging methodically across the sky and so punctual that you could almost check a watch by their flight. To sit at tea and look out from that window gave a sense of belonging to an enclosed world, the society and geography of one's own home, withdrawn from neighbours' homes and differentiated from the common look of the countryside shared by them.

The drawing-room was the heart of Ferns, an informal restful room, almost always lived in, where you could toast your toes in front of the fire and where there was a floor-space behind the big armchair well suited for a child to curl up with a book unseen and forgotten by the grown-ups. But the informality was gracious. I could not come into the drawing-room in muddy shoes and I might not toast my feet on the polished brass fender in any outdoor shoes. I could not make a litter with some messy hobby, and I could not play rollicking games there with my friends. Indeed, apart from any rules of decent manners, the room was fine enough to claim respect and a certain dignity of behaviour from its inmates in its own right. My father and mother built up the drawing-room between them, but in the end I think it reflected mother's personality more than his. I can catch pictures of father in other rooms and in many other surroundings, a vital unresting man radiating energy, so that my pictures of him are more like the shots of a film than stills. Most naturally, I see him striding somewhere, taking a long step with the odd little lift of the hips which was peculiar to all the members of his family and attractive in the males but sadly ugly in the women. He was fairly tall and very lean with broad shoulders and slight hips. He had a rather small head with fine dark brown hair threaded with grey and curly above his neck and ears. His eyes were large and grey and he had a jutting big-boned nose. He wore a small moustache, too thin in colour for his hair and sanguine skin. It did not hide his mouth which more than his eyes registered every change in his feelings in a way that one could never mistake.

But I see mother almost always in the drawing-room, in her small easy chair close by the fire, for she was the great devotee of toe-toasting, with her writing-board on her knee or reading the Spectator or someone's biography or snatching 'forty winks' after lunch. She was short and neat. Her feet and ankles, for instance, were beautifully made so that they looked trim whatever foot gear she was wearing, whether evening slippers or the woollen stockings and thick-soled solid leather shoes which she put on for walking. Her hands were small and neat, too, and she kept them carefully, always wearing gloves outside in a hot sun because father did not like to see tan and freckles on a feminine hand. She had white hair for as long as I can remember and shrewd blue eyes, a clear rose-flushed skin and lips whose thin rather wistful curve could set at times in a hard strength of will.

When she talked one could still just detect the Irish turn of phrase and the Irish intonation of her speech. I see her at the tea-table, coaxing the methylated burner of the silver kettle, or seated at her desk dipping into a drawer for the household keys which were decorated with red tape so that she could spot them easily if they got left about, or doing the household accounts with competence and care. For these were to mother to cope with, because father was a Cambridge Wrangler and mathematics belonged to that part of his mind where intellect and imagination fuse, so that a long column of figures produced in him a boredom which almost always resulted in inaccurate additions, a pleasant source of chaff between them much enjoyed by me.

As for father, when I see him in the drawing-room it is on Sunday afternoons in winter after tea, relaxed for once in the big armchair. The dark green velvet curtains are drawn, the electric chandelier is full on - they always liked it that way and never went in for shaded reading lamps - and father's head is well lighted as he opens his book to begin reading aloud to me. I have emerged from my sconce behind the chair where I have been indulging in uncensored, because unnoticed, reading, the Ingoldsby Legends perhaps, for which I shall pay later in a fear-shot night, and father is finding our place, his big-jointed hands rather clumsy against the golden tooling of the Milton or the padded green morocco of Tennyson. If it is Milton it will be rather heavy going for me at ten or eleven years old; the Idylls of the King are better, but best of all Macaulay's Lays of Ancient Rome, read by father with a rolling lilt so that all those grand Latin names of the fighters at the Tiber bridge or by the shores of Lake Regillus carry me along like beating wings. Later, I shall have to say what poetry I have been learning myself during the week and show my mark book, and then perhaps father will produce pencil and paper and begin teaching me geometry.

I prized the hour after tea with father and was resentful if a visitor stayed so long that I could not have it; the visitor became an interloper spoiling the intimacy of the room so that even the furniture seemed less personal and affectionately disposed. There was the great Donegal rug which covered the floor with soft green and in the embrasure of the south window opposite the fireplace a long low settee upholstered in quiet blue. On either hand of that were the Italian walnut chest of drawers which father and mother had picked up in one of the villages on Lake Como and my Irish grandfather's bureau with the Waterford glass on top. I do not suppose that most of it really came from the authentic Waterford factory at all, but it was always called so and it was thought that you could generally tell by the dull gleam which betokened an extra charge of lead in the formula. Bookshelves ran on either side of the fireplace and under the chandelier there was a round table with more books on it and mother's work-box in the middle. It was a beautiful table, mahogany with a slightly sunk top and carving round the edge. Grandfather's bureau was beautiful, too, mahogany again with two slender columns pencilled with inlay and on the desk flap and doors below more pencilled inlay traced on each rich panel in an ellipse. The mantelpiece carried a pink and blue and white Sèvres lady asleep in her armchair with her legs crossed and one shoe depending precariously from her china toe. She was very charming and elegant and a travesty of the potter's art, and she was flanked by two Sèvres vases equally elegant and even more outrageous for they had each a frill of allegedly real lace at their necks set hard in the clay. Above the lady and the vases hung a large watercolour drawing known as 'The Cardinals', a picture of two graciously ascetic elderly cardinals drinking tea with a jolly Dominican monk at a table spread with a lace-embroidered cloth and appointed with silver kettle and teapot and delicate china. One cardinal was pouring out and the other held a poised fragile teacup. The cardinals and the Sèvres lady matched each other well. Both were altogether charming and neither had the slightest value as art. Then there was the lacquered Chinese work-table which had belonged to my great-aunt Anna away in County Down and which held an assortment of oddments including my great-grandfather's silver inlaid snuffbox and a pair of candle snuffers and a miniature of my great-grandmother whose throat had been so white and delicate that it was said you could see a red glow slipping down when she drank port wine. I expect the same was said of countless other Regency ladies, but it sounded very romantic to me.

Sunday evening, when the lights were on, was not the best time to enjoy the flowers and ferns banked against the cream-painted folding doors which divided the drawing-room from the billiard-room, nor to enjoy the watercolours. Their gold frames and mounts glowed too heavily against the green wallpaper. But in daylight, when the sun slanted just right on the angry-coloured Copley Fielding of a storm off Dover or the unfinished de Wint of King's Lynn which might have been painted by a young-eyed god in love with the lyric earth, then it was clear that father and mother knew how to choose watercolours. There were others, too, in particular a view of Hebron built up to a sure strength from delicate buff and grey tones and a Varley of Snowdon and Llanberis which made one think more of balance and poise and fine manners than of a mountain to climbed. Gissing has said somewhere in *The Ryecroft Papers* that as a child he used to sleep in a room hung round with prints after the English landscape painters: 'I gazed and gazed at them', he says, 'with that fixed attention of a child which is half curiosity, half reverie, till every line of them fixed in my mind ... and I have often thought that this early training of the imagination ... has been one of the emotions directing my life.' I feel the same way about those watercolours, and not only on account of their beauty; there were enough of them to give the sense of a style and a tradition and that, in a world of shifting values, is an item of equipment for which I have been grateful.

No one at Ferns possessed a latchkey. I have no idea why unless it was that father, for all his practical ability, was engagingly liable to lose any keys allotted to him. However, the front door always stood open except after dark and in the very coldest weather because mother liked 'fresh air'. The large circle of uncles and aunts who were always coming and going at the house used to tease her about this, chaff which I enjoyed as much as the chaff about the accounts, for it was always a little exciting to listen to the elders ragging their contemporaries, and the more obvious the occasion the better, of course, I understood it. There was another cause for chaff lurking in the big square porch before the front door. On the right wall there was a carved stone shell bracketed out from the masonry. No one knew whence it came or who had fixed it, but it was suggested that it must have begun life as a holy water stoup, perhaps in Italy. There wasn't the least reason to suppose that it had, but since mother was Ulster Irish the idea of connecting her with 'houly wather' was a good joke to the Ulster contingent of uncles and aunts.

One summer a pair of swallows nested in the top corner opposite the shell. I could watch the male darting in and out on his errands and climb a step-ladder to look at the eggs when the female was taking a breather and later observe the gargoyle-like little fledglings. I waited impatiently for the swallows to come the following season, but they never did, and I hope that this was not owing to the spick-and-span ideas of Grundy, the head gardener, reinforced I dare say by parental dislike of droppings on the tiled floor of the porch. Mother was always having trouble to keep the porch unpolluted and visitors must have wondered why two walking-sticks were propped permanently at the outside corners. Only the intimates of the house knew that this was an ingenious arrangement to counter the determination of Patou, my small mongrel dog, to attend to the calls of his nature in just those two places.

The purpose of the porch was to support the tower, a remote and to me slightly mysterious part of the house because as a small child I was forbidden to go up there alone in case I should fall over the castellated rampart.

During my childhood, the front door was opened, although since the front door was almost permanently open it would perhaps be more correct to say that the inner glass door leading from the lobby into the hall was opened, by Louisa, young, tall and fresh-faced, who played hymn tunes on a Jew's harp; a concert to which she sometimes allowed me to listen in the kitchen. Visitors coming in found themselves in a big oblong apartment, though that sounds rather a formal word for our hall, with a gallery running round at ceiling level from which the bedrooms opened off and lighted by a skylight in the roof whose span almost matched e size of the hall. On the left there was the billiard-room door and then the drawing-room door, straight ahead a charcoal brazier set in a carved and painted wooden stand which father had brought home from Spain and which now held plants. Beyond that there was the dining-room door and a ticking grandfather clock, to the right the stairs and passage to the back hall, kitchen and pantry.

The hall reminds me most of father coming home from Manchester in the evening. He would hang his hat and coat the lobby and then stride into the house calling 'Minnie!' It was always somehow satisfactory to hear that call and now I understand why. Father lived in the world of affairs and practical problems were his battleground. His mind was like sharp sword to attack difficulties, but his judgment was sometimes badly founded because the sword of his mind cut and thrust too quickly for his judgment always to hold firm ground. Then mother with her sober appraisal of a situation would come to his rescue and frequently save him from some mistake. She was prudent where he was impetuous, gentle where he could jostle and fight, but stern where he could be sentimental. Thus that call 'Minnie!' signified a partnership and a complement of personalities; he with his lambent brain among his peers in the big world and she at home ready to give tranquillity and comfort and sympathy when he was worried and tired and depressed, but also ready to give sane and shrewd advice on the problems which sooner or later he always brought back to her for review. Almost all these problems must have had a technical or administrative side to them, for father was the managing director of a big engineering firm and vice-chairman of another adolescent firm which needed skilled and courageous handling to bring it to maturity. And of this side, mother obviously could know nothing. I have often wondered how she was able to help in the way she did. I suppose her clear intelligence and her interest in people must have combined to bare for her the human essentials below the overlay of technicalities.

It was too late, as a rule, for tea when father got home and in summer time he usually took a turn in the garden or played a game of croquet with mother, but in winter he often went up to his study for half an hour before dinner. It was a large and rather gaunt room upstairs, facing west with the desk across the window, but humanized by the litter of papers and scientific and technical journals which lay in piles on the floor, on the chairs, everywhere, with here and there a splash of colour where a blue-print peeped out. For father was lavishly untidy in his study and would not allow anyone else to do the straightening up which was always relegated to a Utopian future when he would have 'more time'. Long and arduous were the campaigns which mother had to wage before he would even give permission for the room to be cleaned. He always threw the rubbish from his breakfast mail on to the dining-room floor. Then later it would sometimes transpire that some precious document was missing and after long and fruitless search in the study it could only be inferred that the paper had been thrown away at breakfast by mistake, perhaps several days before, and then the search would be extended, with the whole household mobilized, from the big old ashpit in the stable-yard to any unlit fires. Finally, mother had all discarded letters and even envelopes parked for a month in an orange box in the pantry before they were destroyed.

Half an hour in the study and it was time to dress for dinner and, though father was disorderly with papers, he was fastidious about his person. I can remember the way he brushed up his curly hair and the clean white handkerchief which was put out every evening on his dressing-table and which he would sprinkle with eau-de-Cologne before coming downstairs in a dress shirt and dinner suit varied sometimes by a black velvet jacket. Of course on any formal occasion, and all dinner parties were formal, he wore a tail coat, but not a white waistcoat. I imagine that white waistcoats were already the fashion in more dashing and exalted circles in London, but they had not penetrated yet to the conservative middle-aged of our society.

Dinner-parties were fun for me because I could lie on the floor of the gallery and peer through the balusters at the guests going into the dining-room and then scuttle down to the back premises in the hope of snaffling a mouthful of succulent food as the dishes came out from the table. Dinner-party food was quite different from the stalwart roasts of and mutton which I ate at midday, hot one day, cold the next and minced up into cottage pie to complete the cycle with spotted dick or jam roly-poly or batter pudding to follow. And because these snacks were illegal I tasted them with attention. With the remnants of an entrée or a savoury I laid the foundations of culinary appreciation much more effectively than if I had been fed on such delicacies for my daily sustenance.

Altogether, dinner-parties were something of a ceremony even for me. Beforehand, well beforehand because she always liked to be ready for events in good time, there would be 'helping mother to dress', a euphemism for hindering mother to dress, which included as the special treat an inspection of her jewel-case and perhaps the extraction for that evening's wear of the diamond pendant which father had given her on their wedding-day and the stiff diamond bracelet which father's chief, Sir William Mather, presented to her after father designed the engine for the first electrically driven underground train which ran on the old City and South London route. That was years before I was born, but I saw the engine with pride after its working days were over in the Science Museum at South Kensington along with George Stephenson's 'Rocket'. Having seen mother safely into the drawing-room to await her guests and warm her feet before their arrival, I might take a stroll round the dinner-table and read the menus and the names of the guests printed by mother on blank visiting cards and laid neatly beside each cover. Perhaps I would be in time to watch Louisa's dexterous folding of the napkins so that they turned suddenly into a lady's slipper or a bishop's mitre. But I had to time to a nicety my installation behind the balusters because a moment too early and my lanky recumbent form might bar the passage to a guest emerging from mother's bedroom where she had left her cloak (I always had a look into the bedroom later to admire the evening cloaks) and a moment too late and I would miss the procession. This timing required the friendly co-operation of Louisa and the housemaid who looked after the guests upstairs, but I could generally rely on that unless during the course of the day I had 'riled' the housemaid who was not quite so even-tempered as Louisa.

Peering between the balusters I first saw Louisa appear, the bows of her starched apron sticking out like propellers from her black dress. She would pause for a moment with her hand on the drawing-room doorknob and glance up at me to enjoin silence, then she would gather herself and swing open the door to announce dinner and in a minute the guests would pass through the hall arm in arm, the black clad men nearest to me and looking rather like the black keys on the piano against the light silk and satin and lace of he ladies. Occasionally a guest tactlessly looked up and caught my eye, then if it was a stranger I would duck quickly and pretend I wasn't there, but if it was someone I really knew I might grin back very secretly. Once a friend of father's, who always pulled my leg mercilessly whenever we met, broke all the rules of my game and all the mysterious formality of the occasion by calling up a remark to me, a horrid embarrassment.

I liked to observe the dresses of the ladies I knew because their evening attire made such a piquant contrast to the tweeds and blouses in which I saw them by day, and I liked to see what the strangers looked like and put names to them. If I was quick I could do this by co-relating the couples with the cards round the dinner-table. And I should probably have been told about the new and able young Liberal candidate whose politics were dangerous but who had married the daughter of an old family friend and was bringing her to their first post-honeymoon dinner-party, or the new territorial adjutant, or the new professor from Manchester University

- on one occasion this was a youngish, fair-haired, blue-eyed New Zealander whose name was Rutherford

The guests were already chattering hard to each other as they passed, a tribute to the well-mannered ease with which dinner-parties were conducted. For they had only just paired off in the drawing-room so that the men must have the smoothest opening gambit ready on their tongues the ladies must have had by heart the correct answering moves. But I wonder how often those orthodox opening bits were developed into a real game of conversation where a witty knight's move counters the keen thrust of a bishop and a couple of rooks bear down with their arguments upon a cornered king. Were the players really intent and interested and out to win, or was it all a polite convention of talk, and what happened to any good conversation when father decided that the moment had come for him to transfer his attention from the lady on his left to the lady on his right and all the other men had to follow suit, whatever their engrossment with their left hand neighbours, with the alacrity of soldiers at drill? That must surely have made real conversation impossible and I suspect that father, who liked good talk, used it as a sort of courtly and amusing game and waited for the real thing until the ladies had departed to the drawing-room and he could send the port on a further round while the drill pattern broke up and cross- table talk began and it was no longer bad manners to listen in silence or to hold single-handed if you could an interested table. I can only surmise, for when I was old enough to attend formal dinner-parties the war had eliminated them ..... the territorial adjutant and the brilliant young Liberal candidate were both killed in France, and Rutherford, perhaps for the first time in the history of science, had mobilized the brains and resources of a great university laboratory for the service of war.

However, perhaps just because it was only a glimpse that I caught from my lair in the gallery, the little procession as it passed in to dinner with the swish and shimmer of the ladies' dresses, has become a symbol for me of that secure Edwardian era which I saw from a child's aloof vantage point as it swept past me into history.

The dining-room needed company to make it companionable. It was an uncomradely room and always gave me a touch of agoraphobia when I had to eat there by myself or even when there were just one or two others. It was long, broad and lofty and the wide walls were cream-painted and hung with mezzo-tints in black frames with gilt edges. The doors were big and heavy, rather ornate and painted chocolate brown. And now, looking back, I can never quite dissociate it from two meals which I ate there alone; one of them a supper of cold roast beef eaten at some indeterminate hour of a January night in 1922 when my father lay dying upstairs. My brother finished his meal and went up to mother as I came down and I hacked first one slice of beef and then another from the joint, wolfing them down hungrily for this was the first time in my life that I had felt strain and anxiety of this kind and it seemed to make me ravenous, yet somehow I felt that I ought not to have a good appetite. But I ate as fast as I could to get away quickly because the empty spaces of the room were uniformly lit by an electric chandelier above the table and there was no comforting fire-glow and soft play of light and shadow. The other was the last meal that I had in the dining-room, no, not quite the last, but the last significant meal. That was years later when I had been sent for from my own home and family in London because my mother had been taken, mortally ill, to a nursing-home in Manchester. As I ate, sitting solitary at the head of the table, the silver and the china and the furniture which were fine rather than intimate yet so familiar and accepted that they seemed subjective and a part of myself detached themselves and drew away, and I knew that the gracious life of Ferns was finishing and that with its ebb my precarious hold on the values of a steadfast civilization would be pulled off.

The furniture was all Regency mahogany, a long serving table at one end of the room which came from father's family and at the other end, pedigree mother's family, a sideboard with eight legs supporting a bow-fronted central drawer flanked by two bow-fronted cupboards. The veneer of its convex surfaces made a stilled swirl of rich red and brown. Opposite the windows and fireplace there was a console table which carried a baroque tea-urn with the Irish family's crest in a centre shield almost polished away. It had always been assumed that the urn was Sheffield plate because had the three bells mark, until one time it was taken away to be overhauled when it was found that owing to the way the crest was engraved it was technically impossible for it to be Sheffield. After some fascinating research into the archives of the still extant firm in Sheffield which had made it, it appeared that it was a piece of very early electro, so early that the craftsman who had put the finishing touches had automatically affixed the Sheffield mark. Sheffield plate, of course, is silver beaten on to copper by hand, electro the same thing but done by an electrical process and much less valuable. However, the story was a good one to tell when visitors admired the urn and certainly with its full generous curves and decoration in relief it made a very fine piece indeed and wasn't it the devil to clean - as I have more recently found out to my personal cost.

Father and mother had picked up the dining table for themselves, in Dublin I think, and the room was welcoming enough when the leaves were put into the table and the glass and silver set out on the glowing

John Hopkinson, the eldest son 1897

Alfred Hopkinson, my uncle 1897

Uncle Charles Hopkinson

Aunt Mary with her mother, Alice Hopkinson, née Dewhurst

1929 Aunt Mary Hopkinson, holding the scroll which was presented to her by the Manchester and Salford Police and Fire Brigade on the 40th anniversary of her founding the Orphanage and Benevolent Fund in 1889.

Aunt Mabel (May) Anson

A later portrait of May
Anson - note the dress

wood, the Waterford decanters and the silver claret jug and the Sheffield egg dish, genuine this time, which we used for sweets. The napkins and the table mats always came from the same firm in Belfast, and after many launderings the inwoven patterns of shamrocks or roses of the damask napkins gleamed like silk. The linen was another of these jokes on mother but from the English side of the family, because she always alleged that you could never buy fit linen in England. If a flippant Anglo-Saxon suggested, for instance, that Robinson & Cleaver was much more convenient and was still an Irish firm though established in England she would snort with contempt and retort that they had long lost their standards through catering for crude and ignorant English custom.

I remember a full dinner-table best on Christmas night, for we always had a house-party of uncles and aunts for Christmas and long before I was allowed to stay up for 'late' dinner regularly, I did so on Christmas evening, sitting between father and his brother Charlie who was then my particular uncle. He had married mother's sister so that there was a double relationship and Auntie May was my special aunt. They had no children and turned over a warm affection to Campbell and me, and they were both devoted to games which suited us very well. Since Campbell was eight years older than me he, of course, got more of the outside games like golf, but Uncle Charlie taught me to play chess and Auntie May was always ready for endless contests at dominoes or halma, and both of them were experts at racing demon or poker patience. Mother seemed to dislike almost all games and in particular could never be induced to take part in the racing demon or poker patience contests, so Auntie May's attitude made an interesting contrast. Campbell usually sat next to Auntie May and then round the table there would be mother's two brothers, Uncle Howard and Uncle Walter, and their wives, Aunt Augusta and Aunt Gladys. Uncle Howard and Aunt Augusta were quieter than the others and took me for walks while the rest played golf. Uncle Walter was a soldier who looked very fine in an early photograph as a Gordon Highlander subaltern, but whose calling seemed relatively dull and unromantic since he had become a staff officer on the 'Q' side. But that was compensated after Campbell emerged from Sandhurst with a scarlet tunic and a crimson sash and a sword whose correct and quick extraction from its scabbard needed a practised hand which he perfected by trying it out with me as a rapt spectator. Aunt Gladys was much younger than the other aunts and came from a different world, the distant and distinguished world of London. I liked her a lot, and so obviously did father for he treated her with a kind of affectionate and pleasant gallantry which was quite different from his attitude to his other sisters-in-law.

The conversation rattled up and down the table for there was no formality in those gatherings. Father liked wit and made fair play with his own. He would dart a remark pointed with crisp humour and then clinch it with his particular smile. His smiles seemed to flash into his face and were completely disarming, but they were not so kindly as Uncle Charlie's smiles which came more slowly and lasted longer, nor so ironical as Uncle Walter's which always ended in a chuckle when he teased mother affectionately and dryly. But it was generally Uncle Charlie who took up father's challenge and then all the other uncles and aunts would egg them on until they lost themselves in outrageous twists of argument, and mother's clear laugh would ring out from the other end of the table, a most infectious and carefree laugh in those days. Yet I think that she must have found the organization of those Christmas gatherings rather a strain, for we never had many servants nor the kind of servant who could share the responsibility with her and she was very jealous of any encroachment on what she considered to be their just times off. We who work at the kitchen stove and sink ourselves are apt to forget that the organization and superintendence of a gracious and full house as Ferns was at Christmas time was also work if you did it yourself as mother did.

When the moment for plum pudding arrived, for several years the laughter turned on me because wasn't it extraordinary that I always got the sixpence! The year that I discovered Louisa inserting it surreptitiously into my helping as she handed me my plate was a major landmark on the road to an adult outlook. But that never detracted from the charm of plum pudding with its sprig of holly and flare of lighted brandy round the dish. There were special and traditional good things to eat at almost every meal during those Christmas house-parties; a shortbread from, Edinburgh, a pâté de foie gras from Strasbourg sent each year by some business connection of father's, a Stilton cheese, a round of spiced beef from Belfast, black-crusted from the super-charged liquor in which it had been cooked. I expect the wine was equally good, but I did not sample that. It was fun, however, to go down to the dimly lit wine cellar with father where dust and cobwebs were actually held in honour as they thickened on the undisturbed bottles in the bins and watch him make his choice and then perhaps be allowed to carry up a bottle with due care not to shake the sediment.

After dinner we went to the billiard-room. It was almost always in use when we had guests, but I don't think mother cared for it as much as the drawing-room. Certainly there was little sense of her influence in it; it seemed to have been furnished without the same loving attention and the result, though comfortable, had no beauty or distinction. The pictures were large gaunt engravings from Landseer and Briton Riviere and Peter Graham with Millais's 'Princes in the Tower' over the piano. I cannot think how or why father and mother who had chosen the watercolours in the drawing-room could tolerate them, certainly I cannot imagine how mother could, for her appreciation and knowledge of pictures widened and deepened through the years, and I am sure that she did not regard them as works of art or even as interesting illustrations. In contrast, there were two humble but charming little prints of Dalton and Joule, the Manchester scientists, above the mantelpiece and near the door a really fine engraving of King Charles the First.

So the billiard-room wore a comfortable but slightly clumsy air, but it won its crowded hour at Christmas and certainly the life lived in it then seemed glorious enough to me as I sat in my chair in a corner and browsed through my Christmas books while I cocked an ear for the repartee which father and the uncles and Campbell shot at each other as the billiard balls slipped over the smooth cloth and buffeted the cushions and cannoned and slid precisely into the pockets. Earlier on in the day the billiard table had been handed over to mother to 'arrange presents' with great secrecy. Everyone had his or her own section and the moment when we were called in was for me at any rate a moment of hardly suppressible expectant excitement.

I was the only child in the Christmas party for Uncle Walter's family was too young for active participation and the others had no children. So Campbell made a good link between me and the elders. His eight years' seniority naturally invested him with all the grown-up privileges, but still he belonged to my generation and we were equals, although he was already out in the great world. I ran after him like an eager puppy snapping up every scrap of attention that was given to me and immeasurably proud when I was let into the secret of any of his gay doings or allowed to share in some rag which he had arranged. No elder brother could have taken a small sister along in a more comradely spirit than he did. He always drew me in when he could and made me feel a partner in the enterprise whatever it might be, but I did repay him, for I fagged for him with unremitting zeal. He and Uncle Charlie taught me to play billiards well enough to take part in a friendly game while I was still in my early 'teens. A good discipline, incidentally, for you can slice any number of divots when you are learning to play golf, yet if you replace them and stamp them down carefully elders will only register disapproval, but if you slice that lovely surface of Kendal green with a billiard cue, then you will have done irreparable damage and incurred a blistering severity of displeasure. Immature hands are not the easiest instruments with which to control a billiard cue, but thanks to my instructors I never cut the cloth.

'General knowledge' was another Christmas game and even mother joined in this. Everyone had a piece of paper and you had to write down a list of subjects such as flower, mountain, battle, statesman, poet, and so forth. Then someone picked a letter at random and in ten minutes of hectic private research into a well- or ill-stored mind you had to find an example of each subject beginning with the chosen letter. The fun began when the answers were read out and the great lark was to set off father and Uncle Charlie accusing each other of fake answers. Uncle Charlie always appeared the worst offender, perhaps because he was more erudite than the others. At any rate, the game ended most happily when Uncle Charlie had surrounded his chair like a defensive rampart with every reference book in the house. Then I was sent unwillingly to bed.

Sometimes after I had gone to bed there would be music and I would lie awake listening whilst mother sang to Auntie May's accompaniment. She had a soprano voice as true and sweet as a bell and I think musical sound affected her as pure emotion so that when she sang she unconsciously invested the old and beautiful songs she chose with sentiment which sometimes troubled me by its very intensity, slipping me from known anchorages of feeling into vague uncharted seas from which I longed to escape in normal childish sleep. But we never had carols at Christmas time; I wonder why and I wish that we had. For thus I did not learn to any of those lovely folk songs of the Christian faith when I was young and my imagination waiting to be lit up. Was it because mother's religion was so deep and personal and to private that she could not bring herself to expose it to the gaiety of a Christmas party? She always took me to church on Christmas morning, slipping away quietly down the hill uninfluenced by the others of the party, most of whom played golf, though one or two usually came with us. Or was it that they did not have glad carols in the North of Ireland where mother had learned to sing and where everything is gay and expansive - except religion and politics.

However, carols or no carols, Christmas at Ferns was certainly the feast of family reunion, and every year the party reassembled, the bags of golf-clubs were stacked in the lobby, the housemaid scuttered along the gallery with hot-water cans at dressing-for-dinner-time, the mistletoe hung over the stairs tied to a gallery baluster, Grundy saved a magnificent show of curly Japanese chrysanthemums to decorate the hall, and I was allowed to join more and more freely in grown-up fun. There was no break until 1914 and then the curtain rang down; the players had scattered and never came together as a company again.

Left: Auntie May and whose baby?

Ethel, Albert, May and Campbell. 1920s.

Ethel (who married Campbell), her mother, Aunt Mary, Mother, Campbell, Katharine and Father

Uncle Howard (Campbell), Aunt Augusta (his wife), Aunt May and Uncle Albert.

Katharine and Patou, 1912.

Mlle Dupuy and Patou

Father, Olga and Albert Hopkinson and one of their sons and Aunty May.

A distant view of Ferns

Ferns showing the tower.

Interior views of Ferns

Views of the drawing room at Ferns

The family arriving at Ferns

Father in the garden at Ferns, 1912

Katharine and Mother at Ferns, 1912

Our driveway leading to Ferns.

Chapter Three
THE GARDEN

Grundy ruled the garden like a grand vizier. He saw to it that weeds were rooted out almost before they had had a chance to declare themselves. His flower-pots were washed with the same care that Louisa bestowed upon the Rockingham tea-service; no pleasant patina of moss or lichen must ever attach to one of them. The greenhouse where he grew the peaches, so lovely when they were just coming ripe and drops of water from the evening spraying glistened on their rosy contours, was kept as sacred as a mosque where the worshipper must put off his shoes and enter with specially slippered feet; and indeed its floor, paved with hard purple tiles, was so clean that slippers might well have seemed more appropriate than garden boots. I dared not pick a flower or eat a strawberry without permission. Once a bold friend of mine offered to show me how to make blackamoor dolls with red petticoats from the big poppies in mother's herbaceous border. You bent back the petals round the stalk so that the black centre stood up clear for a head and then you made a girdle with a blade of grass. It sounded a fascinating pursuit, but I was in two minds what to do. I knew that it was no use asking leave from Grundy to pick poppies for such a purpose and to do it without leave was a trespass whose audacity would be measured up by Grundy's searing tongue if he found out. But I was ashamed of my position and wouldn't confide it to my libertarian friend. So the poppies were duly picked with me keeping a secret and fearful eye in the potting-shed direction lest Grundy should emerge. He did emerge and saw me standing well off the path and on the soil of the border. Brandishing a garden broom, he chased me across the lawn and down the drive until I found refuge in a remote shrubbery near the road, whence panting and wary I made my way back to the house behind friendly bushes.

But fear of Grundy could not prevent me from enjoying the garden and identifying it with my dream self, so that it made the heart of my existence. There was plenty of space where I could roam unchecked, the sloping lawns, the rhododendron shrubberies, the wild bits where the naked sandstone shouldered out of the soil, the dell which was an odd little ravine through which a streamlet must once have wandered down the Edge, the field below the lawn where I was convinced that I could shoot a rabbit with my bow and arrows if I got up early enough and caught it while the dew was still on the grass. I had my particular coign at the top of the rocky bluff opposite the billiard-room windows and from there I could descend as a famished explorer for a hunk of bread and butter with a slice of fresh cheese laid on it which Rose, the cook, would sometimes hand out through the larder window. Or I could retire there when things were not going too well in the world of reality and become an exiled Jacobite chieftain in sapphire-studded armour; the sartorial anachronism did not worry me and I would spend minutes of dreamy anxious thought deciding what precious stones would make the seemliest encrustation on my suit of mail.

But as often as not the world of reality was a good one and every summer in the garden it occupied me more and more. There were trees to climb with the same bold friend who had made the poppy dolls. She lured me to the topmost branches of the big cedar of Lebanon which overlooked the herbaceous border with the kitchen garden beyond it. Up there we could recline in a sort of branchy hammock swaying gently and, so far as I was concerned, a little fearsomely, as the wind stirred the forked bough. Then I could ride my bicycle at speed from the carriage sweep in front of the house round the loop of drive below the rocky bluff and down the long reach with the tennis-court below on the right and trees and shrubs on the left, to a right-angled bend where the drive turned suddenly to emerge between beech trees in a level run out on to the road. The game, of course, was to get round the right-angled hook without a toss. And I had my own garden near the big cedar tree. Pocket money went on stocking it and sometimes Grundy was in generous mood and helped with plants or a rose bush. He tried hard to teach me to keep my tools clean and I certainly had an object lesson in his own which shone like polished cutlery on the potting-shed walls. I wish he could know that at least he succeeded so well that I have always felt guilty when putting away a spade or a trowel with mud caked on it, as if I had insulted a fine tool with slovenly and disrespectful behaviour. For Grundy mellowed with the years and mother's influence and I bear him no grudge for his early terrorism. Indeed, towards the end of his life he was so gentle and forbearing when my own small children came to stay at Ferns that I used to feel almost jealous for my own past!

My garden had a small pergola with climbing roses and a clematis over it and below a brick-flagged path which I had made. On one side of that was a rockery and on the other a mixed flower-bed. I think I was encouraged to become a gardener by 'Meme', my nurse, or rather 'the lady who looks after you' as she preferred that I should describe her to strangers. She was the daughter of an Indian Cavalry major who had fought in the Mutiny and was generally a romantically lit figure in the background of my imaginative life - and of hers, too. She had been 'born at sea' during a storm in a troopship going to South Africa - more romance. Her mother was a well-born county lady from the south who had suffered much in mental and physical health from the hard life she had led as an officer's wife in the sixties and seventies of the last century, knocking about the world and bearing a large family and later trying to make a home and bring up the children at one time in Devonshire and at another on the west coast of Scotland after the major had retired, lost his money and was struggling ineffectively to make a living at one thing or another. So Meme was the typical nursery governess of Victorian times, better born than her charge, having been sent out to earn that living without training or education, because it was the only living that she could earn and retain her standing as a 'lady'. Her first place was in a busy doctor's family where she had no proper times off and was generally put upon and overworked. One year, I believe, they cancelled her sole holiday to suit their own convenience and long after, when I was grown up, she told me without rancour but with a pathetic wistfulness that on Saturday evenings she would be kept working alone in the nursery until eleven at night ironing and goffering the starched dresses and frills of her charges so that next day they might go to church in seemly Victorian rig. I doubt whether the irony of that ever occurred to Meme any more than presumably it did to her employers. They were all Christians together, yet she would never have thought to apply to her own position the story of the snatched grains of wheat nor remembered against her slave-drivers the tart rejoinder which ended the argument. For Meme was meek and unresentful in a beautiful way that would earn her the kingdom of heaven but could only exasperate people who have learned to combine and fight for their better conditions on earth.

I expect, too, that she would have thought such fighting unbecoming to a lady. And she had no professional pride. She did her job as well as she could because she always grew very fond of her charges and because she had a strong moral conscience. But if she had understood, even vaguely, that different conscience which a person has in doing good work well for the sheer sake of the work she could hardly have preferred so indeterminate a designation as 'the lady who looks after you' to the name of her job, however humble it might seem. In short, as the product of a social system Meme was one pretty damning comment on the civilization into which I was born, but as a human being she was like thin panned gold, and I thought her very nearly perfect. I don't think I loved her so much as I loved my mother, but I certainly felt more intimate and easy towards her. She was short and she had silky smooth black hair parted in the middle and brown eyes as soft and trustful as a dog's.

She had a fairly easy time with us and plenty of opportunity to

Meme

follow her own devices with me in tow. I associate her with the garden more than anywhere, for she had a lovely imagination and as we worked and played there she would tell me fairy stories, some of which she had made up herself, with a conviction which communicated itself to a small listener from the first to the last word. Her fairy stories were the stuff of poetry; the magic of

> How many miles to Babylon?
> Three score and ten,
> Can I get there by candle-light?
> Yes, and back again.

was laid on them. And sometimes she told real stories of her girlhood life in Scotland, as good in their different way as the fairy ones. That was where I got the material for my Jacobite dreams, for Meme was devoted to Bonnie Prince Charlie and we set him amongst the lochs and mountains of the western coast which she made as real and grand to me as they were to her, and we shed a tear together when I discovered one day from a little tartan-bound biography which I had acquired that our hero had ended his days in drink and defeat at Rome. But she liked the beauty of small things also. We searched for birds' eggs and we fed the tits and robins somewhat to Grundy's disgust, and on one occasion she brought home from her holiday a pair of fledglings which we managed to nurse through their babyhood until they grew up into a couple of brat-like sparrows and ungratefully flew away.

I was not quite nine when she left and I have never since suffered quite the same feeling of desolation that I did when I knew that she was going. I suppose I needed a wider and more formal teaching than she could give and I suspect, too, that I was getting rather too obstreperous for her gentle handling. So I only had her for three years in the Ferns garden, but the fact that I associate her with it so strongly shows how deep must have been the impress she made. That easy phrase: 'It is a privilege to have known so and so' loses its triteness when I apply it to Meme. It is a privilege to have lived those years when my own burgeoning mind was tender to every impression close to an imagination which was as guileless and fresh as the drops of dew on the flowers she taught me to see and so childlike that I never had the least difficulty in following wherever she led.

I suppose all this accounts for why I find it harder, as I do, to detach myself from the garden and see it as the home of the grown-ups than I find it to stand away from the house. Yet father and mother gave the garden an unfaltering affection and little by little they humanized Grundy so that the flowers became, if not quite familiar friends at least loved personalities rather than the mannequins of a dress parade. But, curiously enough, they never seemed to want to work in the garden with their own hands, though father sometimes went around with a pruning-hook on Sunday mornings. The feel of soil running through the fingers, of a loaded basket of apples at harvest, the sense of fulfilment when a nursling plant has been bred up to sturdiness, these did not appeal to them. Their interest was rather visual and constructive. They saw with sensitive perception, as all good gardeners do, that a garden has a character and temperament of its own derived from climate and soil, contours and views beyond its borders and that a gardener's art consists in drawing out that temperament and character, in moulding and tending it so that its intrinsic qualities may be fully expressed.

I think that mother had most of the new ideas for the garden. It had been rather neglected before we came and was much overgrown with gloomy-leaved rhododendrons whose magenta blooms, when they bloomed at all, she disliked. These were mostly cut down to open up the form of the land and the boles of the forest trees, the vistas and the long views. My guess is that she thought first of clearing the mess of shrubs from the rocky bluff where I had my hideout and planting the ledges and pockets with London pride and whiterock, with aubretia and yellow alyssum and great creamy cascades of arenaria. And it was she who created the long broad herbaceous border which in summer time was a glory of Ferns. As the years went by and her experience grew, Grundy filled it thicker and thicker with clumps of lupin and phlox and delphinium, with poppies and tall helianthemums and globe-flowers and geums, set off by crimson-leaved scarlet-flowered lobelias. In front, she had squat flowers mostly bedded out, violas and scented pinks and jaunty Tom Thumb nasturtiums. She did not believe that there can be discords of colour where flowers are concerned, so the result was a riotous mêlée which even Grundy's disciplinary measures could hardly regiment, glorious to see on days when sunshine darted and danced over the reds and yellows and whites and blues, but more splendid yet on certain clouded days when the flowers glowed with quiet intensity in the heavy light. Until the last summer of her life, mother cared for that border with an increasing love. When she died in mid-August, I cut armfuls of the flowers and wired and trussed them together so that they covered the coffin from head to foot. I could think of nothing else to do for her; it seemed the only natural tribute I could pay.

On an exceptionally clear Saturday or Sunday, father would take any visitors who were with us up the tower. He liked the immense view and to pick out and place the distant landmarks. Quite often we could see the Berwyn hills of Wales on the horizon and occasionally, far beyond through a gap, a tiny blue wedge which father had plotted carefully on the map and was certain must be the Great Orme Head, eighty miles away.

Much nearer, rising from the plain, were the Peckforton Hills and the silhouette of Beeston castle, but still far enough to take the translucent blue of distance except sometimes after a storm when they looked like shadow shapes against a lighted screen. Only ten miles away, it was easy to spot the church spire of Bowdon rising from its hill; Bowdon was the chief residential rival to Alderley Edge for Manchester families and was said to be more intellectual while we were better at games. My grandparents lived there. Then, beyond Bowdon turning through the circle towards the north, father would point out Rivington Pike above Bolton where the grim Pennines came down to the plain. Sometimes we could pick out the Bolton chimneys like delicate pencils of grey. But Salford and Manchester we could not see, nor the moors above dark Woodhead and the High Peak, because they were hidden by a shoulder of the Edge. I liked plotting the distant view with father, but I liked better the bird's-eye prospect of our own garden. I could gaze down into the topmost branches of the tall lime trees near the front door whose height seemed measureless when I stood beside their trunks and looked up through the shimmering layers of leafage. Just beyond them I could see from a new angle my hammock branch on the big cedar of Lebanon with the sprayed colour of mother's herbaceous border below. I could look right into my lair on the rockery top from which there was a small rock-climb down to the drive on the farther side. But that couldn't be seen and the drive only emerged, after its loop round the rockery, alongside the tennis-court and then vanished again between the two rows of beech trees at the bend where I made my cycling tests. They were young trees, not quite arching overhead and incredibly lovely in spring when they were in brilliant leaf, untouched by the creeping grime from Manchester which gradually smirched them a little during the long summer.

When I turned my roving eyes across the lawn which fell away over the breast of the Edge so that it seemed you might throw a stone straight into the village, I could see a corner of the dell; and in the last quarter of the circle I could look down into the stable yard with the big stone coachhouse and stables and the loft and Grundy's cottage and the pigeon-house completing a court. The pigeon loft was empty which was a pity, but pigeons have messy habits and the stable yard was scrubbed with an enormous broom into a pride of cleanliness every Saturday morning. Before that the stable-boy went round with a knife and slaughtered any weeds that showed up between the setts.

Beyond our boundary there were neighbours' houses all around, half hidden in trees and pleasantly fitting into the folds of the Edge. Across the rockery you caught a glimpse of the Crewdsons' roofs, beyond the cedar, the Bles's and Schills', and over our stable yard, there was the

Pilkingtons' cream-brick tower with St Mary's Cliff below, an odd architectural concoction of sandstone and purple brick and black and white gables.

Mother and father shared out their pleasure in the garden. The back drive to the top road and the front drive to the main Macclesfield road which met at the house became a short-cut highway for half a dozen neighbours on their way to or from the village. And any who were intercepted en route were always asked to come and take a look at the border. Flowers and vegetables were taken in to Manchester hospitals, fruit was sent by post to friends and relatives in special baskets so that grapes or peaches should not be damaged. And no premature baby could have been snuggled into its cotton-wool jacket more carefully than Grundy wrapped up in cotton-wool his precious peaches and grapes. At first he didn't much like it that so much should be given away; and with some justification. For he may have felt that he had given his skill and labour to growing the fruit and flowers whereas father and mother had only given money and interest; besides, their friends got the gifts and not his. This point of view they would have found difficult to appreciate, since he who owned the means of production clearly owned the product and had the right to distribute it. So it was hard lines on Grundy that he should have been blamed for selfishness when his attitude stemmed perhaps from some much deeper complex of roots in the social system to which they all belonged. However, mother's generous spirit and care to get him interested in the various recipients steadily broke down his reluctance and in the end I think he really enjoyed filling a hamper or cutting a great bunch of flowers or putting up a smaller basket for mother to take to some friend in the village. It is a picture that I often have of her, setting out down the drive with her sturdy purposeful walk and the basket of fruit in her hand.

She was a natural giver, but also she had a sense of noblesse oblige towards those who were in a less fortunate economic position than herself - not that the recipients of fruit and flowers were necessarily pinched economically; often it was just that they did not have such prolific gardens as hers and would enjoy some little luxury they could not grow for themselves. But I do not think that she ever worried about her 'right' to the way of life which the economics of capitalism had made possible for her. 'The rich man in his castle, the poor man at his gate' each had difficulties and troubles, and mother would spend herself to give help or pleasure if she crossed into the orbits of their lives, but God had ordered their estates as the hymn concluded and it never occurred to her that these could or should be altered. They were accepted in the sense that an assumption is axiomatic or 'given' for the solution of some proposition in

Euclid. Thus the problem of human relations had to be solved for each individual as well as possible within the set terms. Humanity in the mass was too vague and abstract a conception to interest her and her imagination and sympathy were quite untouched by visions of vast social change. Great phrases like 'Man was born free but is everywhere in chains', which a few years later fertilized mine and caused me to question one by one all the social and most of the moral values in which I had been brought up, would have seemed to her mere meaningless rhetoric. Moreover, she hated party politics because she believed in men rather than measures, because she disliked the 'arena' atmosphere and particularly because her sensitivity could not stand the crude and ungracious 'personalities' of election times. Yet for individual human beings she felt a passionate interest and in the climate of a concrete situation her sympathy flowered wonderfully, welled up too strongly sometimes for her own peace of mind. Yet her insight had odd little limitations. For instance, she felt really sorry for Jane, a young cook we once had, who insisted on marrying a lad with a poor job. She could not see that Jane might prefer a husband and home of her own to the easy and pampered servitude of Ferns. For weeks before the wedding mother would refer to it: 'She has been so spoilt here; how she will miss the food and the space and all the hot water and baths. She doesn't know what she is letting herself in for.'

So far as that went Jane, no doubt, knew a good deal better than mother and had put the material benefits of Ferns in the balance and bravely found them light.

But then, again, mother could show a sensitive and beautiful comprehension of some little circumstance that really mattered, but would have gone unobserved by most people on account of its surface triviality. During the war an elderly and simple couple, neighbours of ours, were summoned to a base hospital in France to see their son who was dangerously wounded. Mother packed up a basket of provisions with a thermos of coffee and another of soup.

'You see,' she said to me, 'they are so troubled and bewildered, they will never think of taking food. Besides, I don't think they've ever been abroad before and they won't understand how to fend for themselves.'

I don't know what mother said to them, but I do know that when she handed over the package, the thoughtfulness and compassion which prompted her would somehow be handed over too, so that they could go off in better heart. The postman was another example of her beautiful care for human beings when her imagination was touched; not the postman who brought our letters but the postman who cleared the pillar-box a couple of hundred yards up the road. Mother fell into conversation with him one day when she was posting her mail. People talked easily to mother on account of her genuine and sympathetic interest in their affairs, so without prying she could often uncover the springs of another person's life. In the postman's case it transpired after five minutes' chat that he was cigarette smoking to the financial tune of something like a fifth of his total weekly wage. He was a married man with a young family and knew he could not afford it without trenching on their amenities, even necessities, but he confessed that he had not the self-discipline to cut down. So he and mother talked it over and he made her a promise and she, in return, promised to meet him regularly at the pillar-box and hear how he was faring. For weeks she kept that tryst. But she had her reward, for the postman held to his undertaking, leaning trustfully on her support and encouragement at their weekly confabulations, until he could say that he was all right and that there would be no more family deprivations. I can see mother turning in at the back gate after one of those conferences, walking a little pensively and on her face the recollected look which always took possession of it when she saw her way certainly in some problem of human conduct whether for herself or for others. She would pause at the border on her way to the house and with the same expression still firm on her face would enjoy the riotous harlequinade of flowers before she went indoors. Or she would turn aside to the greenhouses to look for Grundy, and as she talked to him her mouth and eyes would gently lose that recollected air and become animated and immediate while she discussed the destination of the next basketful of fruit or flowers or planned the insertion of fresh patches of colour into that already crowded border.

Mother 1912, in Ferns Garden.

Ferns garden

The drive, Ferns

Father, Mother and Patou.

Tormenting Grundy!

Chapter Four
BACKGROUND FOR FATHER

Father and mother brought two very different traditions to the making of Ferns. Father brought the tradition, if tradition be the due word, of a rising Manchester family, proud of its achievements, proud of its education, whose motto might well have been: 'The world's mine oyster which I with sword will open', except that in the eighteen-seventies it was not cold steel but their brains that he and his brothers were whetting in order to open the oyster. And the process was going on against the Manchester background of business struggle in which their father was engaged as an alert and original engineer and against a home background of fervent Evangelicanism or rather Nonconformism. It was not the harsher and more extreme variety which forbade all amusements to the young, for after they grew up the theatre and other enjoyments were tolerated, but none the less there was a pretty heavy discount on carefree expansiveness and lightness of heart. And the high-spirited sons at any rate must surely sometimes have felt that their parents' constant preoccupation with the progress of their souls and expressed belief that every happening which touched them was specifically designed by Providence as a discipline or a gift for the family made them like plants in a religious forcing-house.

Mother, on the other hand, brought to Ferns the tradition of a long-secured and easy family position, industrial now, but with memories which went back to the ownership of land and carried into the present a feudal and personal sense of responsibility. Noblesse oblige was a favourite tag on mother's lips and she did not mean it in any snobbish sense. She meant quite simply that the better the hand you have been dealt the greater your obligation to play it finely and unselfishly and with dignity. I used to get rather tired of noblesse oblige when I was young, and after I grew up it seemed to me that as a working precept to solve the problems of my world as it had emerged from the 1914-18 war it was about as adequate as a pea-shooter would be to disable a tank. But then ardent young reformers of society cannot wait for personal reforming. They are in too much of a generous hustle and must create their Utopias by mass production methods. For them a life of personal beauty seems to drop into the pool of society without radiating ripples that alter the pool. And it seemed to me, as I saw the slum areas of Manchester mirrored in it, that the pool needed a good deal of alteration.

Noblesse oblige is the ideal of chivalry, but it is also the moral counterpart of good craftsmanship, of the craftsman's responsibility to the thing he creates; and it goes with an age of slow timing. So now that I come to think of it I see that it was not really I and my contemporaries who liquidated noblesse oblige; it was father's men, the technicians and the managers, the remote directors and the financiers who made the big impersonal firms. For better for worse, they tore the surviving roots of feudalism out of industry and with those roots went the sense of personal obligation on the part of a master to his men, an obligation which had operated with the best of the old masters. And with it, too, as the processes of industry became more and more specialized and apparently disconnected, went the sense of personal obligation to your craft. They substituted production on an endless belt, twist the screw here and tighten the bolt there as the grinning aimless bit of some unimagined machine passes your place, for the creative satisfaction of the workman who himself translates the whole idea, or at least some intelligible part of the idea, into material shape. Father understood very well and regretted what was being done to the souls of the mass production workers; I have often heard him discuss the dilemma, but he had no solution to offer any more than his successors have a solution. Perhaps the only solution that can lend dignity to the job of the mass production workers is the spirit of the noble Benedictine motto, Laborare est orare, and we are as far as or further from accepting that solution than we have ever been since first the ideals of Christendom were set up as a goal and a cement for the societies of men.

So noblesse oblige and all that it stands for has come down to me with mother's mark and mother's connotation. I think that even as a child I was somehow aware of the feudal sense in mother's make-up, though of course I could not analyse it. And I was aware, too, that father did not have it. But at home he accepted it from mother; indeed it was mother's tradition far more than father's which set the tone for Ferns. But that was mostly because it suited father personally better than his own, easing his strung temperament, for mother's tradition was pervaded and warmed by a generous Irish glow which must have seemed like southern sunshine compared with the solemn light of his own background. And yet mother had, too, a grave and gentle strain of Puritanism which also laid its light upon Ferns.

My English great-grandfather was, I believe, a mill-owner in the early eighteen hundreds and my great-grandmother was the daughter of a stonemason from Bury. This kind of union was common enough in the opening unstratified social phases of the Industrial Revolution when masters and men shifted their positions from one generation to the next and when the distinction between them was economic much more than social. But there was always an aristocracy of commerce distinct from the social rough and tumble of industry and there were, too, within the rough and tumble stable families who had drifted into industry from commerce or the land and who gave it its feudal touch - families like our neighbours the Pilkingtons whom I shall come to describe later on. I know nothing about my great-grandfather's people, but my guess is that he must have come from such a family, because his father refused absolutely to ratify his choice or receive his lady. He was told that if he married her he would be cut off with the proverbial shilling. Being a weak-kneed fellow he did not. He died when his son was only three. So I could say with some pride that grandfather had started from scratch or indeed at handicap odds were it not that, untrue to the proper lines of a Manchester romance, his father, having played the subservient son, had been able to make a money provision for the family. Still it was very nearly scratch, my great-grandmother had a struggle for there were three girls as well as the boy to bring up and she was left to herself but for the supporting friendship of the minister of the Rusholme Road Congregational Chapel who must, I think, have been responsible in the rôle of family adviser for what chances the young people got. They lived in a humble street off Oxford Road, and of Oxford Road I shall write later, but grandfather was kept at school until he was sixteen, an unusual length of schooling in the circumstances, and there can have been no real lack of money for when he left he was apprenticed for five years to an engineering firm where he had to pay a premium of £400 and received no wages. When he was twenty-four he was able to buy himself a partnership, so his chance to get on was assured for he was not afraid of hard work and had a talent, some have since thought almost a genius, for engineering invention which was much easier to exploit in the eighteen-forties than it is today. I have been told about him in those eighteen-forties when, as little more than a youth and alone at the works, he clanged the gates to and held his fortress against the threats of a crowd of Chartists who were marching through Manchester drawing the plugs of boilers as they went so as to put mills and factories out of action.

Business - the erection of mills and machinery - used to take grandfather over the Pennines into Yorkshire riding on horseback the bleak road which breaks over the moors above Oldham and dips again for Huddersfield along a valley whose smile is never lusty or gay, but always straining through tight lips. He would be making for Skipton where the green of the dales is freer though still bound in by grey stone walls. And at Skipton he wooed and won my grandmother whom he had already met when she was paying a visit in Manchester. She was a Dewhurst and her family spun cotton thread, but the land was in their blood, for two or three generations back they had been yeomen farmers in Wharfedale. They, too,

Grandmother Alice Hopkinson, née Dewhurst

Grandfather John Hopkinson (1824-1902)

Albert and Olga Hopkinson with their children, together with Mother and Katharine.

knew the turmoil of the Industrial Revolution from the employers' side. Their mill had been burned by desperate hand-operatives during those bitter years of changeover to machine production. But the Dewhursts held on and prospered. Only the other day I met a Yorkshireman who reminded me how my great-uncle John Bonney, the grand old man of the firm in its nineteenth century heyday, used to hold a conference every Saturday with his assembled travellers after their week's journeying. John Bonney heard their reports himself, the tale of their successes and failures, the comparisons between their samples and goods produced by other firms. Then, if it was found that a rival firm had turned out something better in any particular line, the brains and energy of the Dewhurst mill were mobilized and kept in action until once again the rival had been outstripped. So, when I read books like Charlotte Brontë's *Shirley* or Phyllis Bentley's *Inheritance*, which picture the lives of those long dead mill-owners of the Yorkshire dales, they are more real to me than literature for my own blood can answer for their truth.

Children came thick and fast to grandfather and grandmother, thirteen of them all told of whom ten survived to manhood and womanhood, five sons and five daughters. It was a hard life for grandmother, the pregnancies succeeded one another with clockwork regularity, there was not overmuch money to spare and poor health kept her nerves constantly at tension. Small wonder that when I first remember her in the early nineteen hundreds it was as a very old and rather remote invalid lady, formidable because she was nearly stone deaf, and holding court in her armchair in the plush and mahogany morning-room at Inglewood. Yet grandmother was not much over seventy then. She had a fine Victorian mind, planted four-square on Milton and Wordsworth, the Pilgrim's Progress and the Authorized Version, but she had never won leisure enough to develop its powers. She loved the English language, and if in my later day I was brought up on Milton and Wordsworth that was because father in his turn had been brought up on them. But I doubt if grandmother ever regretted when she looked back that all her energy had been given to her family. The quiverful - as she would have called it - of home-devoted daughters and tall and handsome and able sons was her life's work, her creation, and she looked upon it and found it good. She was tremendously proud of her sons - such fervid soul- searchings had gone in the past on her and grandfather's part to their shaping - but her pride was perhaps not so good for them, and worse for them still their sisters were led to treat them almost with adulation. Oddly enough, her pride seemed to culminate in the success of their secular careers.

Pride apart, it must have been a relief to grandfather and grandmother when it became clear that John and Alfred, the two elder sons, and Edward, the fourth, could deal with their own scholastic careers by picking up the necessary scholarships. Scholarships took John and Edward to Cambridge and Alfred to Oxford, and I think they knew how fortunate they were. Few lads from their section of society went up to the university in the seventies of last century. John, the eldest, emerged in 1871 as Senior Wrangler in the Mathematical Tripos and first Smith's Prizeman. According to custom he would at once have been offered a fellowship of his college, Trinity. But the presentation to a fellowship still involved written adhesion to the Articles of the Church of England and John refused to sign. The Hopkinsons were quite willing to slip into the Church of England when they felt like it and most of them did at a later date, but no power on earth would have forced any one of them to surrender an inch of religious principle in order to win honour or a job or to satisfy the law. However, the fellows of Trinity who had no wish to lose him met and resolved that the Thirty-nine Articles and not the young man from Manchester must go. Subscription to religious articles should no longer be required as a condition of proceeding to a fellowship. So John became the casus belli for the final fight in this country for religious equality before the law. 'They made a little lion of me', he is reputed to have said, 'and made me roar against the disabilities of the Nonconformists.' The battle for the abolition of university tests raged on for a year and Mancunians took their full share in it. The Northern Church Defence Association passed a resolution exhorting its members to use all their efforts to keep in force the existing exclusion of Dissenters. The *Manchester Guardian* replied with a stinging article in the course of which it castigated the shocking taste of Manchester and Salford Tories who had chosen to pass this resolution on the very day which Manchester had selected to honour her obscure but brilliant son, thereby implying that they approved the withholding of the university's reward. And an angry peer wrote to the press vowing that no son of his would ever be sent to the universities to mix with Dissenters. One wonders whether he held to his oath when a year later the university tests were abolished by law.

Having made this unexpected contribution to history, John swept into the half-explored realm of applied electricity. His work was not the spectacular sort which gets stories in histories of science for boys, but his profession knew him as the near peer of Faraday and Lord Kelvin. He was killed with three of his children in a mountaineering accident in the High Alps, but about that I will write in its due place.

Alfred was a humanist and he has written of his undergraduate days in the Oxford of Jowett and Pater and T. H. Green and Ruskin in a charming chapter of his book of memoirs, Penultima. He became a barrister and later Vice-Chancellor of Manchester University. Charles,

'Uncle Charlie' of the Christmas parties, the third son, had a steadier and quieter mind and his brain was a less brilliant instrument. He stayed in Manchester to support his father in the family engineering works and later became a consulting engineer. The fourth was my father, Edward. Albert, the fifth, came near the finish of the family when finances were easier, so he was able to go to Cambridge and study medicine without having to win a scholarship. And I think that both he and Charlie gained a certain gentleness and restfulness of disposition just because they did not have to live off their own wits and depend on their own wits at an age when any failure would have seemed to them the sack of their ambitions. Perhaps this accounted for the difference I used to notice at Christmas between Uncle Charlie's smiles and father's.

John was too much absorbed and insulated by his science to be personally ambitious, but father and Uncle Alfred were charged up with ambition, and their mother encouraged them by her admiring contemplation of their careers, not to the increase of their happiness. It was also, I think, indirectly thanks to this attitude of hers that they almost worshipped brains and too readily judged a successful life in terms of getting to the top of the tree, any tree, political, scientific, ecclesiastical, military, commercial, academic. An odd sideline, this attitude of granny's to the main religious theme of her life. And yet it was not really inconsistent. It was the Nonconformist version of St Benedict's motto, a version which in its new application would certainly have appeared strange and perhaps repellent to the monks who had deared and drained and tilled Yorkshire dales and sent up their prayers from grey abbeys beside trout streams. For the Nonconformists of the nineteenth century tried to contract for the kingdom of heaven by means of the laborious days they lived on earth. And success was a yardstick of hard work and therefore all too easily a sign that you had lived well and frugally in the sight of God. Their hopes were contained in a very literal and concrete interpretation of the Parable of the Talents. They were all on the side of the man who had multiplied the most the talents entrusted to his care. I am quite sure that granny, who had indeed a rare beauty of spirit, would have been horrified had she been directly confronted by any such philosophy, but I am equally sure that there it was lurking at the back of hers and grandfather's minds, an influence which moulded their outlook though they never formulated it and were scarcely aware of it. Certainly they would not have had very much sympathy and understanding for an other-worldliness which never measures itself against temporal affairs, the other-worldliness of contemplatives, or in another category of a good many artists. Their other-worldliness showed itself in a conviction that if you are not careful most man-made enjoyments lead to self-indulgence and sin. They were afraid, those nineteenth-century northern Nonconformists, of man's capacity for grand enjoyment which is perhaps his compensation for the doom of Adam. Indeed, they no longer regarded man as a son of Adam working in all humility to transform a curse into a blessing. For them he was a son new-born of 'Capitalism and the Protestant Ethic' slaving at full pressure but with a heedless pride, though they did not recognize it as such, which sometimes changes a blessing into a doom. And the doom for which their philosophy was indirectly responsible was the slum cities of Lancashire. Theirs is a point of view which has been growing upon us westerners ever since the break up of the old mediaeval philosophy, but to it we all owe, even the slum-dwellers in the end, a thousand material benefits, so I suppose we ought not to look their gift horse too closely in the mouth.

Since granny fed her sons with sympathy and admiration it was hardly surprising that sympathy and admiration became almost a necessity to them. Father and Uncle Alfred could only work and play at their best when somebody was making it quite clear to them what fine fellows they were. They wilted in a jostle of cold shoulders and father became gloomy and depressed and Uncle Alfred bitter and depressed. But a climate of admiration and sympathy drew out their natural sweetness of disposition and their charm, like those flowers which will open their petals only to direct sunshine. It was worth admiring and sympathizing with them. They could be so very charming when they were feeling happy, and in those moods their companionship was perfect.

All the children were devoted to their mother and those who lived in or near Manchester, sons and daughters-in-law, daughters and sons-in-law, gathered at Inglewood on Sunday or some evening during the week. I don't know at what stage 'late dinner' had been substituted for the mutton chop and tea to which grandfather used to come home when he was a young man, but it was the settled custom by the time they had moved to Bowdon from Grove House on Oxford Road, and at these meals there crystallized an most matriarchal cult which somehow obscured granny's true humanity and beauty of spirit. Not that I ever attended any of them. I just know their feeling the way one does know the feel of things that happened around one as a child even though one was not a direct participant. My visits to Inglewood were with mother for lunch or tea, setting out from Ferns in the waggonette for the ten-mile drive to Bowdon. The waggonette was uncosy because two sat inside like loose peas in a pod, and the seats were high and flat so that my legs dangled. The monotony of the jogging drive was only broken by the hill at Oversley Ford where Paddy, the horse, had to walk and Godfrey jumped down from the box to save weight. I would beg to clamber out also on

Paddy's account and if, in spite of mother's remonstrances, I could contrive to get back as Godfrey did without the carriage being halted, I used to feel that after all the day had held a tiny spice of adventure. Mother would knit since she hated doing nothing and for the drive home on winter evenings she had fixed up a couple of candle-lamps which drew the green from the upholstery and filled the waggonette with fitful liquid light so that inside it became like an aquarium in which mother and I brooded swathed in our rugs. It would have been nicer outside in the starlight and sharp cold on the box beside Godfrey, but that was not allowed.

Inglewood, unlike the big rambling house above the Antrim shore of Belfast Lough which was mother's home, held no romance for me. I am afraid that the only kick which I got from my visits was the consumption of a particular kind of biscuits which Aunt Mary produced from a tin in the dining-room and which were handed to me well-buttered and succulent. But even so the effect was rather spoilt as I had to be so careful not to make crumbs. Mother told me once that she used to be tired out after taking me to Inglewood when I was small, because she could never forget about me for a minute. It was always: 'Don't touch, Kathie', or 'Take care what you are doing'.

Granny sat with her back to the light on one side of the fire in the morning-room. The heavy curtains and furniture, the big table with its serge tablecloth weighted my spirits and I saw her as it were anchored down in concrete to all that. She wore a creamy knitted shawl falling from her shoulders and a lace cap with heliotrope ribbons - heliotrope was the word, not mauve - from which white curls depended and framed her face. Her face was modelled over splendid bones, the big, rather sad grey eyes deep-set below their lintels, the nose jutting at its arch, the wide, thin-lipped and sensitive mouth easing a chin like carving and a strong bony ridge of jaw.

Aunt Mary hovered near and then I would be led up to granny. From that moment my situation was dominated by granny's speaking tube. Its coil was green and gold and the mouthpiece black vulcanite with a faint sour smell. It was like the serpent which entangled Eve, but whereas Eve was entangled of her own free will we grandchildren must talk to granny down this alarming tube which took away all our ease. We were expected to have a recitation ready, a hymn or a poem. Wordsworth's Ode to Duty was a favourite. I would begin: 'Stern daughter of the voice of God' and granny would say, 'A little louder, my dear'. The next attempt would be a bawl and then granny would stop me again: 'Not so loud; I can't hear the words.' It was hopeless. Anyone finds it difficult to speak into a tube and control the voice to a normal conversational pitch, but for a child whose voice isn't much under control at the best of times it is impossible. I never lasted long at the speaking-tube, I was too bad at it, and Aunt Mary would take it from me remarking that granny was tired now. To this day I regret and resent the whole set-up which had been built around granny in her last invalid years, because we younger grandchildren never got through it to the real granny, the sensitive, highly-strung, too introspective young woman who yet had a fountain of gentle fun in her heart ever ready to bubble up and whose spirit had won at last a grave comeliness, disciplined and smoothed where others might have been embittered by the difficult bearing and rearing of thirteen children. My Irish grandmother I could know across the gulf of years as a fellow human being, but my English grandmother I only seem to know at secondhand. Even so I am aware of that particular sort of beauty of the spirit which she had, an austere yet warm light which played over all the harsh and fervent Nonconformist philosophy and touched it to tenderness. It is an outmoded fashion of beauty which has no counterpart in our world.

I cannot remember grandfather and do not propose to write of him merely from hearsay; my Uncles Alfred and Charlie I shall write of again, and of my five aunts there was only Aunt Mary at home, for two had died and the remaining two were married. Aunt Lilian was married to a gentle, yet to us nephews and nieces, sharp-tongued stockbroker in Bristol who loved mountains and built up a magnificent library of rare mountaineering books, some of which are now in my possession. She was by all accounts the gayest of the daughters. There is a letter of hers extant written on her wedding evening from London, amusing for the light it throws on the sentiments correct for a Victorian bride:

'*.... The guard was most kind in keeping the carriage for us and sticking on a reserved label - so it was very much pleasanter as I was able to give way to my feelings which were rather too many for me. However Will was awfully good to me and let me cry my heart out, and then I felt much better and haven't done any more since .... You were awfully brave, Mother darling, and all of you - and it just made all the difference to me, though it was mighty hard work keeping lively and forcing one's own feelings back ..... I am sure he is just everything you could wish. No one could be more loving and considerate than he has been and so far I don't mind being married a bit....*'

Aunt May, the youngest, became Mrs Anson. She had four children, the cousins whom I played with most as I grew up. They lived in Bowdon close to Inglewood except for a spell of several years when they had a large house and garden, glorious for children, in the Lake District, near Keswick. When I was small the Bowdon house rather awed and depressed me because the influence from Inglewood seemed to weigh it down. The drawing-room, so unlike the welcoming drawing-room at

Ferns, was solemn and I would be shown, concealed in a wall cabinet, knick-knacks from eastern lands which had been brought home by missionaries - a room hushed for the suitable entertainment of the missionaries, so it seemed to me. But gradually Aunt May's high-spirited family educated her out of constrained drawing-rooms and into a more liberal outlook on life, and in my early twenties she played on me a practical joke which showed a perhaps new-found astringent humour and which, though it knocked the stuffing out of me very effectively for a couple of hours, raised her many points in my youthful estimation.

I was a guest at a large party collected by the Ansons at a house they had taken in the Lake District, one of a crowd of young cousins and friends of both sexes just let loose from the constrictions of the 1914-18 war. I think Aunt May found us a rather difficult team to control, myself not least, and spent a good many worried hours wondering to what lengths our escapades might lead. So she determined to teach me at any rate a lesson. One morning a note was handed to me written, so it appeared, by a constituent of my father's (he was then the M.P. for the Clayton division of Manchester) in the course of which my correspondent pointed out in no unmeasured terms that my behaviour was not consistent with the dignity required from the daughter of the parliamentary representative of his respected division. He had, so he said, observed the doings of a certain young female and had discovered with disgust her identity. He concluded, so far as I remember, by saying that on his return to Manchester he proposed to complain to my father and if necessary publicize my activities in the division. I spent that morning in a collapse of spirits and a horrified anticipation of repercussions at home. About lunch-time, Aunt May decided to put me out of my misery. She came up to me with her normal gentle smile sharpened to something not far from a sardonic grin and informed me, but with a slight edge on her voice, that she thought I had now had enough and that, in fact, my soldier cousin had written the letter as a leg pull.

As the years have drawn on my friendship with Aunt May has deepened to a trust and love which makes it almost impossible for me to write now while the relationship is still alive of the serious side which was always the foundation and indeed never far from the surface of her being. Her spirit seems to me one of those which are like flowers that unfold slowly and blossom only after a long tight budding, but which when they do bloom show petals so firmly shaped and so gracious in quiet colour and form that always as one passes down the garden path one stops to win a little of their beauty.

Aunt Mary was rather rugged to look at. She had big bones which made her hands and hips and feet angular. She ought to have dressed in rich softening material, velvets or dull satins, but instead she favoured frocks of nondescript stuffs and colours, not too well cut or designed. She ought to have dressed to lead up to her smile. The flesh of her mouth was thin and supple and in repose set in quiet strength, but when she smiled a quiver passed right along her lips and her whole face resolved in clarity and her eyes beamed. She had the sweetest smile of anyone I have ever known, and I think that was because she smiled, not in response to wit or humour or irony, for she distrusted wit and had little humour and did not understand irony, but as a direct expression of some love and sympathy welling up inside her and evoked by some private reaction of her own to what might be going on. But sometimes the quiver of her lips was a little rueful and that was when she felt outside the camaraderie of the young and wanted to be inside. She was a very different proposition from the genial aunts who came to Ferns at Christmas time and I am afraid that as a child, and even long after I was grown up, I found it almost impossible to come to terms with her. For one thing, conversation with Aunt Mary was apt to be conducted on earnest question and answer lines and the young hate to be probed. I remember an occasion soon after I was grown up when she walked me round the garden and interrogated me as to the sort of man I would like to marry.

'Oh, an honest knave, Aunt Mary,' I remarked airily. Aunt Mary chewed the cud of this for a moment and then began her protest and a further attempt to analyse my flippant and incomprehensible predilection. I had really shocked and worried her. Conversation with Aunt Mary always took a moral twist and frequently a religious twist as well and I found it very embarrassing. I could discuss religion in undergraduate fashion with my contemporaries until the cows came home, but somehow with Aunt Mary you were put into that mood of self-consciousness and artificial restraint which a lot of people get at a funeral. And yet Aunt Mary's religion was co-extensive with her life as anyone's religion which is worthy of its premises ought to be. I suppose the real difficulty was that the life and thoughts which were normal to Aunt Mary would have been wildly abnormal for any one of her nephews and nieces. It was not only that her whole life was devoted to 'good works' in Manchester - our neighbour Mrs Schill, for instance, could practise good works and retain a comforting flavour of errant humanity. It was not even that Aunt Mary seemed to make a virtue of austerity. It was much more that she did not express her religion in a way which linked God with the normal beauties and glories and warmths of life, and therefore these seemed to get left out altogether. Perhaps I can explain something of what I mean by recalling the way that she said grace before meals. She made it sound joyless, a constrained expression of gratitude, however sincere, that there was enough on the table to eat. It was never a hearty 'Thank God for good food and good fellowship - thank God for the cook's craft and the hot sun on a vineyard of the Côte-d'or and the vine-dresser's art, for the talk and laughter of friends at your table and the warmth of comradeship.' One could not help feeling that Aunt Mary's Creator, whose earth had nursed the secret sprouting of the petits pois and whose sun was snared in the glow of the burgundy (Aunt Mary was, of course, a teetotaller) might be a little saddened by this lack of appreciation of his gifts. At least that was how I should have felt unless I had modestly taken it for granted that Aunt Mary knew more about her Creator than I did and that therefore he must be a killjoy and a wet-blanket. Not that Aunt Mary was incapable of enjoyment herself or that she really wanted other people to forgo their pleasures. She loved the beauty of wild nature and always encouraged us nephews and nieces in holiday pursuits which involved mountains or the sea. It was rather that she never entered into our enjoyments along lines which did not appeal to herself. Her religion seemed to us young folk like an evangelical Sunday repeated on seven days of the week.

> *Count your blessings, name them one by one,*
> *Count your blessings, see what God has done,*

was a favourite hymn of hers, but the blessings which we nephews and nieces would really like to have said thank you for as we grew up appeared suspect; the larks we had together, the lilting sense of joie de vivre in our young bodies, the excitement when we read some book and crash went a barrier and we marched through into some new realm of the intellect. So instead of saying 'thank you', I, at any rate, was apt to go off rebelliously to bed after an interview with Aunt Mary and relish by myself a piece of Pater's Marius the Epicurean or declaim Swinburne's 'Pale Galilean' lines to the rosebud wall-paper in my room.

I assumed that Christian asceticism is always afraid of pleasure and spurns delight. If I had understood my own mother better, I should have realized that there is another asceticism, one by which gaiety and joie de vivre and intellectual freedom are contained and given shape and form. And if I had known more about Christian philosophy I should have realized that mother's attitude followed its central line and that Aunt Mary's represented a tangent. I should have realized how many battles have been fought and won down the long centuries in order to defend man's gifts of appreciation and enjoyment, in order to maintain the balance of that central line against the tangent makers. And I should, too, have been more charitable about Aunt Mary's tangent since I should have understood it in its historical setting, relating it to Aunt Mary's Puritan heroes and exemplars, relating it also to the other similar tangents which had broken away from the central stream and come to grief sooner or later through lack of nourishment. As it was, my ignorance and consequent intolerance prevented me for years from a full appreciation of the sweetness and sanctity of spirit which really pervaded Aunt Mary's outlook as when brooding mists on a mountain summit are pervaded with silver light before the sun finally dissolves them.

After granny's death Aunt Mary, as I have said, gave her entire life to social work in Manchester. She slaved for the Manchester police and would tramp the slum streets all day from one end of the town to the other, visiting policemen's homes and bringing sympathy and strength to any home which housed tragedy or disaster or even some minor ill. Some of the help might be in cash or kind, but mostly it was not material. She wanted first of all to comfort people's spirits; but of course it all had to be done in the evangelical style and I do not think Aunt Mary would have known in the least how to cope with any problem which had been put up by someone who could not accept a solution in those terms. She was an organizer, too, and spent her evenings in welding the police force by correspondence and administration into a kind of small distinct Christian community with its own esprit de corps and its own tradition. Every summer she brought her police and their wives and babies to Ferns for an 'outing'. They wandered in the garden and sat down in the cleared coach-house to a tea of ham and lettuce and endless plates of bread and butter and seed cake, washed down with heavily sugared liquid from enormous urns. Before they trooped back to the railway station proceedings were terminated by a 'service' at which a number of hymns were sung. I liked the swell of sound in the big coach-house and was specially partial to the crescendo in

Till we meet, till we meet, till we meet
On yonder shore!

You could conjure with Aunt Mary's name among the Manchester police, as I came to know to my advantage, though not exactly to an advantage of which she approved.

There was a railway strike in the late January of 1923. I had been ski-ing in Switzerland and came home to find the car unlicensed and my brother at Ferns with a meeting to attend some miles the other side of Manchester. It would, I thought, be enormous fun to run the gauntlet of half a dozen policemen at the Manchester crossings, and the railway strike plus the alleged importance of Campbell's meeting made a good excuse to have the car out. So off we set, my run-out licence conspicuous on the windscreen. We reached our destination without a hitch and I deposited Campbell. All went well, too, on the return journey through the city. It seemed as if the traffic policemen had been conveniently blinded to the tell-tale hue and shape of the bar across my licence. I was in the suburbs and pulling out for home, the last danger point being a big police station on the main road. As I passed I noticed out of the corner of my eye that there was a policeman standing on the steps. And then an ominous whistle sang out. I decided in a flash that I had never heard a police whistle before, which was true, and that I didn't attach any special meaning to this particular blast, which was not true. I smacked down the accelerator and made for home. Two miles farther on as I drove through the next village I was held up by another policeman standing plumb in the middle of the road. There was no avoiding him and he motioned me to the curb with that peculiar gesture of omnipotence and omniscience which cops affect when they are about to run in a motorist.

'Have you just passed Withington police station?' he said, and he examined the peccant licence.

'Yes' - trying to look as if I wondered what it was all about.

'Didn't you hear the whistle?'

'Well, I heard some sort of a whistle but I didn't know - '

He cut me short, he knew that one.

'Let's see your driving licence.'

I fished it out. By a miracle it was in my pocket and not on my desk at home, and by another miracle it was still current. He studied my name, and then he became suddenly human.

'Hopkinson? Are you any relation to Miss Hopkinson?'

'Rather. She's my aunt,' said I, suddenly seeing a possibility of salvation. And I told my tale about the strike and the meeting.

'Oh,' he almost groaned. 'If you'd only stopped for that there whistle.'

'Well', I said, 'couldn't you possibly let it go this time, now you know the circumstances?'

He kept me in suspense while he went off into a panegyric on Aunt Mary, but when he had finished he shook his head.

'I'm that sorry. I don't like running in her niece. But they rang me from Withington to stop you. It'll have to go through now. But I'll tell you what to do,' and he brightened up. 'You ring up yer auntie and tell her to go to the Town Hall as quick as she can. I reckon she'll get you off.'

It was a hope, but I drove home gloomily all the same. If Aunt Mary couldn't or wouldn't get me off (and you never knew what she would feel about tampering with the august course of justice) the fine would be a heavy one by my financial standards. Perhaps Campbell would go fifty-fifty with me, but even so - I telephoned Aunt Mary. It was not at all easy to explain the situation to her using just the right blend of injured innocence and humble contrition for this flouting of the law. And I think that at the other end of the telephone Aunt Mary was undergoing a moral conflict, torn between her duty to let the law take its course and her sense of family solidarity added to her desire not to have any member of our highly principled clan appear as a defendant in a police court, particularly a local police court. Fortunately for me the family good name won. I believe she spent most of the next day tracking down my summons, and what she said to the authorities I don't know, but she said all that was necessary to quash it. Dear Aunt Mary - if you could only know how grateful I had once been for that excessive and often inconvenient regard which you had for the family name!

It is said that Protestantism breeds social reformers whereas Catholicism breeds saints. Aunt Mary's Protestantism was certainly a hundred percent proof, but she was not even remotely a social reformer. Indeed, after I grew up I found it puzzling to understand how anyone who knew the conditions of the poor in Manchester as well as she did could take so little interest in the politics of social reform. It was useless for mother, who was distrustful rather than oblivious of the solutions of social reform, to say to me in her quiet causa finita manner:

'You can't make people good by Act of Parliament.'

Very likely you couldn't. But I was quite clear that you could prevent people doing a lot of evil by Act of Parliament. If they did not want to be socially just and generous and unselfish of their own accord, you could go a long way by Act of Parliament towards making society, if not the individuals which composed it, behave justly and generously and unselfishly. That might not save an individual soul - it was not a question that very much interested me - but it would save the people of Ancoats and Salford from a great deal of obvious human misery. You could see as plain as a pike staff that Acts of Parliament could get them better houses and a better education and better doctoring and a bit more leisure when they were working and a bit more money when they were past work.

In these discussions I was really up against the old (and unnecessary) collision of function between the saint who gives himself for the love of God to the service of individual men and women and the social reformer who gives, not himself, but his brains and his energy to the service of a cause. So many people must needs take a partisan attitude, favouring one to the detraction of the other. And mother was a backer of the saints because she believed in the kingdom of heaven, whereas I backed the social reformers because I believed in the New Jerusalem here and now in what was left of England's green and pleasant Lancashire after the dark satanic mills had taken their toll of sunshine and clean air and the fresh dew on the fields at dawn.

I see, too, that I had also stumbled on a more fundamental cause of cleavage. I had collided against the uncompromising Christian teaching that the birthright and paramount purpose of a man is to carry his personal integrity unsullied through the adventure of life or in other and more old fashioned words to save his own soul. This was never explicitly stated, but it was implied in mother's and Aunt Mary's attitude of mind. If you believe that men's aspirations and their dreams, their nobilities and their capacities for self-sacrifice are the guarantees and the expressions of a divine birthright, then you cannot at the same time believe that the integrity of mind of a Socrates or the moral and spiritual beauty of a St Francis were implicit in a lump of protoplasmic jelly floating on a fetid sea an indefinite number of aeons ago. And if you do not consider that St Francis and the protoplasm are exactly the same in kind but different only in degree, then it is unlikely that you will be made dizzy by the social crusader's slogan of 'Progress' as the magic marching orders of mankind. You may like the idea of mankind on the march as a metaphor, but it will not take you far because you will want to know before you agree to fall into step exactly where man is marching to at the moment and where he last bivouacked and whether perhaps he is not doing a temporary turn after his own tail or marching through a fog in a circle back to his last starting-place or merely doing a route march for exercise out of sheer exuberance of energy. But you will not see life seriously in terms of a march, however spectacular, from the primeval sea to the Promised Land of a race of demi-gods. Because you will believe not in demi-gods of the uncovenanted future, but in men and women as they are here and now and have been since the dawn of history, men and women who wring your heart with their griefs and their sufferings, men and women who brace your heart with their splendour of devotion, men and women who light your heart with their love and their charity and their humbleness and men and women who break your heart with their arrogance and their cruelty and their lust. You will believe in men and women who will create a foul ugliness or the most glorious beauty and in men and women who will use their minds to confuse the plainest issue or to discover the most difficult truth and split the hardest paradox, because such is the nature which has been conferred upon them.

The beliefs of Christianity are not formulae for the erection of some prefabricated New Jerusalem; but at twenty-one I was firmly convinced that they ought to be, and that was where I fell foul of the philosophy of mother and Aunt Mary. I was baffled and exasperated by this notion that the first duty of a human being is to see after the soul God gave him. It seemed to me the height of egotism, and worse when the rider was added that the conditions in which people had to live were essentially irrelevant to the process. For that seemed to imply a tacit acceptance of social conditions however sordid and evil. If saving your soul was the prime aim of existence and you could do it perfectly well in a slum, then it was only logical to conclude that the people who believed this would not have very much incentive to abolish slums. And to a considerable extent I was right. It is true that the doctrine of personal regeneration does sometimes tend to make those who hold it lukewarm about 'causes' however eager they may be to care for individuals. But conversely, theories of social evolution, whether the New Jerusalem is to be a land fit for heroic amoebas to live in at some climax of their long upward struggle, or more simply the kingdom of heaven on earth, tend to make men neglectful of individuals in their ardour for a cause. The ranks of the social crusaders are not manned as a rule by people who minister to individuals for the love of God. Nor are the ranks of the saints manned as a rule by people who believe in the apotheosis of an amoeba.

Indeed, the saints are the realists and the social crusaders the idealists; and that perhaps is why youth is apt to enlist with the latter. For a belief in the New Jerusalem sorts well with the generous enthusiasms of youth. It is good for the young to handle a bow of burning gold, even though their arrows are tipped, as Blake sang with sublimely unconscious irony, only with the wishful thinking of desire. But it is also important to grow up some time and demand the actual blue-prints of the New Jerusalem. For it is only then that you realize that there are no scale-drawings and that no one has ever seriously intended that there shall be. For the New Jerusalem is not a real city; at best it is a crusader's noble dream, a shadow of those age-old aspirations and visions and nobilities of man projected on to the screen of the future; but too often it is a subconscious device to keep men on the move and distract their attention so that they shall not ask too many questions nor struggle in detail with their circumstances.

I think that I grew up in this regard when many years later I read William Morris's *News from Nowhere*. As I laid down the book I realized with a pang of disillusion two things; firstly that Utopias of this kind are merely escapist dreams since they solve none of the problems of society in terms of actual human nature, and secondly, how I should hate myself to live or have my children live in Morris's Utopia. Because his people could be no longer real men and women since it seemed that they had lost adventurous desire and spurs for endeavour and the salt of suffering. Morris's projected England was a country of static beauty, no more and no less than a lotus-eater's land. In cordibus aruerat. In the hearts and minds of his people those great dynamos which drive human history were silent.

Perhaps if the social crusaders would admit the dreams for what they are they would find the partisans of the saints less sceptical and more co-operative when they appeal for their help in the solution of some specific problem. For the real job of the reformer is strenuous, never ceasing and of desperate importance. There are plenty of specific positions held by the soldiers of evil and ignorance for the social crusaders to assault. There are other positions which we have won from evil and ignorance during the course of long centuries. But always and ever we have to hold and consolidate them. We are learning that there is no respite to sit back and preen ourselves about progress. Surely we are like workers at a dyke ever struggling to keep back the wicked lick of the tide. Here there is a breach to be filled to protect threatened land which we have already reclaimed and elsewhere there is a new sea-wall to build so that we can take in some fresh piece of marsh and sweeten and till it. We need captains and foremen on that job; they are the social reformers. But we need too, and perhaps more desperately, comfort and compassion, cherishment and inspiration. It is given us by the saints. There is no need to make a clash between them. They are all on the job. But the saints are rarer and more precious and their quality is a holy thing.

I think Aunt Mary was very nearly a saint.

When she was elderly and already very deaf she was knocked down by a tramcar while crossing a Manchester street. The injuries were serious and passers-by carried her to the pavement and laid her there until an ambulance could be fetched. Someone called a policeman to the accident and when he came up and knelt beside the torn body to do what he could he recognized her and showed his own distress so plainly that she noticed in spite of her pain. He rolled up his policeman s tarpaulin cape and placed it under her head for a cushion.

'I'm afraid it's very hard, Miss,' he grumbled, 'but it's all I've got.'

Aunt Mary looked up at him and the smile quivered along her lips and her drawn face lightened and relaxed; she had to comfort the policeman.

'Oh, no,' she whispered, 'I think it's the softest pillow I've ever had.'

That story is cherished among the Manchester police. I heard it years after the event from one of the heads of the force. It had been passed along from mouth to mouth and had become almost legendary, but a true legend. I am glad that I can record it here if only so that I may make up a little for the many years during which I misunderstood Aunt Mary's quality - and I think that father would be glad that I should close with it this chapter in which I have tried to describe his family setting.

Mother c1905

Grannie Campbell

Grandpa Campbell

Chapter Five
BACKGROUND FOR MOTHER

Mother's roots were bedded deep in the bitter soil of Irish history. Her forebears, all of whom bore Scottish or English names, were scattered over the north of Ireland having drifted in with one plantation or another. One of them, the Reverend George Walker, Rector of Donoughmore in Co. Tyrone, was a maker of history. In 1688 when Londonderry was invested by the army of James II, and the Governor, Colonel Lundy, was anxious to capitulate even before the siege had begun because he was short of supplies and pusillanimous by nature, the Rev George supported the citizens whose ardent wish was to defend their town and raffled the troops who were bewildered and discontented because they feared they were being deserted by their officers. He slipped the cowardly Governor out of town in disguise and proceeded to organize and conduct the defence himself. He and his garrison held 'Derry for a hundred and five days of semi-starvation, and on the hundred and fifth they had left to eat 'only nine lean horses and among us all one Pint of Meal to each man'. On that day, the Rev George preached a great sermon in the cathedral exhorting the defenders to maintain and increase their courage and resolution since 'they need not doubt but that God would at last deliver them from the difficulties they were under'. And then, as the weak and weary garrison came out of church, suddenly they sighted three English ships sailing up the Lough, two merchantmen and an escorting frigate. There was a great boom across the mouth of the River Foyle placed there by the investing army to prevent the arrival of any relieving ships. The Mountjoy and the Phoenix crashed through the boom in the teeth of the enemy's gunfire and fetched up in the harbour. 'Derry was free - and the Rev George, who had probably done as much as any one man to establish the House of Orange squarely in these islands, went quietly back to his parish, remarking with a deprecating modesty that 'the part he had acted in this service might more properly have been done by other hands, but that necessity had thrown it upon him and would he hoped justify him before God and the World from the irregularity of interesting himself in such an affair, for which he was neither by Education nor Function qualified'.

Another of mother's forebears, Alexander McCulloch, was killed at the battle of Ballynahinch whilst fighting for the United Irishmen during the '98; and mother used often to tell me as a child the story of how her great-grandmother, carrying her baby in her arms, took refuge in the little church at Killala from the soldiers of the Revolution when Hoche made his landing in 1796.

The McCullochs were my grandmother's people. Originally they had owned good land in Co. Down, some of it land from which considerable wealth has since been derived from quarrying rights which I believe are now owned by an aristocratic Anglo-Irish house. But the McCullochs were typical Irish squires. They frittered away their land in payment for gambling and other semi-reputable debts, and by the end of the eighteenth century they had drifted west to Co. Mayo, whence my grandmother came back to Ulster to marry Mr John Campbell of Mossley, Co. Antrim. You could tell at once that granny was not a northerner. She had an exquisite skin, the gift of that emollient air of the western seaboard, and she had the soft western speech; I can hear it still in the tiny lilt which she used to put into the long 'a' of my name - Katharine, which other people made short and hard.

The Campbells, too, had once owned land in Co. Down. I do not know how or when they came to Ireland, but I suspect that a certain Captain Campbell, who fought in the army of William of Orange and was afterwards granted Irish land in recognition of his services, may have been their forebear. At any rate, at some time or another, they had come from Argyllshire, for they had the crest of the Campbells of Argyll, a boar's head on a platter with the lovely motto Ne obliviscaris. Towards the end of the eighteenth century one, Michael Campbell, was living as a country squire at Ballyalton and I think it must have been his sons who decided that the life of a small squire did not offer golden prospects to young men of enterprise and that they would find better openings in the rising business world of Belfast. They began to spin linen thread at Mossley a few miles outside the town and founded one of those feudal family industries whose atmosphere is directly derived from the relation of a squire to his tenants.

The family lived in a pleasant Regency house with the mill to one side of it and the mill dams a stone's throw away. Sons grew up to take over from their fathers in the same spirit that their ancestors had taken over from father to son the little estate at Ballyalton. Capitalism at Mossley has never become a rank growth fed on the unanalysable manure of financial ramification; it is still at the feudal and human stage. There are no semi-absentee directors whose criterion of value is the dividend they must produce to hold the market price of their shares and content a scattered host of shareholders whose absenteeism is total. The master at Mossley is an individual known by his worth and his idiosyncrasies to all his workpeople and the workpeople are individuals known each of them by name and character and function to the master. His children know the mill almost as well as he does. When I used to stay with my grandmother, my cousins and I would spend hours at Mossley. And that was years after the family had left Mossley House for higher ground above the Lough, for my grandmother had been threatened with T.B. and Mossley was thought too low- lying to be safe for her. We would fish for eels and perch in the big dam and I can still see my green and white float squatting all too tranquilly on the opaque greenish surface. And then we would run off to see George Gibson, who was one of the clerks or a foreman, I forget which, and who had made my brother a marvellous model of a cutter like the ones we saw scudding down the Lough in a blue sparkle of sky and shining sea. And we would go home sometimes in the Mossley farm cart with old Devinney (I have never seen his name spelt), jogging slowly and dreamily along a road where hobbled goats grazed on the verge and old women sat at the cottage doors smoking stained clay pipes. Perhaps we would call in at Devinney's cottage for slices of soda bread hot from the baking and thick spread with butter. And we would eat them sitting round the fireside where the turf fire smouldered away and fowls strutted in to peck for crumbs in the cooled ashes on the hearth.

Master and man share a living tradition at Mossley, a tradition which is vitalized by the loyalty of each succeeding generation of Campbells to their mill. Five generations have served Mossley, but to-day for the first time in more than a century there is no Campbell in charge. My cousin, whom the men at the mill called 'Mr Dermot', was killed in the last war and his elder brother whom they called 'Mr Lawford', was killed in the first World War. But Mossley is waiting for young Garry, Dermot's son, to take over and Garry, though he is only a boy, has I hope begun already to shape his life for Mossley. If you have the sense of the past it is easy to sentimentalize and idealize a relationship which has run into five generations. I do not want to idealize Mossley. No doubt there are still scores of family businesses scattered over these islands with traditions as old and as fine and as vital as those of Mossley. There have been many more which have gone down, crushed out by the financial pressure of new combines or starved out through the incompetence and sloth of the masters who served them. There have been others, thousands of them, which had no good tradition, where the masters drove their men like galley-slaves and the men paid back with hatred and cunning. Mossley has been lucky in a succession of able and energetic and just and devoted masters. And in a civilization where the collision is head on between the mammoth undertakings of a dehumanized capitalism and a young socialist experiment which has yet to prove its ideals in practice and show that it can make great scale industry a human thing worthy of the dignity and freedom and goodwill of the men and women who work it, Mossley has an ideal to offer. Because it stands for personal leadership as against impersonal direction, for the spirit of a team as against the principle of a wrestle of clashing interests, because it stands quite simply for human relationships, imperfect though they may be, against an age which is infected even to its metaphors by the idolization of efficient machines.

I know that orthodox socialists have tended to dislike and despise the feudal type of capitalism even more than they dislike the great impersonal firm, simply because the feudal type is based on a personal relationship which gives the masters a hold and an influence over their men unknown in the relations of the big limited companies to their employees. On the masters' side it is easy for such an influence to degenerate into interference with and organization of other people's lives, and on the men s side it is easy for it to degenerate into dependence and near servility. More serious still, the solidarity of labour has perforce been maintained on the principle of clashing interests and the victories of labour have been won mostly as the front became wider and more impersonal. I concede all that and I see, too, that today Mossley is becoming an anachronistic survival; none the less I submit that it is an anachronism to cherish and learn from while we can.

My Irish grandfather I can scarcely remember at all. In my recollection, granny lived at Rathfern with my Uncle Howard who was then a bachelor; every summer while she was alive I went to stay with her. Nearly everything that I have got from Inglewood I have got by hard thinking as I look back from my adult standpoint to the way of life for which Inglewood stood. The only part of Inglewood which is instinctively a part of me is an absurd reaction that anything which is hard and distasteful to do must automatically be one's duty, but anything which is easy and agreeable will almost certainly be a reprehensible self-indulgence. But with Rathfern it is far otherwise. Rathfern nourished and expanded the tiny roots I was striking down into life. Every scrap of its atmosphere and its activities that I could lay hold of with my child's emotions has fused with my self, and my difficulty as I write now is not, as my difficulty with Inglewood, to look back and disengage the good that I never discovered there as a child, but rather to build up an objective picture of Rathfern out of specific memories perhaps meagre in themselves and not out of the instinct for living which is part of mine because I got it there.

Rathfern was a grand place for a child, the sort of place where you would expect a fresh adventure to happen every hour of the day. The house stood on a rise of ground well above and away back from the Lough and you looked out first across the tennis court and some flat lawn with trees to the right under which autumn crocuses thrust up their pale lobes, if I was lucky, before my visit ended. Then came the curl over of the big hayfield dipping to the road which you could not see, and beyond was the crisp blue lough fringed on the far Co. Down shore by tiny white houses strung out like a row of lumps of sugar. In the distance you could see dim blue silhouettes of shapely hills which were the mountains of Mourne.

The drive wound down beside the hayfield and I see it with my grandmother's victoria bowling down, the horse's coat brown and sleek as old brandy and patterned with brown harness wax-polished till it gleamed even against the glossy coat, the dark green carriage paint shined with patient rubbing to a lacquer finish. They say Vermeer learned how to produce his smooth surfaces from the technique of painting coachwork. I think the Rathfern victoria would have pleased him. On the left of the drive there was a paddock memorable to me because I took my first toss there from a pony's back. Father was over for a visit and insisted on having me up, bareback I think, on the lively pony. He ran alongside half holding me on and everything was great if rather fearsome fun until an extra joggle canted me well over beyond my centre of gravity and off I came with a bump which I did not like at all. The little episode was regarded as rather typical of father who was always too apt, so mother thought, to 'take risks' - uncovenanted risks.

Smells recall for me the Rathfern garden more vividly than anything else. I always stayed there in full summer when the hay was being cut and the scent of new-mown hay invariably flashes that view from the top lawn into my mind's vision. Then there was the kitchen garden off to the left with its box borders simmering in the hot July sun. I happened once to catch the scent of warm box whilst exploring the grounds of a half ruined château in central France. Something from the far past was conjured up in my mind, but I could not tell what for it was an emotion rather than a picture. And then suddenly it was clear; the small child in that Antrim garden had been called to life again by the fragrance of a French box hedge.

Behind the house were the stables and the farm. You took the former very seriously, and on Sunday morning after church at Carnmoney there was a ritual walk round when I would be handed a fistful of strong peppermint discs, one for each of my uncle's hunters and one for each of granny's carriage horses and one for the black pony. I liked, too, the sombre saddle-room with the bits gleaming from hooks on walls faced with dark green cloth and the whips with their long knobbled stocks of bamboo and grips of whipcord and springy lashes. I liked to stand there and enjoy the mixed odour of beeswax and leather and horseflesh. I liked to handle the harness, the elegant bridles with their brass buckles, the long supple traces, the cruppers which were greasy to touch from the oils of the skin below the horses' tails; and the strong curving shapes of the polished saddles and collars became imprinted on my mind as forms of beauty. I am glad that I was born into a civilization which was still dependent on horse transport. You cannot enrich your life very much with memories of a motor mechanic's bench. You can from a carpenter's shop or a coachman's workroom. I think it is because metal has never had organic life, whereas the genius of the forest tree is still imprisoned in a plank of wood and the living warmth of an animal's hide still vitalizes a piece of leather. Nor can you learn a discipline and a code of behaviour from a motor-car which you can thrust into the garage muddy and wet and cold, whose engine you can neglect or overrun by careless driving without violating my principle of living more important than the wastage on your own pocket except in so far that it is always ill-behaviour wantonly to spoil a piece of good workmanship. But the men who care for horses cannot behave like that. Like the captains of ships or the commanders of soldiers, they must learn to put a principle of selflessness before the satisfaction of their own comforts and convenience and caprice. No doubt sociologists would tell me that the origin of this is a self-interested motive derived from the supreme necessity of horses to mankind and the difficulty of rearing and maintaining them through long ages of history. I do not mind; I am still glad that as a child I was shown the code of behaviour, whatever its origin, of the men who look after horses.

The Rathfern cows were big beige-coated Alderneys with the gait of a heavy fishing smack getting under weigh. Their tongues gritted one's touch like a mouthful of sand and their breath smelt of meadow flowers. It was in their byre that I first drank milk warm from the milking pail and watched the cowman at work coaxing a strong white squirt from the udder with the practised drag of his supple hands. And then I would watch the butter being churned and when the yellow globules were collected and patted I was told that the reason the butter was so yellow was because the cows had been eating buttercups, a pleasant notion that I am still in two minds whether or not to believe.

We had their products at breakfast, the yellow butter and a jugful of cream to pour into the hole you had scooped in your porridge, to pour so lavishly that the cream brimmed over and the whole plateful was covered. On top of that you could sprinkle as much as you wanted of a peculiar light brown sugar, very sweet, which I have never met again. Granny sat at the head of the table with a copper kettle on a high stand beside her dealing out the good things, not ostentatiously but with a natural bounty, an unconscious assumption that plenty is normal and gracious. At the other end of the table Uncle Howard would be eating his breakfast rather silently, but with a peaceful deliberation which in itself set the Rathfern breakfast table in a class apart from the breakfasts of Ferns which were always rushed since father had to catch an early train for Manchester. In fact each weekday breakfast at Rathfern had the quality of a Sunday breakfast at Ferns.

In the house there were various interesting oddments to engage the attention of a child, a spinning-wheel in the hall with a hank of flax fixed to the spindle, a stuffed monkey on the back landing, an elephant clock on the drawing-room mantelpiece, the clock face being the howdah on the china elephant's back. And there was granny's stillroom to which she would sometimes call me in her gentle western voice in order to pop some delicacy into my mouth. But on the whole the house did not excite me like the grounds and the outbuildings, and I remember it mainly as a generalized pattern of chintz drawing-room and masculine leathery billiard-room with the big sunny bedroom dominant where Meme and I slept and where I would wake in the morning to listen to Meme's yarns of a fairy life which intertwined with our own. I remember it, too, as the scene of mother's stories of her own girlhood when the house was filled with the gaiety of young people, her sister, her four brothers and their friends.

It must have seemed a warm hospitable home to the young English engineer who was building the Portrush electrical railway and who had come over with an introduction to grandfather in his pocket which opened the way to repeated visits to Rathfern. I think mother regarded those times before he carried her off to England as a sort of golden preface to her life, an overture to the more complex and serious English music of her married years; but that English music all the time was shot with little tunes reminiscent of the Irish melody. So much so that she always made me feel that I wanted to be Irish rather than English. But when I would ask her gravely whether I could consider myself Irish she used to answer with a teasing smile: 'Ach, maybe just the tip of your little finger's Irish.'

I think it is very hard for the English to comprehend the attitude of Ulster Unionists towards their country. They cannot understand how people who have made it quite plain that they would sooner plunge into a bloody civil war than break the political union with England and align themselves with their own compatriots can at the same time express pride in their Irish birth and a kind of contempt for the English way of life. Mother was typically Ulster Irish in this respect and her reactions came out in all sorts of amusing ways.

As one example I remember the census, I suppose, of 1910. Father was filling up the form and in the section reserved for religion was automatically jotting down 'Church of England'. 'No,' said mother, 'I belong to the Irish Church which your politicians robbed and disestablished. Put me down Church of Ireland.'

Yet she had lived in England since her early twenties and from every practical point of view was a most loyal member of the Anglican Church. 'Your politicians' and 'You English' - how mother enjoyed beginning some comment with one of those contemptuous if generally good-humoured apostrophes.

She never concealed her conviction that England was nine-tenths responsible for the disastrous course of Irish history. When the English had governed Ireland with a mailed fist they were behaving like tyrants. Ulster Protestant though she was, a bitter sad note would harden her voice when she referred, for instance, to what Cromwell had done to her country. And sometimes when we had music I would coax her into giving us the 'Wearing of the Green', and then she would sing about the wrongs of Ireland at English hands so that to this day I have never been able to read Irish history objectively, because I cannot cut out the sense of tragic destiny which she used to put into:

The most distressful country that ever yet was seen
For they're hanging men and women, too, for the Wearing of the Green.

But when the English were governing Ireland, as she thought, in a weak fashion, as under the Liberal administrations of Campbell Bannerman and Asquith, then their conduct was ignorant and vacillating and they were breeders of unnecessary trouble. In short, mother forestalled the slogan that the customer is always right but altered it to 'England is always wrong'.

I have often wondered how to explain this attitude which superficially looks hypocritical enough. Perhaps it is to some extent analogous to the feeling of Theodoric the Goth for the broken Roman Empire. Theodoric would never have allowed his Goths to be ruled by Italians any more than the Protestants of the Plantations would submit to be ruled by the Catholic Irish, but at the same time Theodoric and his Goths were settled in Italy and had a sentiment for Italy which was deep and genuine because it was based on a half-conscious desire to be at one with the civilization they had conquered. For the Ulstermen it was an unresolved dilemma, for culturally Ulster and the rest of Ireland were too different. The commercial and industrial enclave round Belfast was tinctured with the spirit of 'Capitalism and the Protestant Ethic'. Historians like Weber and Tawney have uncovered its growth through the centuries with fascinating insight and have shown how Protestantism moved away from the scale of values set up by mediaeval Europe and came to identify merit with thrift and money-making and hard work for hard work's sake, with business enterprise and success. I have already made reference to this spirit in regard to my English Nonconformist grandparents. It is a spirit which has never found encouragement from the

Catholic Church. In Ulster its influence was less obvious because the Ulster people did have some flavour of the southern attitude to life, but nevertheless I think it explains more nearly than anything else the aversion of Ulstermen for southern Irish rule. Where economics and religion are fused in one ideology the two strongest motive powers that can shift mankind are in action together.

During bouts of the 'Irish Trouble' mother was always careful to particularize herself as 'Ulster Irish'. One day, during the summer of 1914 when the Irish trouble was at its most serious, mother and father happened to travel up to London in the same compartment as Lord Sheffield, the chief landowner of our district. Now Lord Sheffield was an ardent aggressive and doctrinaire Liberal as well as a very able man. He liked travelling up to London with father because he enjoyed rummaging the latter's brains. Father did not altogether appreciate this process when he needed the time to work during his journeys, so finally he began to tell the porter: 'See that you put me into a different compartment to Lord Sheffield.' But on the occasion in question solitude had not been achieved and the talk was directed by Lord Sheffield to the Irish question. He produced the usual Liberal Home Ruler's invective against Ulster. Mother stood this for some time and then she said quietly:

'I am an Ulsterwoman you know, Lord Sheffield.'

'Really? Well, don't you think they are the most disagreeable and difficult people you have ever met?'

'On the contrary. I think they combine the charm of the Celt with the common sense of the Anglo-Saxon.'

Father grinned and his lordship subsided. But I can see the little flush of red that would have spread over mother's cheekbones and the fighting light in her blue eyes.

I do not suppose that she went on to tell him that her nephew had been one of the band of young Ulstermen who ran guns and ammunition from a German yacht which had fetched up off Larne one night in the early spring of that year, nor that all through that spring and summer when the forces were mustering for a civil war which would have made 1798 look like a child's picnic game, her youngest brother was alleged to sleep with a revolver under his pillow as a sober and common sense precaution. In 1913 and 1914 Irish politics were in one of their most bitter phases, but throughout mother's girlhood feeling was relatively easy. It was relatively easy also when I was a child at Rathfern; the Ulstermen thought themselves secure. And yet I see that clear free life against a background of smouldering fires. I think that no one who has been brought up exclusively in either country will ever quite understand the difference between them. More than two hundred years have passed since

Englishmen have felt constrained to fight for their way of life and an English boy or girl knows the meaning of civil war only from history books. In England men have not only sheathed their civil swords, they have hung them up in their halls with the blades unset. In Ireland the swords are sheathed from time to time, but the blades are kept set and no Irishman's hand is far from his sword-hilt.

Grandfather and grandmother were as staunch Protestants and Unionists as anyone could wish, but they did do all that they could to keep the swords sheathed. Grandfather was not, I think, on principle a member of an Orange lodge, and he did not encourage the parades and demonstrations on the 'Twalfth', the famous July anniversary which marked the victory of the Boyne Water. I would dearly have liked to go and see the Orangemen marching, but was never allowed to do so. Incidentally the day always ended in a row, sometimes a minor row and sometimes a near riot, and my elders would breathe a sigh of relief when it was over without any serious disturbance. Nor was any differentiation against Catholics or discourtesy to Catholics tolerated at Rathfern. The jeering Orange jingles which the street-boys used to chatter on the quays of Belfast were taught me surreptitiously by my cousins. I would never have dared to repeat in public:

> When we go into battle
> The cannon will rattle
> The Protestant boys'll be there with the gun
> Holy water, Holy water,
> Sprinkle yer Papishes i-ver-y one.

or

> Oh there came along a man
> With a shovel in his han"
> An' he said, 'Boys go no farther
> For we'll tighten up the rope
> An' we'll see they swing the Pope
> When King William crosses the wa-ther.'

sung with a grand slurring drawl on the first syllable of water. These were among the more polite and I quote them from memory, but I dare say verbal accuracy is of little account since like other folk-songs they can, I think, muster several rival versions. But I have never been able to discover why the exuberant prospective hangman went about with a shovel.

On the Catholic side, light relief was provided at one period of my youth by 'Orange Billy', a revolting ginger cat of no fixed domicile. He was lanky and huge, far larger than any self-respecting domestic cat ought to be, and at appropriate times you might see him with the great bones knobbed and moving under the fur of his shoulders loping down the road with a mob of little boys in pursuit yelling suitable slogans. He was a gift to them with his heaven-sent ginger hue and his unpleasant habits.

In mother's day the young people had grown up with intimate Catholic friends. It was odd in a way, for a mixed marriage would have been regarded by the parents on both sides as a disaster and there were two attractive daughters and four eligible young men at Rathfern. Granny's medical man, Dr Gumming, was a Catholic and his children and a friend of theirs, Lucy Hall, were always free of the house. Indeed, Lucy Hall and Florence Gumming remained two of mother's closest friends to the end of their lives and used often to come and stay with us at Ferns. I remember them all through my childhood and well into my grown up years. Mother treated these two and her other Irish friend, May Sims, who was gay and vivacious and a great favourite with father and my uncles, quite differently to the way in which she treated her English friends. Her natural shyness and reserve operated, I think, on her English friendships and made them a little formal, as if she were withholding something; it was symbolized in her habit of withholding Christian names. But with these Irish friends of her youth she was always free and at ease and for that reason I used to get a lot of enjoyment for myself from their visits.

Miss Hall was a relative of George Gavan Duffy who years later would come to London along with Michael Collins and Arthur Griffith to negotiate the 'Irish Treaty' which gave birth in 1921 to the 'Free State'. She was tall and dark with rather indeterminate features and a gentle personality made vivid for me by more than a touch of brogue. When she and mother sat over the drawing-room fire chatting together, I noticed how Miss Hall's accent and the rhythms of her diction revived the Irish lilt and turn of phrase in mother's own speech. She had a rich alto voice and there was always music when she was in the house, a turning over of the songs which she and mother and the rest used to sing in the old days at Rathfern, for they were all musical, all except Florence Cumming who, as mother explained, defending her, took out an aesthetic appreciation in poetry. This gave me a fellow feeling for Mrs Russell as she had become when I knew her, for though I learned music I could make nothing of musical sound and used to feel when I was laboriously practising and heard mother call out from another room: 'Kathie, you're playing a wrong note; it should be F sharp,' that she was deliberately queering my pitch since she could see neither the keyboard nor the sheet of music. I, too, took out my appreciation of sound and rhythm in poetry.

Mrs Russell was of tougher fibre than Miss Hall and had a much better brain. Like mother, she was short and neat, but with black and silver hair when I knew her, dark bright eyes, a sanguine complexion and a rather small pointed nose and chin. She had a clipped cool voice, a northern Irish voice, which made her a little more formidable than Miss Hall. She had married the eldest son of Lord Russell of Killowen. The climax of Lord Russell's career at the bar had been his defence of Parnell in the famous enquiry of 1888, which led to the exposure of Piggott's forgeries and cleared Parnell of the charge of condoning the murder of Lord Frederick Cavendish in Phoenix Park and shielding some of the murderers. So that was another piece of Irish history that was alive for me. Mrs Russell's husband had died before I remember her and she had no children or ties. So she gave up her life to prison relief work in Liverpool and London. I used generally to feel a reaction of antagonism to 100 per cent practitioners of 'good works'. There were a number of them round Manchester and they almost always dressed badly and generated an atmosphere of indifference or even hostility to the more gracious and agreeable things of life. But I never felt that way towards Mrs Russell any more than I did towards Mrs Schill whose 'good works' also took the form of prison relief. She could and did live hard herself, but she did not make a principle out of indifference to agreeable living. She remained completely human and completely a woman of the world though she never scaled down her values or compromised her judgments. When I was older and more in mother's confidence she would sometimes compare Mrs Russell's attitude with Aunt Mary's and regret Aunt Mary's indifference to ordinary pursuits because it cut her off from so many interests and subjects for conversation. Yet of the two I think that Aunt Mary was essentially the more lovable and it was she who was the near saint.

Mrs Russell would sit over the fire at Ferns and talk about her prison work in Liverpool. In her cool dispassionate voice she would describe the most appalling crimes and build up the character and motives of the women who had committed them. For her, evil was not an unnatural phenomenon but an endemic condition of human nature to be tackled intelligently with the instruments which her religion had put into her hands. She reminded me of a surgeon, and after I grew up I tried to contrast and analyse the difference between her approach and Aunt Mary's. For Aunt Mary was also concerned to fight evil, but she was so much more shocked and emotional about it. Her tactics were those of Perseus who had to decapitate the Gorgon with averted gaze.

Mrs Russell accepted humanum errare est as a necessary basis and proceeded accordingly without any illusions. But with Aunt Mary you felt that a fresh illusion was being shattered every time that she was brought up against some example of evil, and not only serious and nasty evil, but all sorts of venial and pardonable lapses. My generation for its undoing substituted a sentimental empirical humanism for the clear-cut principles of right and wrong to which our parents subscribed. My quarrel with Aunt

Mary is not that she had clear-cut principles but that her application of them sometimes confused the issues instead of clarifying them. Because she had no sense of proportion in the application of her principles. If she found out that a young nephew got drunk occasionally on convivial occasions she would be as much upset as a normal person would be whose nephew had committed a felony. So far as I was concerned, the result was simple. I am afraid that if Aunt Mary had given a moral judgment against me I should have assumed that the judge was finding on a code of law which I did not recognize. But if Mrs Russell had done so I think that I should have attended to what she said. For with Mrs Russell you felt that she knew exactly where she was and her way about in all the tangled messes that human beings can make of their lives.

I dare say the difference between them was partly one of individual character, but it had also something to do with race. It is the English and not the Irish who have a romantic and emotional reaction to life - as Shaw has pointed out in the brilliant paradoxical preface to *John Bull's Other Island*. But primarily this difference between Aunt Mary and Mrs Russell was a difference of emphasis in their religion. 'The Church has steady nerves,' says the shrewd wise old curé of Torcy in Georges Bernanos's *Journal d'un curé de campagne*, 'The Church has steady nerves, sin does not frighten her, on the contrary, she looks it straight in the face, tranquilly, and even, after the example of Our Lord, she carries it over to her account, she takes it in charge.'

That was Mrs Russell's point of view. But Aunt Mary derived her philosophy almost exclusively, I imagine, from her own very personal religious experience, and in the light of that contact with any sort of sin and in particular the more spectacular sorts involved a shrinking away of her whole being.

I think that almost everything I have ever learned about human nature tallies with the few but vivid impressions which I got from Mrs Russell. She was never didactic and she was very reticent about her religion. Cardinal Newman remarks somewhere in his Apologia: 'At that time I knew nothing about the inner life of Catholics.' This 'inner life' Mrs Russell kept strictly to herself, but the results of it were apparent in the poise and assurance of her personality, a poise that was unconscious and an assurance that was never aggressive or dominating because both poise and assurance were more than personal.

I do not suppose that it entered her head for a moment that I was storing away these impressions in my mind for consideration long afterwards. For that matter I was not aware myself that I was doing so. It is only when you delve back into the past and try to place the people you have known in their niches in the long history of human thought and human endeavour that you begin to realize the complex strands of your own heritage. I look back with gratitude to those evenings at Ferns when I would sit as a more or less silent third half consciously garnering impressions between mother, who had her small chair drawn up close to the fire for toe-toasting, and Mrs Russell who would be sitting rather upright in father's big armchair on the other side of the fire. And I wish that I could recall one of them so that I could say to Mrs Russell: 'Now do I see.'

Before passing on from the homes from which father and mother had come in order to make Ferns, I must complete the tally of the Rathfern family. My Uncle Howard was the eldest, then came my Uncle Garrett who was married and the father of the Irish cousins whom I knew best. He was an able cultivated man, a fine linguist, rather dominating and also withdrawn into himself and not sharing his interests as father did; and I regarded him with some fear on account of his irascible tongue which sometimes flayed the young and obscured the deep kindliness and justice of his nature and the wit which reminded me always of the flavour of fresh nuts. My mother was the next and then my Uncle Walter who broke with family tradition by choosing an army career and whom I have already called up for a moment from the past as one of the Christmas party at Ferns. He left his regiment early to become a staff officer on the administrative side and finished the 1914-18 war as Allenby's Quartermaster-General in the Palestine campaign. Later, he became Q.M.G. at the War Office. He and Uncle Garrett both had a reputation for 'accuracy' in our branch of the family. When they asserted a fact, it almost inevitably turned out to be a fact. Father, who was given to exaggeration in friendly argument and to ranging statements, used to find himself sometimes neatly potted and brought to earth when one of his flights had been taken au pied de la lettre. He would, if this happened at dinner, raise his napkin to his mouth in a peculiar way he had which also exaggerated the size of the linen to about twice its actual number of square inches and remark with a mixture of mock and real discomfiture: 'They're not only accurate but aggravating.' In Uncle Walter's character the Scottish strain was predominant and there is a neat reference to the Scottish characteristics of the Q.M.G. in Lawrence's Arabia when that wayward genius came up against the granite Ulsterman on some matter which occasioned a difference of view. Yet granite is scarcely the term to apply to Uncle Walter for in his own circle his affectionate humour could be very endearing. By contrast, Uncle Lloyd, the youngest brother, who gave a rather divided attention to Mossley, was something of an Irish playboy and we young ones thought him a very gay dog. I met him once with mother for lunch in London and was much impressed by his meal of stout and oysters. But he had his serious side and when the Irish troubles were at their height in 1913 and 1914, he plunged into politics and was deep in the counsels of the Ulster Volunteers. It was he who was said to sleep with the pistol under his pillow. That, too, I found very impressive. Finally there was Auntie May, who married father's brother Charlie, and of them I shall write more later for in my life the place they filled most perfectly was during holidays.

Mother and our motor, c1910

Father c1905

Chapter Six
FATHER AND HIS COLLEAGUES

Father had emerged from Cambridge as tenth Wrangler in the Mathematical Tripos of 1882. He had lived frugally, perhaps a little too frugally for his health, for he did not have much money to spare, he had studied hard and he had cultivated his spare athlete's body, for he had stroked his college boat, won college cups as a sprinter, skated from Cambridge to Ely and climbed crags in the Lake District. After his Manchester upbringing, so intense morally and intellectually so definite yet circumscribed, Cambridge must have been for him an experience like that of the young eagle which trusting its wings suddenly becomes free of the sky. Men whose names have come down to us as makers of intellectual history were working at the university in his day. Lightfoot and Hort and Westcott were teaching divinity; Clark Maxwell and Lord Rayleigh, physics; Seeley, modern history; Fawcett, political economy; Skeat, Anglo-Saxon. F.W. Maitland was examining for the Moral Sciences Tripos. It was an exciting world of intellectual fermentation and before father went down Thomas Huxley had been elected to the presidency of the Royal Society and Darwin, with that engaging unconcern for the beliefs of the deceased which marks our national interments, had been honoured by burial in Westminster Abbey.

After some uncertainty father had determined to become an engineer and soon after going down he joined the Manchester firm of Mather & Platt and before long was put in charge of its electrical department, a fine chance for the brains of an alert young man since the senior partner, Sir William Mather, was always keen to seek out adventure in the newly discovered realm of applied electricity. And here I must try to sketch in the portrait of the head of the firm.

Mather & Platt was a private firm in those days with two partners, Mr Mather and Mr John Platt. I know nothing about Mr Platt's youth and antecedents. Mr Mather, who had become Sir William by the time that I knew him, was a son of the founder of the firm. He must have been a lad of original mind and much physical toughness for at twelve he announced his desire to leave school and enter the works at once as an apprentice. His father agreed and young William stuck it as a volunteer apprentice for three years. One of these years was 1851 and he took a holiday to visit the Great Exhibition, that astonishing landmark in the Victorians' lives. He went by himself and travelled by stage coach at the cost of a five-shilling fare. When he was fifteen he suggested to his father that he should now be sent back to school for a while, and again his father complied. This schooling only lasted for a twelve month in a formal way, because the school was wound up and the headmaster took a group of his remaining pupils to Germany for a year, William among them. Back from Germany he resumed his apprenticeship and continued his book education by attending evening classes. The works at Salford were about four miles from the family home at Greenheys - in those days a home amongst fields - and he had to leave at five in the morning in order to be on time at the works' gate by six o'clock. Twelve hours later the gates clanged to, releasing him and his fellow-apprentices to freedom, but for William not to leisure since he went home merely for a wash and a big tea and then set off once more to the Mechanics' Institute for his night school which was not over till nine. The day ended with nearly an hour's walk home; he was only seventeen.

I have often wondered whether he looked back on that strange boyhood of strenuous work and oddly enriching haphazard education when in late life he was wealthy and at ease in his country home in the New Forest, a privy councillor and honorary doctor of his city's university, the chairman of a great business built up by the men whom he had chosen and guided and captained, a figure in public life with a long career of political and philanthropic and educational work behind him. Would he have had his youth otherwise? Would he have changed places at seventeen with the young man, son of another engineering employer, who would later become his lieutenant in the business and was then winning his scholarship to Cambridge? Would he have changed places with his own son when years later the latter was enjoying the last phases of an immaculate education as he walked up 'the Hill' in flannels warm flushed by a lowering sun from the playing fields of Harrow? I rather doubt it, and I doubt, too, whether a more leisurely and formal education would have added anything to the stature of his personality or the virile and imaginative grasp of his mind.

He was always a Liberal in politics, sitting in more than one Parliament for a Lancashire division. Gladstone was his hero. He was present in the Speaker's Gallery when Gladstone spoke in the debate on the despatch of the British Fleet to Constantinople in 1878 during the troubles between Russia and Turkey - the action which produced the famous music-hall jingle:

We don't want to fight
But By Jingo! if we do,
We've got the ships, we've got the men,
We've got the money, too.

He stayed from four till nine, 'riveted by the masterly and almost supernatural powers of Gladstone' who was thundering with all the guns of his rhetoric. 'Inspired', so Sir William thought, 'by the love of truth and goodness with a logic so keen and a clearness of vision so full, he placed before the country the great issues at stake, for all posterity.' He followed his hero with equal enthusiasm during the Home Rule struggle of 1886, telling his electors of South Salford that the age of the grand atonement had arrived and exhorting them to show that the English nation preferred the justice and freedom proposed by Mr Gladstone for the downtrodden Irish to the fetters and chains of Lord Salisbury. It must have been fun electioneering in those days; rhetoric went a long way and hecklers did not ask for unexceptionable statistics to be produced like rabbits out of a hat. In 1900 he was telling the electors of Rossendale that 'the nineteenth century has been distinguished beyond all other periods in the history of our country for the triumphs of peace, liberty, industry, commerce and knowledge, yielding national prosperity and contentment, affecting all classes of the people'. But he was not proposing that his electors should sit back crowned with these nineteenth-century laurels. His address forestalled the great radical programmes of 1906-11 and indeed some of the legislation which has had to wait until our own day. He asked for good working-class housing and improved poor relief, the abolition of plural voting, the reform of the Land Laws so that land might anywhere be acquired for the public welfare, the reform of the House of Lords by a restriction on its power of veto.

It is hard as a mid-twentieth century commentator to think oneself back into the atmosphere of moral fervour generated by those Victorian Liberals. Calloused as we are by unremitting tales of horror and cruelty and oppression, Gladstone's grandiloquent indignations seem to us farfetched and Acton's rolling aphorisms ring down the years with a rather hollow sound. We have learned to play down noble sentiment in the harsh school of ignoble fact. There is nothing very new in the divorce between noble sentiments and harsh facts. That separation was just as apparent if you looked for it in Sir William's day as it is in ours, in this country it was a great deal more apparent. But he and his kind saw it through the rosy spectacles of pride in their triumphing century whereas we like to think of ourselves as tough-minded hard-headed realists. That is the compensator if not the corrective for that too tolerant humanism which in fact decides most of our judgments. Accordingly, we suspect moral, fervour of sentimentality and hypocrisy. Things do not get done by waving the magic wand of high-falutin' sentiment. They are done, and optimistically so we believe we do them, by getting down to the spade-work of practical thinking. Up to a point we are right, but beyond that point it seems to me as I try to read myself back into Sir William's mental atmosphere, that we are lamentably wrong. Because the high sentiments of men like Sir William expressed a consistent outlook on life and created a standard. The actions often fell far short of the standard, personal actions, political actions, diplomatic actions. Often they were used as an unconscious cloak for meanness and hypocrisy. But always the standard remained as a yardstick of reproach. And if you scale down precept until it tallies with performance you lose your gauge. We have nearly lost our yardstick of reproach.

Sir William's Liberalism drew its inspiration direct from his religion. He was always a man of religion. But he disliked creeds because he suspected them of side-tracking energy which should be used for the improvement of men's lot and of generally impeding the flow of the milk of human kindness. 'As you grow older with a pure heart', he wrote to his son, 'you will see God in all things, not in one form of church, not in one road to salvation; but you will see good in all forms of faith which result in deep veneration for God in all His works and words.' Apparently it never occurred to him that a faith is apt to lose its cutting edge unless it is firmly held in the haft of a creed. And he mistrusted, as I did half a century later, the Christian belief that 'it is the first right and duty of every man to use his mind and will to achieve his destiny which is eternal life' (the quotation is not his) not because he disbelieved in eternal life, but because he had seen this belief so often construed by the congregations and clergy of the various and numerous north country churches and chapels into a selfish absorption in winning a place in the ticket queue for heaven regardless of the mess and misery that needed cleaning up on earth. Since men had been taught to pray: 'Thy will be done on earth as it is in heaven', then surely, he argued, their first and obvious duty on earth was to apply themselves to promoting the kingdom of heaven here and now, leaving their personal future to their Maker. But this attitude was not that old and unnecessary antagonism between saints and social reformers. Sir William's anger was in the spirit of the scornful indignant opponent of the Pharisees. And in practice, though he may not have given all of them theological credence, the great Christian beliefs flashed like steel blades from his splendid and generous philosophy.

His Liberalism and his religion combined to form his outlook as an employer. When he took over the captaincy of Mather & Platt the legacy of the early phases of Lancashire industrialism was being collected from the sordid streets of Manchester in wizened bodies and stunted minds:
'What does Let him Be Poor mean? It means let him be weak. Let him be ignorant. Let him become a nucleus of disease. Let him be a standing exhibition and example of ugliness and dirt. Let him have rickety children. Let him be cheap and drag his fellows down to his own price by

selling himself to do their work. Let his habitations turn our cities into poisonous congeries of slums. Let his daughters infect our young men with the diseases of the streets, and his sons revenge him by turning the nation's manhood into scrofula, cowardice, cruelty, hypocrisy, political imbecility, and all the other fruits of oppression and malnutrition .... Money is the most important thing in the world. It represents health, strength, honour, generosity and beauty as conspicuously and undeniably as the want of it represents illness, weakness, disgrace, meanness and ugliness. Not the least of its virtues is that it destroys base people as certainly as it fortifies and dignifies noble people. It is only when it is cheapened to worthlessness for some and made impossibly dear to others that it becomes a curse.'

Nearly forty years before Bernard Shaw had produced that invective with its finale of glittering devilish paradox in the Preface to *Major Barbara*, Sir William saw that the children born of those fathers and mothers with wizened bodies and aborted minds and reared in the squalid streets would grow up through no fault of their own to 'perpetuate the misery, degradation and criminality of their parents'. He might be proud of his triumphing century but he was not blind to its short-comings. He lashed his fellow-employers with an invective as scathing as Shaw's:

'Our children are well educated, respectable, prosperous; we are industrious and amass larger means than we can or need to spend; we give tithes of all we possess - a sigh for the wretched, a prayer for the wicked and, committing both to God's care, take shelter in the spiritual and social delights of our Church' (I wish I could know Sir William's opinion of the clergy of Trollope's Barchester; I doubt if any but old Mr Harding and poor Mr Crawley would have escaped the whip) 'and thus the world rolls on; men come and men go, but the black and putrid stream of human misery, want, ignorance and crime flows on for ever. The state of social life in England below the upper working class is a disgrace to civilization, a mockery to the religious fervour of which we boast, and it is the badge by which, among other nations, our own is distinguished, or rather notorious.

He was never meanly afraid, like so many of his contemporary business men, that education for working men would prove the dangerous dynamite which could explode the society in which he was himself so comfortably placed. In season and out of season he fought and planned to get a finer and wiser and sunnier education for working class children because he believed that they had the same right as his own sons and daughters to nourish and ripen their shooting faculties from their country's heritage of culture and intellect. To-day that belief seems a self-evident truism hardly worth stating. But the truism of to-day is often the struggling truth of yesterday. The truth becomes a truism only after long battles fought by men like Sir William to force its acceptance.

In his own business he was always planning for better conditions for the workpeople. They were his fellow-workers not his 'hands'. They gave the dignity of their labour as their capital in a joint moral partnership - a partnership that he would fain have made in some way financial as well as moral. In 1893 Mather & Platt, first among British engineering firms, introduced the forty-eight-hour week. Sir William's speech, when the idea was put up to the men, was typical of his insight:

'I have long felt that some rearrangement of hours is necessary .... Various considerations make the first quarter of the day unprofitable to employers and not very enjoyable to workpeople. We have now many recreations and amusements, and very properly so, for the people after the hours of work. It is not quite so easy to go to bed at nine or ten o'clock as it was twenty or thirty years ago. There was nothing much in those days but work and sleep. There were few night schools, or education in the way of lectures or rational recreation for leisure hours .... These pursuits naturally occupy some time and probably you may not get to bed until ten or eleven o'clock, instead of at nine, as your fathers did. The changed circumstances render it especially difficult for boys who have to attend night schools.

'I wish to make it possible that there need only be one meal hour in the working time of the day. I think it would be better for workmen if they could start their work after enjoying a good solid meal with their families before leaving home ....

'Now what you have to do is to devise a scheme of working time which will be advantageous both to you and to us.'

He left it to them. The scheme was devised and after a year's trial was voted a roaring success from the point of view both of the workpeople and the management.

It was the same with wages. In 1918, when I was electioneering for my father in a Manchester division close to 'The Works', I fell in with an old engineer who told me how, many years before, when he was a young man working for the firm and an engineer's wages were counted in shillings a week, Sir William had decreed that no engineer who worked for him should go home on payday with less than a golden sovereign in his pocket.

No doubt his attitude had more than a touch of paternalism. Workpeople had a right to be consulted about the conditions of their work, but he would have brooked no interference with the broad conduct of the business; and for years he jibbed against the conviction of his younger lieutenants that the time had come to turn the private firm into a limited company. This was finally done in 1898 when father was appointed the managing director.

My direct recollections of Sir William centre on his numerous visits to Ferns. He filled the house with an atmosphere of lavishness; his personality was so ample and so vivid. Even a child could sense that atmosphere of overflowing largesse. In concrete ways it overflowed in his gifts - and also in his scale of tipping. This last was sometimes a real embarrassment to younger and poorer men who had to follow on his heels. As for his gifts, sometimes they were magnificent and costly like that diamond bracelet which he gave to my mother after father had successfully pulled off the first run of his electric locomotive on the old City and South London with the Prince of Wales on the footplate, sometimes they were modest like the plain visitor's book which he gave to my parents when we moved to Ferns. The money side of them did not matter, it was the sincerity, the thoughtful appropriateness which counted. He gave me my christening bowl and a gleaming sovereign, a musical box which I still have, trinkets brought back from his travels which were better than pretty. But he was not exactly an easy visitor.

There was a spice of the grand seigneur in his disposition when he came to Ferns as the guest of his lieutenant. Father was always Edward, the young man whom he had chosen for Mather & Platt, and it was not always easy to differ from him either on some matter to do with the conduct of the business, or on politics where the cleavage between Sir William's ideas and father's widened as the years went on. There were other practical little difficulties as well. Sir William was a chronic cigar-smoker and every curtain and drapery in the house stank after his departure with a brooding odour which mother very much disliked. In order to get rid of it windows and doors were recklessly flung open and we lived in a whirlpool of draughts until the curtains and the upholstery had been successfully deodorized. Then when he grew old he wanted to bring his valet. This was another difficulty for mother, because there was nowhere at Ferns considered suitable and decorous to sleep the valet or to feed the valet. Our maids had communicating bedrooms rather cut off on the top floor and we didn't possess a servant's hall. They ate and sat in the big kitchen. Admittedly, a valet could hardly share their sleeping quarters, but it appeared that he could not decently share their eating quarters either. I have never been quite clear whether this latter trouble arose because it would have entailed some infringement of etiquette in the domestic hierarchy, or just because mother was afraid that the maids would giggle and flirt.

Mother was very particular about anything which symbolized decorous behaviour as between males and females. The downstairs lavatory, for instance, was sacrosanct to the men of the family and their guests, the upstairs was reserved with equal exclusiveness to the females. Woe betide me if I was ever found slinking into the downstairs to save time. Conversely, the good breeding and social knowledge of any male guest who was suspected of having used the upstairs while dressing for dinner was immediately called in question.

It was all a part of the complicated code of manners, the corseting customs built up with half-conscious carefulness in order to keep a seemly look on our personalities and prevent them from spreading and slopping over at uncomely points. There were so many of these little rules to remember, but we were drilled so that it was no effort to remember them, and indeed a breakage of any one of them meant conscious and premeditated rebellion. Those connected with meals required the most careful distinction in their application. We could, for instance, make our entry to the dining-room for breakfast within reason when we liked; we could come straight to the lunch-table, brushed and clean, of course, from whatever activity we had just given up. If we were a few minutes late that was less a breach of the general code of good manners as a breach of mother's particular code of consideration for the maids. But at dinner we had to approach our food formally, assembling first in the drawing-room, silk-frocked or dinner-jacketed according to sex. No slipping into your chair when the rest of the company was seated.

'You're not leaving yourself time to dress for dinner,' mother would call down from her room as the clock ticked minutes after seven. When Campbell was at home with one or other of his friends and we had been out on some frolic, the helter-skelter rush to change, compose oneself and reach the drawing-room as the first gong rang always put a finishing touch of piquancy to the day.

It was often a nuisance and always a discipline, but it did make for order and leisure and a certain grace of fellowship at the meal. Indeed, most of those troublesome taboos and observances touched some real value however remotely. I think most of them referred ultimately to a consideration for other people, a sense that the ball-bearings of your society will not run smoothly unless a film of lubricant is kept between them. They were very much a part of Sir William's visits and looking back it seems to me that I associate the meaning they had below the exasperating surface artificiality with him. For he was so naturally at ease in an atmosphere of fine and gentle behaviour, and in spite of the grand seigneurial touches his warm generous personality made polite manners come alive and attain significance.

I have been lured away from Mather & Platt in this attempt to convey the meaning of his personality. Perhaps I have given him too much space, but this has been done deliberately since he, together with our neighbour Mr Pilkington whom I shall shortly try to describe, represent for me the finest flower of Manchester's Edwardian civilization.

The other partner, Mr John Platt, a small rotund man with a bristly beard, was much more the shrewd natural-witted Lancastrian, wiry fibred and less urbane in manner, very kindly, a little greedy of his food, in short rather gritty to the mental touch compared with Sir William. He usually brought his wife when he came to Ferns and she made a contrast with her slightly aloof manner and her admirable figure and clothes. Children are often unconscious psychologists, hardly aware what they are doing but, in fact, analysing and classifying the people who cross their path, letting the simply planned characters go by default but always returning to pore over the more complex ones. In this way perhaps I let Mr Platt go by default and really remember very little about him. It was the same with Mr John Taylor, another of the directors, who was a burly full-blooded self-made Lancashire man with a northern accent and a large house near Windermere and much drive and ability.

A fourth Mather & Platt personality who came frequently to Ferns and whom I continued to see for years after I was grown up was Mr John (after the 1914-18 war, Sir John) Wormald. He was in charge of Mather & Platt's London office and his was one of those complex characters which youth watches with unconscious fascination. He had a hawk's nose and a chiselled sensitive mouth; a little more look of weight to the cranium, a little more lift to the arch of forehead and he would have had a very fine head indeed. He was a Scot by origin and still retained a faint agreeable Scottish intonation in his speech. He had made his own way in the business world from some lowly start hidden from the friends of his success and prosperity, but I think always for himself a memory which followed him down the years like the beam of a torch playing over his success and his sincere but rather pathetic efforts to buy himself a life of beauty and culture, playing over all that quite mercilessly and showing him to himself, a lonely, able and successful man with a craving for culture and no notion how he might satisfy it except by buying expensive bric-à-brac and period furniture. He was sensitive enough to guess that there was something phoney in that kind of satisfaction but he could not shake free from the illusion that the more money a thing costs the nearer will be its approximation to excellence. So his approach to beauty was at once humble and crassly arrogant. His true natural instinct was overlaid by his taste for opulence, symbolized for me by the fat pearl studs of his dress shirt. And I doubt whether the Chinese pots and the period pieces which filled his house on the banks of the Thames ever opened for him more than the chink of a vista into that world of art which he coveted so wistfully. That vista might have become a prospect if only Sir John could have forgotten that he was a rich Edwardian capitalist and thought himself, for instance, into the point of view, so frank and spontaneous, of the ordinary men and women of young Renaissance Florence who celebrated as a communal triumph the completion of the bronze doors made by Ghiberti for their baptistery and headed by their signoria, who never left the Palazzo della Signoria in an official body except on the greatest occasions of state, turned out en masse to inspect the doors and honour the sculptor; if only he could have thought himself into the point of view of the sculptor, the maker of beautiful things, who had worked for twenty-two years on his doors casting and recasting them in his struggle to express ever more perfectly his idea; if only he could have thought himself into the point of view of the batch of young Florentines whom Ghiberti employed to help him and who each and all made their eager and subordinated contribution to the central purpose of their leader.

It is well known that the perfume is usually bred out of large and exotically coloured and stylishly formed garden flowers, sweet peas and roses and the like. I wonder whether Sir John, strolling on his groomed lawns with the roses about him and the warm summer sun drawing the smells from the soil and the humbler flowers ever noticed that his finest blooms were scentless; and drew the conclusion?

He was very likeable and very fond of father and mother. Mother always said that at heart he appreciated simplicity. Perhaps that was why he liked Ferns. Not that life at Ferns was exactly on the lines of sancta simplicitas, but it certainly was completely without pretension and it had integrity. I suspect that Sir John contrasted it in his heart with his own smart and elaborate home dominated by a smart and elaborate wife and added the contrast to his store of wistful hankerings.

These four, together with father, were the leaders of Mather & Platt during my childhood, and the fact that one or other of them was so often at Ferns made a link between father's working life and his home which produced somehow a sense of strength and unity in our set-up; not the feudal unity of Mossley, for I never played in the purlieus of Park Works or made friends with the workpeople, but a satisfactory feeling that mother and I were not cut off and held separate from father's activities as a professional and business man.

Bright young men from Cambridge were an innovation in the engineering world when father had joined Mather & Platt. Conservative firms preferred the lad who had been through the works and could base his aptitude for design and invention on practical rather than theoretical knowledge. But Sir William saw that the days of firms were numbered whose designers were still being bred in the tradition of Arkwright and Watt and Stephenson, and that the future lay with men who could bring the brain of a trained scientist to the problems of engineering design. Today, 'the application of science in industry' is a creed, in my youth it was a slogan, in father's youth it was a daring and revolutionary conception. Father's line was applied electricity, partly, no doubt, because that was the line of his brother, John. Sir William had brought home from a visit to the United States the rights of manufacturing Edison's dynamo. Upon this dynamo father and Uncle John got to work, altering and improving it, until between them they were able to produce what became known throughout the world as the most perfect electrical machine of the time. A few years later Sir William, always ready for adventure, signed a contract to equip the first London tube trains with electrically driven locomotives instead of a clumsy system of haulage by wire rope. It was pioneer work in an almost virgin field, though some of the problems involved had already been tackled by father and others for tramways and light railways, and it fell to father's department to make the daring contract good. Backed by Sir William's unflagging encouragement, they experimented for two nerve-racking years and at the end of them father had produced his locomotive. This, with the dynamo, made his original contribution to engineering science.

So many boys and men seem to have a magician's touch for the practical handling of a machine, but they can never become great engineers because their mental and imaginative grasp of principles is not deep enough. With father it was the other way round. He always used to say that he regretted never having served an apprenticeship in the shops, but I think he would have hated it had he done so. He was no good with his hands; they looked loosely knit and clumsy and he did not care for doing things which involved a neat use of hands, except that he liked to make watercolour sketches on his holidays. I never knew him want to tinker with a bit of machinery. When we acquired a car, fairly early in the motoring era, and embarked on the usual series of breakdowns which marked the progress of the internal combustion engine, he always let the chauffeur fiddle along as best he could, having never bothered himself to learn the practical details of the working of a motor-car engine. But our chauffeur was no Shavian character proper to the lusty aggressive atmosphere of the new mechanical age. Father and mother would have loathed to be served by such a one as Henry Straker. They regarded the new type chauffeur as a pert, cocksure fellow with an unsuitable manner for 'service' and a probable absence of pride in polished paintwork and brass. Ours was an ex-naval petty officer who had been discovered by Campbell. Richardson's taste in polished brasswork was impeccable, his manner a correct deference humanized by a tincture of naval breeziness, though sometimes the breeziness predominated a little too much for father's liking. But on the whole he passed muster as a 'gentleman's servant' (the phrase is not mine) and that was regarded as more important than natural talent for handling a complicated piece of mechanism.

The combination of father and Richardson when one of the frequent breakdowns occurred was comical and ironic. Father, the fine engineer, would stand about in the road, rather impatient and impotent, making a suggestion now and then, but never with his head bent over the bonnet and his hands busy with the innards. Poor Richardson, whose real affinity was with sailing ships, had to muddle through as best he could, struggling with the mysteries of the ignition system and the complexity of the carburettor. Nor did father ever learn to drive. He never wanted to until the war when Richardson, who had been called up as a reservist, was a prisoner with the Naval Brigade in Holland and his temporary successor, an ex-gardener this time, was away making munitions. Then one day it occurred to him that he would have me teach him to drive. The result was a strain even on my youthful nerves though not apparently on his more than middle-aged ones. After three or four lessons we swept down the great 'S' curves of the road which descends from the 'Cat and Fiddle' to Macclesfield and missed an army lorry by a hair's breadth when the accelerator was applied instead of the footbrake. The driving experiment was short-lived, fortunately perhaps. He never acquired a 'feel' for the controls.

The fact of the matter was that father had the mind of a mathematician rather than that of a practical engineer. Mathematics made his intellectual element, but because he had nothing of the student in his character and tastes and needed an outlet for his energies in the world of affairs, it was natural that he should think to apply his mathematics to industry. As he grew older the manipulation of affairs claimed more and more of his interest and energy and seemed to open a wider field for his ability. Although he always maintained that no one can manage the business side of engineering or conduct large-scale salesmanship without a sound technical training, yet he drifted steadily away from a personal solution of scientific and technical problems. And that side of his mind shrank. During the war I remember that some Government official stayed with us at Ferns who had come to Mather & Platt to seek the invention of an apparatus for disinfecting ships or something of the sort. Rather sadly father indicated to me that for himself he could no longer be sure of solving the new and difficult technical problems involved. That faculty of his intellect had fallen into disuse and refused now to function with the old imaginative sweep. Perhaps he realized then for the first time that he had lost some value of the spirit. His personal creative capacity had been used up in the pursuit of business power and the architecture of a great business.

He got plenty of recognition from the business world yet, significantly enough, he once told me towards the end of his life that the one honour he would really have prized was to have been elected a fellow of the Royal Society as a young man. A year or two before he died he was chosen president of the Institution of Mechanical Engineers, and I think that tribute from his fellow-engineers pleased him deeply.

In the latter half of his business life father became interested in the Chloride Electrical Storage Company which had made a modest entry into the industrial world shortly before his connection with it. He was appointed vice-chairman and it was mainly through his drive and vision, coupled with the keen intelligence of the chairman, Mr Bannister, that the Chloride battled through its early years, steadily enlarging and strengthening its position until at last it could claim one of the leading shares in the world market for accumulators.

In those days the firm was run by an oddly assorted quartet. The chairman, another visitor to Ferns, was known to us as 'old father Bannister'. He was a gnome-like figure with a long profuse black beard and he always wore a black frock-coat. Walt Disney would have appreciated him as a prototype for one of the dwarfs in Snow White. He came from the south of Ireland and was a warm-hearted 'black' Protestant with a child's lovable simplicity of outlook - except where business was concerned and in that field he had plenty of shrewd acumen. The company's secretary was Mr Daniel Patrick Dunne, another southern Irishman who had, I think, been born and bred a Catholic, but that had not prevented 'old father Bannister' from fishing him out of an obscure boyhood and planting him on the road to success in the Chloride. In addition to outstanding business wits, Mr Dunne had the wits and the manner to become a man of the world and he could be very good company indeed. He knew exactly what the naive English expect of an Irishman in the way of social entertainment and over a cigar and a good bottle of wine was always prepared to give it to them. The works manager was Mr Naylor, a sound and prudent Lancastrian whose qualities later brought him the chairmanship of the company. Finally there was father.

The excitement, the dangers and vicissitudes attendant on his work as one of the leaders of two expanding firms took their toll from father's athlete's body and from his temperament, naturally sunny but always strung to concert pitch. As the years went on, overstrained organs which should have been given rest, gradually collapsed in chronic ill-health; and the flashing smiles that one watched for like rapiers of sun cutting through clouds came ever more rarely. Worry and overstrain seemed to generate a fog of depression and abstraction which drifted into every cranny of his being and drew down the lines of his face and made his eyes unhappy.

'Don't they look the personification of woe?' mother would say half teasing, and coupling father with his brother Alfred and his sister Mary who shared the same oblivious disregard for the expressions which they allowed to possess their faces.

But the strain on her was an increasing one, for as his ambitions became more complicated and his temperament less resilient, father demanded ever more of the sympathy and moral support which his own mother's attitude had taught him to crave for and expect. Mother never failed him; her character deepened and toughened to meet all the demands made upon her. Throughout their married life she had laid upon herself the plain first duty as she conceived it of carrying father through his troubles and difficulties. It was a duty of love; I am quite sure that she never thought of herself for a moment as a sacrificing female and I do not think that a questing psycho-analyst would have found any evidence in her make-up whereby he could reduce her impulse of love and protection to masochistic self-indulgence. But she did, in fact, contract her own interests and pleasures and capacities lest they should ever interfere or conflict with father's. Her time, her energy, her judgment and sober intelligence were always at his service. Sometimes he would embark upon a course of action of which she disapproved, but if she had tried to dissuade him and failed, then she let the matter drop. I never heard her nag. And she did get her own way about a number of things by a tactful use of the strategy of the indirect approach, a use so unobtrusive that even I imagined for long enough that it was invariably what father said or thought that 'went' at Ferns. He certainly was masterful and a leader and in all groups that I knew of took the initiative. And he expected to be waited on and obeyed. When he travelled, porters were prompt to carry his luggage and waiters to serve his table. Even on holidays abroad he was always well served although he was a shocking linguist and used to cause mother amused but excruciating discomfort by his murder of French syntax and pronunciation. It was his personality that gave to Ferns its vivid light. He was always, for instance, a stimulating host. He liked to have men guests who were setting their mark on affairs, and he liked women guests who looked well and could combine at least some measure of wit and charm. Women of that sort evoked his own wit and charm and the sword-play of personality between them was a delight to watch. Even through his final illness in the years succeeding the 1914-18 war something of this vivid stimulating light remained. It went out when he died, but then the deeper and quieter glow of mother's influence became more clear.

Gradually, during the years of their long marriage, the relation between them had been transformed. Father had brought a girl over from

Ireland, shy and gentle and dependent. When he died, mother was still shy and reticent, still gentle, but her personality had been annealed. The basic, vital pulses of her life beat, so it seemed, independently of any human being. Father might be outwardly masterful, but mother was inwardly the mistress of her own being. She had always seemed to hold her innermost self secret, but after father's death she withdrew a little more whilst at the same time transferring her sympathy and her supporting strength to a wider circle of her friends and protégés. As I think of her I am reminded of a rock to which tired and uncertain swimmers can cling for a time and get rest and warmth in sunshine and a renewal of strength. When she died it seemed as if the rock had been submerged leaving only a flux of waters and no anchorage. I was to become a good few years older before I realized that the self-pity of a generation which committed itself to a philosophy of empirical and ad hoc moral judgments (unrelated to any standard of values more precise than a belief in generosity and tolerance) had been at work, at any rate in my own case, in this foreboding half-articulate sense of a lost anchorage. For it was not only sympathy and support that mother gave out to those around her; the integrity and the steadfastness of her standards shone through her personality compelling an influence of which one was only properly aware after it had been withdrawn.

Sir William Mather c1885.

Firwood, home of the Pilkingtons.

Chapter Seven
NEIGHBOURS

As I look back it seems to me that the life of Ferns never interlocked or fused with the life lived in our neighbours' homes with the exception of two where friendship dated from times before the three families had been geographically neighbours. Father and mother were on friendly terms with most of the families who lived on 'the Edge' and I lived in happy camaraderie with the young of several houses. But none the less Ferns, with so much coming and going of relations and friends of mother's and friends of father's, who were linked to him through one or another professional tie, had a certain self-sufficiency of its own; and not only a self-sufficiency for even as a child I realized that this elusive sense of apartness was really a sign that Ferns belonged to a wider world than that of Alderley Edge, and that though outwardly father lived the Manchester life of his neighbours the range of his mind and activities mostly out-distanced theirs and thus drew in to Ferns a richer nourishment than was offered to most of the Alderley Edge homes. Perhaps I realized, too, that mother's personality had a certain timeless quality and that although outwardly she was conditioned by the society in which she lived, in herself she would have fitted any setting in which gracious manners and her sense of noblesse oblige could prevail. She would have been very much at home, for instance, as that 'gentle' cavalier Lord Falkland's lady presiding at Great Tew in 1642, and I can see her sitting rather reluctantly for Holbein as the mistress of St Thomas More's household which she would certainly have run with more sympathy and understanding than it ever received from the great Chancellor and martyr's actual wife. It is therefore with a sense of stepping out of the personal world that really mattered to me as a child that I turn for the time being from Ferns in order to try to sketch the likenesses of some of our neighbours and the lives they lived in Manchester and at Alderley Edge.

Every morning in my childhood the business men caught the 8.25 or the 8.50 or the 9.18 trains into Manchester. The times are graven in my memory. Anyone out early would see them hurrying to the station, one lot down the 'back hill' - Dr Hopkinson from Ferns, Mr Schill from Croston Towers, Mr Bles from Underwood, Mr Lees from St Mary's Clyffe, Mr Chesney from Redclyffe and Mr Pilkington from Firwood. And then there would be another stream down the 'front' hill, the Macclesfield road; this would include Mr Crewdson from Springfield, Mr Worthington and his sons from Broomfield, Mr Roby and funny old Dr Wilde who was a distinguished scientist. At the station other streamlets would converge from roads which struck out into the plain from the village. In one of these would be found Mr Cobbett, a grandson of the great Tory-Radical pamphleteer.

The business men travelled, of course, in the first-class carriages, dividing easily into groups so that compartments were made up between more or less particular cronies. The young men who got together in this way made, I fancy, a boisterous journey; the elders probably read The Times or the *Morning Post*, but most frequently the *Manchester Guardian*. But I can only tell by hearsay, for any wife or daughter who had to go into Manchester by one of those trains always travelled third; to share a compartment with the 'gentlemen' (we were taught never to call them just plainly 'men') would have been unthinkable. Indeed, the ladies always avoided the business trains if they possibly could. It was highly embarrassing, a sort of indelicacy, to stand on the platform surrounded by a crowd of males who had to be polite but were obviously not in the mood for feminine society.

There is a common belief in other parts of England that the Manchester business man every time runs true to type. You obtain him by running the good human metal into the standard Manchester mould and the result is a mass-produced human being with the easily recognizable characteristics of a mass-produced motor-car. Southerners, lunching at the Midland hotel and looking around them, have perhaps some excuse for endorsing this belief. Yet our neighbours were certainly not struck from one pattern or run into one mould. They had, however, one common and dominant characteristic which perhaps accounts for the Manchester myth. This was their acceptance of the economic system which had produced Alderley Edge. Indeed, acceptance is too passive a word for they believed positively in the system; it was for all of them a fundamental article of social faith. A socialist was unthinkable in that company and had he got there he would have been treated with a mixture of distrust, contempt and fear. Yes, fear, but a fear born of exasperation at the waste of energy from interference with the system rather than a fear deriving from any surmise that the system might be successfully overthrown. He might have made them afraid, too, for a subtler reason which they would hardly have recognized or admitted. A socialist's scheme of social values is expressed in material terms, but it is, or should be, derived from moral and even spiritual premises, belief in the innate dignity of each individual man and woman and the fundamental rights and safeguards and equalities which spring from that. The Manchester men's scheme of social values was also expressed in material terms, but first and foremost the scheme was valid for themselves and their families, and it was argued from the alleged

Alderley Edge station

Basil Jeuda collection

Wilmslow station

Basil Jeuda collection

necessity of the battle for success and from the odd confusion of thought produced by marrying that old puritanical conception of thrift as a virtue to the utilitarian idea that the self-interest of one is really the best long-term interest of all. They thought of laisser-faire economics almost in terms of a cosmic process and would have been horrified at old Thomas Huxley's sad conclusion that the evolutionary cosmic process has no sort of relation to moral ends and is even in conflict with them. Thus a socialist on the station platform at Alderley Edge would have implied a criticism, even if an unadmitted criticism, of the whole set up of social values. For that matter the same galling effect of criticism from a non-material standpoint would have been produced by the inclusion in the station group of some impoverished member of the old Cheshire landed gentry who fulfilled, as some of them most faithfully did, Lecky's rules for the functions and justification of an aristocracy.

However, within this framework, beyond which most of them never looked, our neighbours were as diverse in their interests and characters and as civilized often in their manner of life as any other well to do section of the community. Old merchant and shipping families of Liverpool may have had a certain metropolitan polish which a number of the Manchester men subtly lacked - the Liverpudlians certainly took this superior view of themselves - but none the less the belief in the boorishness of the Manchester man as a recurrent trait in his pattern becomes just a part of the myth of standardization when you try to generalize it. Novels like Mr Howard Spring's *Fame is the Spur* give a totally wrong impression of the Manchester society of forty or fifty years ago. Spring's hero, Hamer Shawcross, who climbs to political fame from a back street in Ancoats, the blackest of Manchester slums, never meets a single educated and civilized product of the Manchester bourgeoisie in the course of his long career either as friend, patron or foe. The moneyed types whom he does meet, the warm-hearted, vulgar, unschooled pilers up of 'brass' are certainly true to life and so is the 'intellectual' Aunt Lizzie, sister to one of them. But they are only a part of the truth and using them exclusively distorts the picture out of recognition. Sir William Mather was also a Manchester man. And let us see how some of our near neighbours on the platform at Alderley Edge themselves squared up to a more polished standard.

There would be Mr Rothstein peering his elderly hook-nosed Jewish face over his newspaper, the back inner page of the Guardian where the financial reports were printed, but it would not be surprising if he had looked first at the musical criticism of last night's Hallé concert and it would not be surprising either if, had he the knack with his pen, he could have dashed off quite as informed and perhaps a more meaty criticism himself. Mr Rothstein's father had helped to found those concerts. He had been sent over from Germany as a youth to foster business connections in Manchester, had married an English wife and stayed on to found a Manchester family. But he had never quite lost touch with his friends and relatives in Germany and as a young man our Mr Rothstein had visited them in Frankfurt. Mr Rothstein senior had been a Liberal under the golden aegis of Bright and Cobden and Gladstone; the starker fighting Liberalism which had rocked his old city of Frankfurt in 1848-9 was as remote from him as it was from his Lancashire contemporaries. But he retained his German way of life. Lavish German food and drink were piled on the dining-room table of the big house fronting Oxford Road, and the sound of German music drifted chronically through the rooms as one or another member of his family sat down to the piano.

As for our Mr Rothstein, in so far as he was interested in politics at all he professed a conventional Free Trade Liberalism which might or might not survive the audacious budgetary career of Lloyd George in 1909. For the rest, our Mr Rothstein was no longer, like his father, a practising Jew although he was still loosely attached through his private and exclusive pride of race to the faith of his ancestors. He had been educated at Manchester grammar school and spoke English with a slight Lancashire as opposed to his father's German accent. He had sold most of his father's German books, but retained all the well-marked opera scores and sheets of music, for he could read a score as easily as he could read a book, indeed more easily for he was not an adventurous or assiduous reader. You never saw many books lying about in his house. He had reduced the groaning German board, or his wife had, to a more English weight, but he still drank half a bottle of claret every evening at his dinner. His sons, who were my contemporaries, had no Lancashire accent and a reduced pride of race. They went to Rugby; his daughter went to Roedean.

Then there would be Mr Swinside whose manners were pleasant but who had no interest in the world so far as I knew beyond marketing cotton cloth and bringing down his golf handicap on Saturday afternoon. No doubt he had observed that his wife was the best dressed-woman in Alderley Edge and was pleased and proud about that, but then his wife was a possession and it was always satisfactory to possess something of a rather better class than your neighbours could boast. In addition, perhaps he had an interest in his garden for he spent time in it on Sunday, and this so far as it went must have been a genuine interest in flowers for their own sake, because he had no talent as a gardener and therefore his garden was not among the best examples of Alderley Edge horticultural art and so could not minister very effectively to his competitive pride.

Mr Chesney came from a line of Irish soldiers and I do not know how or why he had settled in Manchester as a young man. Certainly he had no affinities with the men of the Manchester myth. It was he who read the Morning Post. Most of our neighbours found the Morning Post too much concerned with the doings and outlook of London and county society which were essentially more alien to them than the doings and outlook of Ancoats. Very few of them to their honour wanted to buy their way into that society, but most of them knew very well how Ancoats lived and realized dimly that their forebears had either created Ancoats or struggled out of it as the case might be and that they carried some responsibility to mitigate its harshness. The sort of things they did to discharge that responsibility I will try to describe later. Meanwhile there was Mr Chesney, the descendant of soldiers, whose dining-room walls were darkly decorated by ancestral figures in heavy gilded frames and whose wife came from the old merchant and industrial aristocracy, the kind of family which had given Peel and Gladstone to English politics. His elder son carried on the military lineage and went into the army. So it was quite in order for Mr Chesney to read the Morning Post because it represented his tradition, the conservatism of the pre-1914 army paired with the conservatism of the Church of England of Trollope's novels. He was the solicitor to the Bishop of Manchester.

Mr Lees was another solicitor whose connections had taken him to the Balkans and other outlandish parts of Europe. He was a big heavy man with a clean-shaven face and rather ponderous jowl. Not long ago I found in an old trinket-box a couple of rings made of brass wire and tiny bright beads which he had given me after a visit, I think, to Bucharest. Bucharest and the other Balkan capitals sounded to me like places where adventures could happen, but I doubt whether Mr Lees, waiting each weekday of the first decade of the proud twentieth century on the station platform for the 9.18 train, for all his knowledge of the Near East, surmised that in one of those capitals an adventure was gestating in the belly of time whose direct result, so far as he was concerned, would be to drown his only son in a torpedoed troopship off the north-west coast of Africa. Jasper was a good deal older than I was, Campbell's contemporary, and he went to Eton and New College. We thought both rather unnecessarily 'posh'. But the Lees were not social climbers. They had their own satisfactory standard of manners and culture, manifested by the Scottish shooting holidays which they took quietly and naturally most summers and by the books which lay about Mr Lees's billiard-room, the curios from remote parts of the world which were dotted about all over the house, and the lovely delicate china ranged in the drawing-room cabinets and along its shelves. Besides Jasper there were four daughters, all older than I was, but all my friends. One of them was the daring comrade with whom I had made the poppy dolls and climbed the big cedar of Lebanon. So I used to go to that house a lot. I have already mentioned it as a concoction of reddish sandstone patterned with purple brick, Gothic mullioned windows and Tudor gables slashed with black and white. Indoors it was a rambly place with long passages and rooms unexpectedly leading out of each other, marvellous for playing bears and hide-and-seek, but captivating also because as you turned a corner or flung into a room you would suddenly see one of the fascinating curios or better still a group of exquisite cups and saucers or a row of plates wired up on a wall. Dashing past on our wild games, these glimpses were snapshotted on to my mind without my being in the least aware of what was being done to me, and I am sure that those snapshots have given me a standard, and a true standard, by which to measure grace and charm, if not the greater and nobler preserves of beauty.

Mr Bles was a Dutchman by descent and he had made a collection of old glass which contained some of the finest pieces held in private hands; part of it is now at South Kensington. He was, too, something of an expert on prints and engravings. I am afraid I remember best their black and gold frames, but I also remember the elegant feel of his house produced by the mixture of mellowed furniture and patterned chintzes. His son was in the Indian Civil Service and on his rare leaves was welcomed by father as a sort of young ambassador from that wider world outside Lancashire from which father was always anxious to draw his intellectual food.

Mr Tulloch and Mr Hutton - I have forgotten to mention them at the outset - came to the station with the group which emerged on to the Congleton Road and the former was manager of one of the big Manchester banks and reputed to present the dessert, when he and his wife gave dinner parties, on gold plate. This opulence was not envied by the sensible, but on the contrary caused a good deal of derisive mirth. He had, however, other more sensible and also more engaging characteristics including a sprite-like capacity for turning Catherine wheels for the delight of his neighbours' young. Mr Hutton was a distinguished fisherman and was said by those who knew to be one of the greatest authorities on the ways of salmon in the country.

Then there was 'old Mr Worthington' a notable Manchester architect with a patriarchal beard. As a very small boy he had been taken to the opening of the Manchester to Liverpool railway on that famous occasion of which we had read in our history books when Huskisson was killed while trying to climb from one carriage to another. And he had, too, seen European history in the making at the romantic beginnings of two revolutions. When he was a young man he found himself in Paris on the eve of the insurrection which broke the bourgeois monarchy of Louis Philippe. They told him what was brewing and advised him to clear out, so he left for Marseilles by the last diligence to get away from Paris. It was a hopscotch sort of journey for every now and then the coach wheels were unpinned and the vehicle lashed on board a truck to travel a few miles by the new railway. When the length of track came suddenly to an end the coach was put together again, the horses harnessed and away they went with the horn going full blast until they came to another stretch of railroad in action. More unpinning and hoisting aboard and so on to Marseilles. There he took ship to Civitta Vecchia and arrived in time to find Mazzini's revolution about to explode. He saw Pope Pio Nono drive about the streets and heard him speak to the crowds. From Rome he went to Naples where the British fleet rode at anchor in the bay on the watch for complications, and the ships were three-decker sailing ships, sisters to the men-o'-war which lay off Naples when Nelson was making love to Lady Hamilton to the detriment of Mediterranean strategy. Yet when I was a child of eight 'old Mr Worthington' was stalking about Alderley Edge with the patriarchal white beard cascading over a voluminous ulster. I think he is my best 'link with history'.

In a sense he and his two architect sons hit Alderley Edge life at a tangent. Where they touched the circle they merged with it completely and wholeheartedly, but there were vital sections of their lives outside it where a scheme of values operated - Ghiberti's scheme of values - which had nothing whatsoever in common with those of our neighbours. Their purpose was to create fine and fit buildings, but the purpose of the other 'makers' on the station platform was to create saleable commodities or machinery to make the commodities or even machinery to make the machinery, and all would eventually be judged by their fellows the merchants (who found the markets) in terms of expanding trade and a money return. It is true that the industrialists mostly stood for good workmanship, but that was partly because the standard and tradition of the old hand-loom and the old hand forge still survived precariously and partly because they were obstinate and would not compete with cheap and shoddy foreign lines. Thus an aesthetic standard had nothing to do with the core of living. Perhaps this was the key to Sir John Wormald's failure to win a fundamental satisfaction from his pursuit of objets d'art. You could appreciate watercolours or old prints or eighteenth-century glass and china as sensitively as any connoisseur, but that belonged to your leisure. And because your appreciation touched only the surplus after the essentials had been dealt with on a different scale of values, the contribution of the creator of beauty, the artist or the craftsman, was not a matter of basic seriousness. His profession was essentially frivolous. There was no bite on life in it. No one would have liked his son to become an artist. The Worthingtons did not come into the frivolous category because they created solid and useful things, Manchester buildings, so the difference in their approach, went unobserved. You did them the honour of not thinking of them as artists. Yet behind the scenes, so to say, where the business men did not penetrate, they were artists. For them art was not a decoration for the leisure hours of a sensitive taste, it was the core and purpose of their working lives. For them the men and women who created works of art were doing the most serious thing that a man or woman could do. It was this that set the vital sections of their lives apart. Except the Worthingtons, whom I did not recognize as such, I never met a live artist until I was twenty-two. Then suddenly I recognized the Worthingtons by analogy and began to work out for myself what I have been trying to analyse here. When I had done so I found that I had effected a major revolution of outlook.

Another and very different Alderley Edge character was Mr Crewdson. He was a surviving specimen of the gentle mid-century type of Manchester man. His place was in a novel by Mrs Gaskell who would have domiciled him exactly where he was in fact brought up, in a solid and dignified town house on Ardwick Green within a stone's throw of the family warehouse. He was a short man with slightly bowed legs and appeared like a very neatly dressed groom. He wore a flat-topped bowler hat, stock and white collar and smooth dark grey suit. He had a shrewd clean-shaven face with humour in the eyes and a smile whose sweetness I remember now. Father liked him and he often came to tea on Sunday afternoon and father would listen more patiently than he sometimes did to guests who 'stayed on' while Mr Crewdson talked in a rather thin high-pitched voice. I doubt whether he had any aesthetic sense or intellectual standards, but I think he was sincerely and simply religious and he was certainly compact of public spirit and practical. intelligence. Perhaps the combination was a result of his Quaker breeding. His family of spinster daughters were like him (his sons and married daughter lived elsewhere), public-spirited, intelligent, practical and staunch.

This public spirit of which Mr Crewdson was so fine an exponent was a very definite characteristic of the best among the Edwardian business men and its outlet was philanthropy. Numbers of them were enthusiastic philanthropists. Manchester hospitals depended upon their money and upon their services on the boards of management, their womenfolk sat on the subsidiary hospital committees and the town teemed with a heterogeneous crowd of 'charities'. There were charities to look after your body and charities to look after your soul and charities which aimed at benefiting both. These last were the most frequent; I think the Nonconformists saw to that. Indeed the ramifications were so complicated that if the system of charity had broken down social conditions in whole districts of Manchester would have come very near collapse. Charity (and not planned and comprehensive schemes worked out through the city government) was the piecemeal and incoherent method they chose to discharge those responsibilities for the slums of Ancoats. Much of it was an honourable generosity springing from a simple-hearted desire to help the weak and the unfortunate. But the rest derived from more complicated motives and smacked too much of 'conscience-money'. Charity was the oil used to lubricate the frictions of a social and economic system whose machinery divided society between the few rich and the many poor. But there is this to be said. Since to their minds the system was a law as certain in its working and as unlikely to change as the law of gravity they were not seriously afraid about their own privileged position because they took that for granted. So they were not trying to buy immunity with a Danegeld. I would say that the series of bitter strikes which studded the pre-war years scarcely disturbed this belief and that a book like Mr Dangerfield's *The Strange Death of Liberal England* reads into the employers' psychology a fundamental uneasiness which was, in fact, simply ad hoc and superficial. They happened to have hearts and consciences and they satisfied their decent feelings by squirting their charitable oil-cans where the frictions of the machinery had made the worst human scars. And sometimes, not often but occasionally, one or another of them like Aunt Mary entered Ancoats in humble imitation of the solacing spirit of a St Peter Claver or a St Vincent de Paul.

Only, I think, in the matter of education did they feel fear. Sir William's attitude to education was a rare one. So far as I know there was no charity to give a working man a straight education in the facts of his history and of the world in which he lived. The Workers' Educational Association, for instance, was not much supported by them; it relied on the university. Indeed, I seem to remember that it was regarded as a suspect organization designed to throw a spanner into the machinery, a wasteful proceeding since the machinery, thanks to its impersonal majestic law, must inevitably go on somehow however many spanners were hurled into it. Perhaps, too, they subscribed half-consciously to the comforting if dubious theory that fed and mended bodies and souls on the way to salvation are politically innocuous. But a fed and mended mind on the way to mental adventure; there is a most perilous dynamic.

Two specimens of the Manchester man I have kept to the last and must now try to draw rather more fully since without them the station platform at Alderley Edge would have lost notably in richness and variety, the cross-section of Manchester character would be incomplete and out of balance. Mr Schill and Mr Pilkington came from those two homes which I mentioned at the beginning of the chapter as interweaving with the life of Ferns more closely than any of the others. I find it much harder to draw them than the rest and am much more concerned as to whether I have got them true, I suppose because I knew them so much more intimately and from a different angle. The others were geographically neighbours and relationships though friendly enough were derived from that, but Mr Schill and Mr Pilkington merged with their families as old friends of my family and they and their wives had been companions of my parents in the days when they were all young and their children are still my close friends. So this interlacing intimacy nets them in a long tangle of memories, but as I look back it is symbolized by the little intimate circumstance that I was on terms to go straight into their houses without ringing the front doorbell.

Ringing the front doorbell and having the door opened by a trim maid meant beginning the visit with a certain formality which made for shyness. The houses of Alderley Edge depended on the style with which their front doors were opened. There were no butlers but the maids were excessively trim, clad in starched print of a morning and in black or brown with finely woven aprons in the afternoon and always, of course, wearing a cap as a badge of office, and those few houses which produced untidy maids gave an impression of a slatternly home which I find ineradicable, partly no doubt because it was scored in by mother's comments. None the less, the trimmer the maid and the more distant her manner the more intimidating the formality of one's entrance; so being able to run into the Schills or the Pilkingtons to find my friends as I would into my own home meant a fundamental differentiation of contact for me as between them and the other neighbours.

Mr Schill was a merchant in the South American trade by occupation but he was, in fact, quite out of place as a business man and that he was a business man was in its own way a comment on Lancashire customs. I suppose that as a lad he had slipped almost automatically into the place waiting for him in his father's firm. It was difficult to refuse the allotted place in a family concern and a lad had to be very sure of what he wanted to do and how he proposed to do it before he broke the tradition. He had to be ruthless and self-confident, but Mr Schill was gentle and sensitive and no fighter, so he had not stood up for his own things at the outset of his career. Neither, during the course of it, had he grown the leathery epidermis to his character and feelings necessary to anyone who would shoulder successfully through the scrum of business life. Even his physical characteristics were wrong for his part. He had mild and rather timid grey eyes and a winning diffident smile, and his voice was muted and soft in contrast to the normal harsh Lancashire voice. You might be shy of Mr Schill, and I was a little bit, but you could never be afraid of him. You could only be afraid for him. His life was full of interests and they were absorbing interests, not mere decorative foils to work. But they were the interests of a recluse and an escapist; at least, I feel that he pursued them partly because through their magic he escaped into a more serene and easy world. I see him standing before his drawing-room fire for a few minutes after he had come home from Manchester, smoking a cigarette and smiling with that rather lost look on his face, and then fading off to put on an old jacket and go out into his garden or into his billiard-room. He was an erudite and passionate rock-gardener. His love of gardens was quite different from that of my father and I find it illuminating to compare the two of them. Unlike father, it was not the general look that Mr Schill really cared about. He would never have tried to lay out a garden with an eye to the overall pattern. The sense of large design which produced the noble gardens of eighteenth-century country houses was lacking in his make up. He would never have employed 'Capability Brown'. He liked detail in all his enterprises whereas father hated detail and throve on large schemes which he could plan and initiate but need not carry into every-day application. So it was the feel of the soil when he drove his trowel into it which gave pleasure to Mr Schill, the joy and triumph of tending successfully some tiny exotic plant which he cared for as he might have cared for a delicate child, some plant from the Himalayas or the Alps which by all rules should have died in the raw damp atmosphere of Alderley Edge and which could only live when all sorts of minute artificial conditions of environment had been created for it. Indoors, Mr Schill was a stamp collector, a very special and detailed stamp collector, for he was only interested to collect 'whole plates' and these had to be South American plates into the bargain. The billiard table was covered with the trays awaiting completion. And then he made watercolour drawings mostly of trees and very meticulous, but he handled his finicking technique with competence and strength.

As a young man, when he was out representing his firm in South America, he had made an expedition up the Amazon to collect butterflies and moths. He would have made a fine biologist, a patient and adventurous collector of specimens and also a good dissector, for his watercolours showed that he had command of his hands. But he would never have correlated his finds and like Darwin produced a great key theory. Father, on the other hand, might easily have seen some Darwinian synthesis in a flash of mental insight, but he would never have had the patience to be a fieldworker and he had not the controlled hands neatly to dissect a rabbit.

I do not know whether there were many misfits like Mr Schill in Manchester, but I do know that the family business was often like a trap whose spring snapped home for life before a son had the strength of will or the knowledge to extricate himself.

Mr Pilkington was by lineage a cadet of one of the oldest families of Lancashire, a family which had lived for many generations at Rivington Hall near Bolton. Tradition asserted that his ancestor had fought for King Harold and during the storm of the Norman invasion had needed to go underground disguised as a mower, whence the family crest of a man holding a scythe. An eighteenth-century forebear figured as the hero of 'The Spectre Horseman of Rivington Pike', one of the eeriest ghost stories in Robey's grand book, *Traditions of Lancashire*. When or why the branch to which our Mr Pilkington belonged had drifted into industry, I do not know. His family owned the glass-making firm at St Helens, but as there was no place for him and two of his brothers in the glass-works they had gone to an uncle who held collieries at Clifton outside Manchester. So our Mr Pilkington was brought up to be the captain of a colliery in the days when it was all an intimate family concern and the master lived in the big house near by the pits and knew his miners as closely as a huntsman knows his hounds. Indeed that is not an inapt metaphor for the whole relationship. There was the same kind of rough warm affection on both sides, the same turbulence, and as with the huntsman, the same art of handling and the same sense that he must look after his hounds before himself in all weathers and in all circumstances. But with that, too, there was on the part of the master the huntsman's sense of obvious and unquestionable superiority and leadership. Hounds course the fox but they do not interfere with the strategy and rules of the hunt, nor do they dictate when and how they shall hunt or what kind of kennels they shall inhabit. From another point of view it was a feudal relationship and perhaps Mr Pilkington's ancestry enhanced that aspect in his case as it did with my Irish uncles and grandfather in their conduct of Mossley.

The relationship was very different to that of my father in regard to his industry, and the contrast is worth dwelling upon for a moment because it is an epitome of the change which came over Lancashire during the eighties and nineties of the last century, a change which was at the same time a cause and a result of the Limited Liability Acts which shifted financial responsibility from the individual employer to an impersonal collective entity called 'the Company'. Father had begun his career with Mather & Platt when the firm was still based on 'the family' but was shortly destined to become a limited liability company and thus lose to a considerable extent its intimate and patriarchal quality. His Cambridge mathematical degree and outfit of brains won for him the opening and later a leader's place in an industry which, as Sir William saw, was beginning to find inadequate the empirical knowledge and traditional experience of the craftsman. He was the trained scientific expert, the precursor of the modern managers whose type and functions are so brilliantly analysed in Mr J. Burnham's book *The Managerial Revolution*. He brought a new outlook to Lancashire at once differentiated from that of the unlettered youth who would build his own business shilling by shilling from a capital of a few pounds by sheer dint of energy and native intelligence and from that of the scion of an old merchant or industrial house with an assured career ahead of him and no need to make his own way. In this sense father was an adventurer, there was nothing feudal as I have already remarked in his personal feeling of relationship to his industry. He was more like the free captain of Renaissance times who put his sword at the disposal of any prince or monarch, but then fought with gallantry and skill and loyalty. Father's loyalty was to 'the firm', an impersonal loyalty compared to that of my uncles for Mossley or to that of Mr Pilkington for his colliery. Workpeople did not refer to father as 'Mr Edward', in the way that they distinguished my Irish uncles by their Christian names, but they did refer to Mr Pilkington as 'Mr Lawrence' (with the 'Mr' affixed as a mere matter of form) because he had played among them as a boy and they had seen him grow up into the firm; besides he had several brothers and how else could a distinction be made between them except by the familiar and friendly use of a Christian name?

The impact of father and his like upon Lancashire resulted in an odd paradox, a sort of contradiction in the system. It was not only that by their improvements in techniques and managerial efficiency they stepped up the pace and volume and even the standard of production whilst at the same time they left further and further behind, stranded in history, the qualities of the hand craftsman; it was also that their methods and ideals brought a paradoxical. loss and gain in human relationships. The old personal relation between master and man began rapidly to die out, the master became an 'employer' and the firm a depersonalized concern, a concept like 'the state' rather than a collection of human beings. The loss in human values was obvious, but at the same time there was also an offsetting gain which may even have transferred a good deal to the credit side of the account. The socialist thinkers who preferred an industrial structure of impersonal firms to one of family enterprises like Mossley or the Clifton Colliery had good reasons for their preference. For the impersonal firm made an opponent better suited for collective bargaining and in the upshot the workpeople, if they no longer received some feudal consideration from their 'masters', won far more real independence from their 'employers'. Working conditions and wages could be treated from a broader point of view and were no longer at the mercy of an individual's caprice or fortune. These arguments were in my mind and in fairness had to be recalled when I was finding so much to admire in Mossley. In this transition or revolution in Manchester father represented the new and Mr Pilkington the old régime.

It must have been some fifteen years before I was born that father and his brothers while on holiday in the Lake District had carried Mr Pilkington on a farm gate down to Wasdale Head from Piers Ghyll on Scafell. They were all mountaineers in the days when rock-climbing was still a young and golden sport and almost all the Lake District crags awaited exploration and conquest. Mr Pilkington had been making a route up the deep clefts of Piers Ghyll when a fall of stones had caught him and smashed his thigh. While one young man clattered down Wasdale on a borrowed horse to fetch a doctor the others did what they could to make the injury comfortable. That was how the friendship between our families began and I was born into it.

Often it happens that the associations bequeathed from one generation to its successor grow outworn and tedious, but in this case the friendship deepened and expanded so that as the years passed it came to mean something important in my own ripening life. Thus when I try to describe Mr Pilkington I am thinking of him not so much with an adult's critical faculty playing on the child's vision, but rather as I knew him when I was just grown up in the years after the 1914-18 war.

I can see him now sitting in his big armchair in his music- room which was also the family sitting-room, with his head resting against the chair-back and his hands on the two arms with the fingers drumming a little as he talked. I think he had the most beautiful head and hands of any man I have ever known. His skin was rosy and his eyes a clear grey-blue. The short beard and moustache, white when I knew him best, did not hide his lips which were strong and delicate, moving often into a smile of grace and sweetness, which spilt over sometimes into a puckish grin. His nose jutted a little and the nostrils were finely cut. The forehead was high and broad with a little sinking on either side of the temples. As for his hands, there was power in them as well as delicacy and the fingers were very long with broadish tips.

I could listen for hours to his tales, of the colliers and their wives who had made up the pattern of his Lancashire working life, of fishing off the west coast of Ireland, of pioneering adventure in the Alps. He would have been a great mountaineer but for that disaster on Scafell when he was twenty-nine. As it was he had made the first ascent of the Meije without guides, the prize of the Dauphiné Alps, and in conditions - the rocks were plastered with ice - when none but the most daring party would have set out. I have often thought that I should like to have seen those fine fingers of his taut on some handhold of rock or curved about the shaft of an ice-

Neighbours Mollie and Lawrence Pilkington of Firwood

My friends, Dorothy and Margaret Pilkington

Pilkington family group in the
window of Firwood
Courtesy Phyllis Redding

Lawrence Pilkington in his
later years

axe and that chiselled profile set against an Alpine snow slope with the clear eyes scanning for a route.

It is significant that many of the great pioneers of mountain climbing, men like Leslie Stephen or, in a later time, Geoffrey Winthrop Young, have been persons of rich talents and interests. Mr Pilkington was one of these. I believe he could have been a distinguished musician had he wanted to dedicate his powers to music, but he found enthralment at too many points in life. He was a sensitive amateur painter. I have possessed for years a watercolour of his of the Cairngorm mountains; it never stales but is always satisfying because it exhibits so deep an understanding and love of wild mountain scenery. He wrote poetry, too, and had he set himself earlier in life to learn and submit to the discipline of the poet's art his sensitivity of emotion and impression would have carried him to an honourable place among poets. His mountain poems were like his mountain drawings. A mountain meant far more to him than a simple agglomeration of rock and earth cast in a fine or fantastic form. Indeed, I think that the beauty which he found in all nature was, for him, a reflection of the mystery behind the visible universe. I doubt if he had any formal religion; I think his was one of those rare souls, brave and ranging, but with an innate self-containment which enables and even requires them to seek and keep touch with the Infinite without the compass of a creed or a church. At any rate, I have never met another human being who made me feel more certainly that man does not live by bread alone. It was when he was speaking seriously that one realized, though perhaps not very consciously at the time, that youth has no greater privilege than admittance to the wisdom and goodness of a finely strung mind. When he was not being serious, fun rather than wit sparkled through his talk. He told his stories with whimsical humour and a boyish delight in pretending to shock his audience.

But for all that he was also and all the time a seasoned Lancashire master. The tough tissues which had failed to grow and protect Mr Schill were firmly knit in Mr Pilkington's makeup. Thus, when the talk drifted on to politics I did find it difficult to admire him wholly after I grew up. For he possessed in full measure the aggressive individualism of the nineteenth century Lancashire master, the automatic and unquestioning belief in the system, the acceptance of his own position and that of his class. He gave his time and money unstintingly to serve the Manchester poor - he was chairman of the Salford Royal Hospital - and he would go to any length of trouble for individual Tom, Dick and Harry among his workpeople, but if Tom, Dick and Harry got together and tried to alter the balance of industry then his resentment was aroused. It was aroused equally when any action of government could be construed as interference or when outside persons of authority dared to express opinions about an industrial dispute. I remember his bitterness when the late Archbishop of Canterbury, William Temple, who was then Bishop of Manchester, made pronouncements which favoured the miners' case in the coal disputes after the last war. Men of religion had no business to set up ethical standards for industry since they could not understand the conditions under which industry was run. This kind of conversation sent me home smouldering and rebellious and more determined than ever to equate the Lancashire order with Blake's dark satanic mills. I could not understand Aunt Mary's attitude of indifference to the politics of social reform, but Mr Pilkington's hostility to any suggestion from outside for industrial reform made me indignant, particularly when the suggestions seemed to my youthful comprehension only reasonable and just. In this mood I would never have understood what a perfect example Mr Pilkington was of the flower of our Edwardian bourgeois civilization, nor known how to equate that perfection with the harsh economic system in which the flower was rooted.

Mather & Platt advertisement 1911

Oxford Street c1937, viewed from the balcony of the Central Library.
Chris Makepeace collection

Oldham Street 1905

Chris Makepeace collection

Chapter Eight
MANCHESTER

When the business men reached Manchester they all dispersed to their several offices and factories, but they met again for lunch at the Union Club. At least, those who were socially elect did, for membership of the Union Club was a passport even to a good marriage. There was racial selection, too, for a discernible dash of anti-semitism flavoured the club. Mr Rothstein, for instance, was not a member, and I recall ominous feelings being aroused when Mr X desired to join and had it conveyed to him that he would not be acceptable on account of his Jewish blood. Mr X was a civilized and cultured gentleman. My father could not stand this and talked about resigning. He and his brothers were always threatening to resign from clubs on crusading grounds. They threatened to resign en bloc from the Alpine Club along with some other stalwart Manchester members - I think Mr Pilkington was one of them - when that respected mountaineering institution which then epitomized all the social prejudices and predilections of upper middle-class England was about to blackball their Manchester friend Hermann Woolley, who was a fine climber but unfortunately a wholesale chemist. And their political affiliations with the Manchester Reform Club were shot with resignations.

However, as to the Union Club, it was to the other Manchester clubs what the Guards are to the rest of the army; and it was a masculine sanctuary. The community quarters of a monastery are not more jealously withdrawn from outsiders than was the Union Club from feminine penetration. No one among our ladies would have dared enquire for her spouse at its portals. That would have been spectacular immodesty. But I inquired there once. I inquired for my father on Armistice Day of November 1918. The bells were ringing in Manchester, the crowds were milling about the streets. My daring, absurd though it may seem, was a measure of the sense of profound release which was slowly spreading through one's being as the minutes passed on from eleven o'clock when the 'cease fire' had sounded away in France. I brought father out from his lunch. I think he wondered, but he smiled and understood.

The established men, the heads of firms and offices, returned by the 5.7 or 5.45 trains, the younger ones usually failed to get away before the 6.28. And after their departure the centre of Manchester became a city of the dead. There was life in the side streets and at the theatres and at the Midland Hotel, but the streets of warehouses and offices were silent and empty. Then it seemed that against a twilight sky the Gothic beauty of the cathedral was awakened, magically released from the spell of the beast. The gates of factories had clanged to and their gaunt walls appeared to wait for the breeze of dawn to soothe the smarting touch of daytime airs. But round about them the life of tired and harassed men and women who relax for an hour went on behind the walls of houses joined one against another in countless rows of streets whose dismal lamps led up gloomy perspectives to some brightly lit public-house at a corner which seemed by contrast the rich and inviting creation of an entertainer.'s art.

The bread-winners behind those walls did not catch a 5.45 to Alderley Edge and a garden breaking into spring. So far as that goes, it is likely that many of them did not want to. They preferred the comradeship of little houses cheek by jowl. But that is not the point. There are two points. Firstly, they did not have the chance to choose, and secondly the exodus of the well-to-do into Cheshire produced a vacuum in the city life which had not existed before and which began steadily to spoil the looks and to a large extent the character of Manchester.

The exodus spoilt the looks of Manchester by emptying the homes where the merchants and industrialists had lived close to the city centre. The square built houses of dark red brick along Upper Brook Street and at Ardwick Green were evacuated first. They were Regency houses or at least so early Victorian as to have escaped with years to spare the sham Gothic infection which Manchester took very badly about the middle of the century. They had clean lines and no frills, a solid and suitable dignity of workmanship and design. Ardwick Green had been the fashionable town quarter, and there is a good description of it as it looked in its fine feathers in Mrs Linnaeus Bankes's novel, *The Manchester Man*. It was from one of those houses that Lawrence Aspinall, her flash hero or villain, sallied forth in his laced uniform of an officer in the Manchester Yeomanry, to charge the crowd at Peterloo. That was in 1819; perhaps thirty years later our Mr Crewdson, who was, as I have said, brought up in Ardwick Green, was sallying forth from a similar house with his school books under his arm. Today Ardwick Green is a squalid square with a music-hall as its architectural feature. And for as long as I have known them, the Upper Brook Street houses, those of them that remain, have been a draggled travesty of former worth. They have been turned into cheap offices and shops and tenements and some of them even built up together so that you can only just trace out the members of the old façades. Occasionally you see one smartened up with a fresh coat of paint for some reason and then you realize what a fine and pleasant approach to Manchester Upper Brook Street must have been in the days when all were turned out in like manner and private cabs with spruce coachmen on their boxes took up their owners and

Upper Brook Street in the 1960s.

Chris Makepeace collection

The Central Library with the Midland Hotel in the background

Chris Makepeace collection

Owens College, now Manchester University c1901

Chris Makepeace collection

The Infirmary 1918

Chris Makepeace collection

The John Rylands Library
Chris Makepeace collection

Left:
Manchester Grammar
School

Below:
The Art Gallery 1905

Chris Makepeace collection

Art Gallery, Mosley Street, Manchester

Mosley Street c1857and the Portico Library

Chris Makepeace collection

The Art Gallery 1911

Chris Makepeace collection

drove them with a show of dignity to their offices.

The Ardwick and Upper Brook Street evacuation was complete when I was a child. After that came the Oxford Road flitting. Oxford Road runs out to Cheshire through the once villages of Rusholme and Fallowfield and Withington. The houses which flank it are larger than those of Upper Brook Street, symbol of the growing power of Manchester 'brass'. Most of them were built rather later and are, therefore, more florid and varied in design and a good many are faced with stucco. They stand, or stood, in bigger squares of garden. But now the gardens with their plats of lawn are blackened and seedy where they have not been built out altogether, the grime-stained stucco is scaling off, the windows with their great panes look like bleared eyes.

My own grandparents typified this process of 'moving out'. They moved in sequence from York Place behind Upper Brook Street to Grove House on Oxford Road where the Whitworth Art Gallery now stands, and then to Bowdon in Cheshire.

The process spoilt the character of Manchester because it left her without her natural leaders. These obviously were her merchants and industrialists. In the mid-nineteenth century when they 'lived in', the city was the centre of their lives and they formed it to express the way of life for which they stood. They did have a culture of their own and they did have civic pride as distinct from philanthropic and charitable zeal. One of them founded the Owens' College, which later became the university, another left money to trustees for the formation of the Whitworth Art Gallery which now houses perhaps the finest collection of watercolour drawings outside South Kensington. A third endowed the Rylands Library, a Gothic revival building quite unsuited in style to the character of a rising industrial city, but whose interior grace made you forget the incongruity when you were reading lovely books in its little elaborately panelled recesses. A group started the Portico Library and housed it in a small and unpretentious neo-classical building whose proportions are aptly gracious and a joy to single out as one passes along Mosley Street.

These Manchester men had the walls of their Gothic town hall decorated with Ford Madox Brown frescoes - it is there that you will find the final version of his famous 'Work'. And they bought the pictures of the pre-Raphaelites for their art gallery. This is significant, for when the pre-Raphaelites were contemporary it must have needed a certain serious and even daring care for art to purchase their works. They had the wit and the generous vision to welcome and support the efforts of the German and German-Jewish colony when these immigrants wanted to enrich the life of their adopted city by founding the Hallé concerts. Their new compatriots brought with them an instructed love for music and they learned from them with avidity so that Manchester became the most music-loving city in England. So they made of it a city almost in the Greek sense, coherent in culture and temper - perhaps all too Greek. For the slum-dwellers were the equivalent of the Greek slaves; they had no share among the democracy of citizens.

But when the sons of these nineteenth-century citizens moved out they could no longer carry on the tradition. The city became the place they worked in by day and abandoned in the evening as quickly as might be. Their leisure interests and recreations were elsewhere and the time they gave to civic duties dwindled. The city was no longer the centre of their cultural lives and though, as I have said, they still contrived to run a host of charities, they tended to withdraw their services from the city council. They grumbled enough about its quality and would sometimes make a comparison to the detriment of Manchester civic public spirit between their city government and that of the Birmingham of the Chamberlains, but it never occurred to them that they as individuals were perhaps to blame. Again, my own family typified the process. My grandfather was proud to be an alderman and mayor, but not one of his sons sat on the council. On the other hand, my father and my Uncle Charles certainly shouldered a full share of that charitable responsibility which all the best of them felt. Father was for years a treasurer of the Salford Royal Hospital and chairman of a colony for epileptics out in Cheshire, and Uncle Charlie sat as chairman of the Building Committee of the great new infirmary on Oxford Road. It was really a rather odd and illogical condition of mind.

I believe the same tendency of 'withdrawal' operated against the Chamber of Commerce. The leading business men seldom liked to serve on its executive body and this was left largely to the 'self-made' types. The result was a vicious circle; the more the Chamber of Commerce came to represent the brass-piling element the less the aristocratic merchants wanted to have to do with it. The Chamber of Commerce was never mentioned without a faint innuendo against its social composition.

Manchester's contribution to national politics suffered from the same drift. When I was a child the old Liberal tradition was beginning to weaken, even 'free trade' was being questioned by some of the more unorthodox spirits, and an alarming proportion of the business men were showing a readiness to vote Conservative. Yet Conservative Party managers despaired of inducing them to back their politics by standing for the city divisions. They left that to carpet-baggers with an easy complacency which contrasted badly enough with the political public spirit of their Liberal fathers.

The fate of Miss Horniman's repertory theatre is a good illustration on the cultural side of the final results of exodus. In the early years of this century the Gaiety put on a fine run of plays; Shaw, Galsworthy, Harold Brighouse, now and then a Shakespeare or a Sheridan and at Christmas time something suited to my contemporaries and me, such as *Alice in Wonderland* or *The Blue Bird*. But the Gaiety never properly paid its way. For years Miss Horniman waged the most gallant struggle against financial loss, but shortly before the outbreak of the 1914-18 war she had to admit decisive defeat. The Gaiety was closed down and later reopened as a cinema showing the usual fatuous programmes of the low-brow picture theatre of the inter-war years. The Prince's Theatre and the Royal suffered the same fate a little later. To-day the Opera House is the only commercial theatre in Manchester which puts on a straight play, but in the precincts of the City Library and partly subsidised by public funds there has recently been started a small theatre which has revived the spirit of the Gaiety, a sign perhaps to show that Manchester's municipality is ripening culturally.

Of course, it can be pointed out that a town the size of Manchester should not need an aristocracy of merchant princes to keep three theatres going. Numerically this is obviously true. There are quite enough people with quite enough money still living close enough to the centre of the city to keep half a dozen theatres going. But qualitatively it is not true. Perhaps it might have been had the merchant princes been less Greek in their exclusiveness. But it is not practical to breed a proletariat in the slums of Hulme and Ancoats and then expect that by and large their sons and daughters who have come up a bit in the world will be hungry for and able to digest without more ado the cultural food which has been denied to their forebears for generations. The glamour of a film story and the clash of noise and colour in a music-hall derive in a direct line from the gin palaces where the workpeople of Disraeli's *Two Nations* bought forgetfulness. When I was a child it was still necessary for many of their descendants to buy forgetfulness. In the years after the 1914-18 war, when the promises of politicians were extinguished one by one like the lights of the public-houses at closing time, the unemployed could only dream of forgetfulness. The need is gone now, but the inherited craving is there and must be educated out of the people's souls before enjoyment won from mental and aesthetic effort can be substituted for enjoyment derived from an opiate dream - and that will be a long business.

The City Art Gallery is another example of the cultural impoverishment due to 'moving out'. It has been undernourished both as regards money and interest. Except for the co-opted members, its committee has been largely manned by councillors whom their fellows, with unconscious cynicism, have regarded as too feeble to be entrusted with important services such as tramways or sewers. The men who had the vision to make the pre-Raphaelite collection in their day have not had enough worthy successors. Successors of their character would have taken a chance and filled a room with the works of painters like Renoir and Cézanne when these could have been bought for reasonable sums. So far as I know there is not a single major work by either of these painters in the gallery. A few years after the 1914-18 war they had the chance to acquire Degas's 'Jeunes Spartiates' and they havered and haggled and lost that to the Tate Gallery. I do not think that they can even show a great Sickert to represent England.

Again, it may be said that the Art Gallery of a city like Manchester should not have to depend upon the services of a handful of enlightened merchant princes. It should not, and it would not if... It will not when the curse of Disraeli's *Two Nations* has been finally worked out. Meanwhile, since the educated bourgeoisie progressively withdrew its services from the city council, the council was left in too great a proportion to men whose roots were twisted in a soil too harsh and insecure for an appreciation of art to flourish. A councillor whose grandparents or even parents had lived perhaps in a back to back house on the banks of the Irk or the Medlock, streams whose waters stank to high heaven, would be an exceptional man if he thought that the purchase of a picture (about whose artistic quality he was already doubtful and dependent for a verdict upon the professional curator who was his paid servant) was of equal importance with the laying of a new main sewer. He would give his full and intelligent attention to the sewer and not to the Cézanne. The point is driven home by a comparison with the Whitworth Gallery which houses the finest collection of watercolours, as I have already remarked, outside South Kensington. For the Whitworth is not a municipal collection and its trustees and governors and executive are recruited from the best that cultural Manchester can give. Here the distinction holds between the willingness that the more cultured sons of Manchester have always shown to serve their city through one or other private enterprise and their unwillingness since their exodus into Cheshire to serve her through her city government. It is of no use to pretend that a city like Manchester can do without the services of her educated and enlightened business men without suffering great loss. And by educated and enlightened I mean men who have had a tradition of style and culture at least for a generation or two. It is of no use to romanticize 'the people'. That throws on the people a responsibility which it is not fitted to carry. Public school and 'ancient' university intellectuals will have a right to hand over that responsibility only when they have cured by a new and truer education the blight which their forefathers laid upon nine-tenths of the population of the great towns in the interests of the Industrial Revolution.

'Moving out' strangely enough never killed the Hallé concerts. Every Thursday evening the Free Trade Hall was crowded; low-cut dresses and opera cloaks, boiled shirts and dinner jackets with an occasional tail-coat on the floor of the hall, and Sunday best upstairs in the cheaper and less exclusive gallery. People came in from Bowdon and Hale and Alderley Edge and half a dozen other residential ex-villages at considerable inconvenience when transport was by horse- carriage or rail. All the railways ran a 'Hallé train'. Week after week there would be the same absorbed faces in the same seats and the interval was a pleasant social interlude when the listeners moved about and greeted their acquaintances. On the vast platform there would be the same faces too. The sardonic melancholy-visaged man at the drums, Brodsky the first violin; Richter conducting. And some time after the reign of those two, Arthur Catterall, young and tall with a body swaying to the strokes of his bow like a wind-buffeted sapling, and Beecham with his gleaming band of collar below crisp grey hair and his back with the superbly tailored shoulders and the arrogant cut of his features when he turned to the audience to acknowledge its applause. An exciting Mephistophelian face, very pale, with high cheekbones and a pointed beard. Later, there was Hamilton Harty, the big-chested red-haired Irishman, whose face shone with a film of sweat while every muscle of his body seemed to come into play as he led his orchestra through some great passage. He reminded me of a charioteer controlling splendid galloping horses. Performers and audience were interlocked on those Thursday evenings by the power over them of the music. They were like two teams playing their game regardless of the outside world.

The Hallés went through some hard times in the inter- war years and their conventions have changed. The economic blizzard of 1931 and the loosening up of 'style' all through the twenties was reflected in a flight from evening dress. Only here and there one of the old guard appeared with a satin or velvet cloak or a white shirt-front. Their social axis has altered, too; and that is a reason for taking heart, since perhaps it means that a new and educated democracy is on the move to cultural freedom. Some day perhaps the new audience will recall the style, even though it was only a provincial style, of their predecessors and decide that this, too, had a certain merit.

But the Free Trade Hall has gone, all but the comely neo-Gothic shell smashed by German bombs. It is sad, for it was a good building, one of the few along with the City Art Gallery and the Portico Library and the Bank of England in which Manchester got away from its curious obsession that Gothic expressed the temper of an industrial age. It is a pity, too, because of its associations. These were political as well as cultural. An earlier generation had heard John Bright and Gladstone thunder from its platform supported by the leaders of the great Liberal families, the Ashtons and the Philips and the Gregs who, in their day, had made the political strength of Manchester a national watchword. Great foreigners had spoken there also; Kossuth was one of them.

There is a pleasant story about a visit of Gladstone's when he was the guest of the Philips at 'The Park' at Prestwich. The Philips 'equipage' met his train at London Road - liveried coachman on the box, groom at the door with the rug over his arm, and Mr Robert Philips alert to receive his guest. They drove down the incline and along the level to Piccadilly where a big crowd had collected sprinkled with men from the Philips's warehouses which faced on to the square. As the carriage entered Piccadilly a tremendous cheer went up. The great man put his head out of the window, removed his hat and waved it to the crowd. When suddenly the roar subsided and a solitary voice rang out:
'Put tha bloody 'ead in. It's Bob Philips we're shoutin'!' Neither did 'moving out' kill the Manchester Assemblies, a kind of club ball held every so often during the winter months in a lovely dance-room decorated with flowers and sometimes faintly hazy with the acrid fog from Cheetham Hill outside. Here the more exclusive and gilded youth danced with a decorous enjoyment under the eyes of numerous chaperones.

Any civilization must be judged on its 'form'. And form is a collection of diverse and sometimes contradictory facts studied so intimately and in such a way that eventually they coalesce and produce in the mind a criticism which derives not from argument but from the 'feel' of the subject put up for judgment. I have been trying to convey something of the 'feel' of Edwardian Manchester and I am not under correction because a critic could tell me with accuracy, for instance, that a number of the old families still lived in or as near in as makes no difference, and that a number of the merchants and industrialists who lived out still contrived to serve their city through its government. I know very well that the Ashtons still lived in Didsbury and the Philips in Prestwich, which are Manchester and not Cheshire suburbs. The large house where the Ashtons lived became the Regional Headquarters for the north-western area during the war and it was strange, a grim irony of history, to connect up the organization for combating air-raids and governing the area in case of an invasion which should cut off the north from London with the secure and ample Victorian and Edwardian life which once had filled those big solidly built rooms. But the last of the Philips, a little great old lady of terse manner, was still holding generous court at Prestwich guarded by her butler until her death a year or two ago.

I know that C P Scott, the great editor of the *Manchester Guardian*, lived until he died in a comfortable fog-ridden house in Fallowfield still nearer the heart of the city. I went to see him there once shortly after the 1914-18 war when I thought that I wanted to become a journalist (I did not get much easy encouragement out of him) and before my mind's eye, as I write, I can conjure up, as clearly as if the scene were actual now, against a setting of heavy Victorian furniture, the alert, still tense old man's body, the white hair and beard and elegant moustache with a half twist to its ends, the shrewd keen eyes, the features at once so sensitive and strong, reminding one of the delicate cutting of a cameo and the gathered strength of oak. Epstein's bronze head of him caught the character of oak but altogether missed the incisive delicacy of the cameo flint.

C P Scott

Then, too, when I was a child a group of lawyers and doctors and professors from the university still lived in Victoria Park in houses surrounded by gardens, yet even in those days the gardens were bleared with soot so that it seemed almost cruel to the flowers to plant them in that unwelcoming soil. But all pictures which seek to convey a truth must be simplified. That is where form comes in as the fusion of differing facts so that for writer and reader the true feel of a period can be built up. The form of Edwardian Manchester is now a matter only for memories and what I have written are mine.

The Union Club, Mosley Street c1870-1886
Chris Makepeace collection

Peter Street showing the Theatre Royal and the Natural History Museum c1855.
Chris Makepeace collection

The Free Trade Hall during the 1880s.

Chris Makepeace collection

The Whitworth Institute - now the Whitworth Art Gallery.

Chris Makepeace collection

Gaiety Theatre

Princess Theatre 1936

Manchester Town Hall

Chris Makepeace collection

The Entrance Lodge, Victoria Park c1900

Chris Makepeace collection

Barlow Moor Road

Basil Jeuda collection

Wilmslow Road, Didsbury

Wilmslow Road, Withington

Palatine Road, Withington 1909

Basil Jeuda collection

Withington station 1905

Basil Jeuda collection

Business train arriving at Withington station

Basil Jeuda collection

Didsbury station

Basil Jeuda collection

Central station

The imposing Midland Hotel c1908

A slightly later view of the Midland Hotel

Basil Jeuda collection

The Royal Exchange 1908, heart of Manchester's world wide textile trade

Basil Jeuda collection

Two early views of London Road station, now renamed Piccadilly
Basil Jeuda collection

The back to back 'rows' which were hastily thrown up to accommodate the growing
Manchester workforce as industry expanded

Chris Makepeace collection

The beginnings of the demolition process following the re-housing programme which began
in the 1960s

Chris Makepeace collection

Further examples of the poor housing conditions endured by the workers.
Top: Lee Street and above, Stone Street

Chris Makepeace collection

The Cottage - a favourite Alderley Edge picnic site

Alderley Edge Cricket club with Edward Hopkinson second left

Chapter Nine
ALDERLEY EDGE LADIES

If the 'moving out' process damaged Manchester neither did it do any real good to the 'reception areas'. Alderley Edge had been woodland and isolated farms with a hamlet at the bottom of the hill. The traditional centre was Alderley, two miles away, where the old parish church with its squat tower and the eighteenth century rectory were at one with meadows humanized by centuries of toil. There, too, was the water-mill where for generations receding into the mists of the past corn had been ground for the lord of the manor as a feudal due. Every year the mill wheels still turned in order to fulfil this duty and secure the tenant in his title. The miller's house was charming, old rosy brick and sandstone with a bloom on them like grapes, and the walls rose straight out of the mill-pond so that house and water were married by the reflection of one in the other. The Stanleys were lords of the manor and lived in the hall across the park. For some reason which I now forget they had had to take over the Sheffield title a generation or two before, and the Lord Sheffield of the Macclesfield to London railway compartment was now the reigning squire. A Victorian wit of the family had dubbed us ex-Mancunians, 'the Cottontots', and they had all been much put out when the railway was built from Manchester. And if one of us should drop the 'Edge' in referring to our village when in conversation with any Alderley man, we were made to feel that we were mushroom growth in no uncertain terms.

Alderley Edge became a good-sized village. As I remember, it contained a number of nice tradespeople, but its purpose of existence was solely in relation to the big houses on the Edge. The tradespeople battened upon the big houses. The preferential treatment these received when any preferential treatment was going was offset by permanently preferential prices. This was the sort of thing that happened. The gardener's wife who cooked for the Schills was sent one day to buy a kettle from Mr X, the ironmonger. She chose her kettle and said: 'How much?'
Mr X was quite frank: 'Is it for you or Mrs Schill?' he enquired.

There is a new generation of residents on the Edge, but Mr X still runs the ironmonger's shop and I doubt whether in his ripe old age he has abandoned his discriminating price lists. He was affable and obliging to me when I was small. I can see him, when I came in to buy a pennorth of nails, amid the metallic clutter of his shop, smiling down at me, leaning with both hands on the scored counter, his bony red wrists emerging from too short jacket sleeves. So I refrain from mentioning his name. But this is a pure convention of loyalty. For everyone understands the game, and in any event he has an ironmongering monopoly. If people want a kettle they still have got to buy from Mr X unless they go to town. Poor people, indeed, often did go elsewhere. They found it worth while to shop several miles away in Stockport. For all prices were high. As between Mrs Schill and her gardener's wife it was simply an exercise in relativity. The poor people were almost exclusively the personal retainers of the Edge houses, the gardeners, the coachmen and later the chauffeurs, so there was no chance for them that the shopping pattern would be shaped according to their needs.

As a social institution the village was bad, for it had no life-blood of its own. It was a parasitic growth. It was not even the vestigial remains of a feudal village grouped around one big house. It was grouped around several dozen houses whose masters' roots and economic interests lay elsewhere. There was no feudal interlocking of function and dignity of status. No one at Alderley Edge understood that conception of the distinction between a man and his office which can enable human beings to hold their essential dignity and equality in a hierarchic society. How could they understand it when there were no local offices except the parson's and the policeman's, and the only outward differences they saw derived from material possessions?

Perhaps the masters of the big houses suffered in their souls most. For they had lost a city community life, without I think knowing it, and still ignorant they did not understand that they had won no village community life to take its place. The lads' club that some of the younger ones ran had no roots in a shared life and many of them were almost living in a civic vacuum. In that way it was better for their womenfolk, who at any rate spent their days in the place. As for the tradespeople, they were to their credit neither servile nor sycophants. I think they probably accepted the situation with a sort of agreeable cynicism which enabled them to get out of it what they could without unpleasantness.

After the 9.18 train had pulled out of the station the Edge became exclusively female. You never saw a man on the hill roads unless it were the doctor or the plumber, and you never saw a man in anyone's home except the gardener or the coachman. And yet it was a man-made and a man-lorded society. When I tried to sketch the neighbours on the station platform, I was thinking exclusively of the heads of families and their sons. That was partly because there would be no females on the platform except the occasional embarrassed one who had to catch an early train and partly because the womenfolk moved across my daily scene and I cannot detach them so easily from it. But I was also thinking about the men exclusively for a subtler reason. I could not sketch the ladies on the same plane as their husbands and fathers and sons because it would not come natural to put them on an equality. For the men were the money-lords, and since for almost every family the community values were fundamentally economic, it followed that their women were dependents. They existed for their husbands' and fathers' sakes and their lives were shaped to please masculine vanity.

Of course, since human beings remain individuals in spite of the economic system in which their lives are fixed, in private it might well happen that Mr A deferred to Mrs A, leaned upon her advice and respected her separate personality. But Mr A would never have admitted that as a proper pattern for the relations of the wife to a husband who toiled each day in the grime of Manchester to keep her and his female children in affluence. Still less would he have admitted the right of his wife to produce a set of activities of her own which in any way threatened the vested interest in her time and personality which he had secured for himself It might also happen that Mrs A had an income of her own which could make her independent, but this, in spite of the general economic criterion, would prove only a paper emancipation; in reality she would be as dependent as the others who had not a penny to bless themselves with. I do not remember any woman in our circle who had a career or a paid job of her own, either a married woman or a spinster. A paid job for one of his womenfolk would have cast an unbearable reflection of incompetence upon the money-getting male. What is more, if any wife did try to stake a claim for herself, all the other women bunched together on the side of the challenged male. Even Mrs Schill, who was probably the most advanced and able and intelligent woman of our community, and who really did believe that women have duties and privileges as citizens in their own right, and that daughters are not dedicated like vestals to the home from the moment they leave school to the moment when they put on a wedding dress and drive to church with their fathers - even Mrs Schill drew the line at paid jobs, and no tentative line either but a thick black chalk Rubicon which it would have taken a female Caesar to expunge.

I think the first girl in our circle to get a paid job was Eileen McElfatrick, a doctor's daughter. Her father had died and the family finances required supplementing so she went into a bank. And this is what happened. She was a keen tennis player and had entered as usual for our Alderley Edge tournament which took place in the middle of July when the evenings were long and lasted about a fortnight. There was a rule that all ladies' matches had to be played off in the afternoons so as to leave the evenings free for the men when they came home from Manchester. Eileen was, of course, now no longer free to play in the afternoons. The situation which had arisen was without precedent. The committee cut the impasse by ruling her clean out of the ladies' events. And so far as I know all the other girls accepted that ruling without a protest.

So most of the women were idle in the sense that there was very little real work which they had to set their hands or minds to do whether they liked it or not. Like a large house and garden, a wife or daughter with nothing to do was an emblem of success. There were plenty of servants and nurses about so domestic chores were mostly limited to ordering the meals and doing the shopping, and domestic responsibility to captaining the staff. Of course, on the nurse's half-day, mothers with small children inexpertly looked after their young and usually longed for the nurse's return. For the rest, they all 'filled in time'. One method was paying calls; they all paid calls, not because they liked doing it or because they really thought that social good accrued from it, but because it was an accepted social duty and the only way open to them of getting to know a new neighbour. An introduction on neutral ground could never be followed directly by an invitation to tea or dinner. An invitation issued in so casual a way would have been a social heresy, an attack on the true faith which the invitee would probably have discussed later with her husband and countered with a polite but firm refusal. And that was not the end of it. When a dinner invitation had been issued and accepted in proper form and the dinner had taken place then, a week or two later, the female invitee had to pay a 'dinner call' on behalf of herself and her husband. Wretched bachelors had to pay dinner calls, too, and waste a precious Saturday or Sunday afternoon in the process. And it was essential to leave the cards in correct numbers. To get this wrong showed ignorance of polite manners and therefore brought the caller's whole social position into question. So far as I remember, the visiting lady left one of her own for the lady of the house and two of her husband's, one for the gentleman and one for the lady. If there was a grown-up daughter, that made a further complication. But I dare say I have got it all wrong; only I remember so well mother working it out for each house rather as if she were playing a complicated game of patience.

Those like mother or Mrs Pilkington or Mrs Schill, who did respect their time and had plenty of occupations on which they would have been glad to use it, ordered the carriage or later the car, and went forth about three o'clock in the spirit of drilled and disciplined soldiers parading for fatigues whose necessity they do not see, but whose performance they cannot question. Even the tone in which they would announce their intentions at lunch betrayed their real feelings:
'I must pay calls this afternoon,' mother would say and go upstairs with stern determination to change into her calling things. On the whole it

would be a more successful afternoon if most of her hostesses were out. That meant getting through more in the time, because the cards could be left and the score counted just the same. Mother would come home about half-past five and say with relief:

'Mrs X and Mrs Y and Mrs Z were all out, so I've got through five this afternoon. Now I can read to you for half an hour.'

And then something real would happen. Mother would take off the best clothes which I hated and settle down in the nursery chair and in five minutes we would be well away with the Scarlet Pimpernel, rescuing romantic aristocrats from the clutches of the guillotine.

As for my contemporaries and me, when we grew older, if ever we had to accompany our parents on these expeditions, and some of my senior contemporaries went through two or three years of it before the war released them, then we felt like soldiers who undergo worse than unnecessary fatigues; for we were driven into battle to suffer for a cause which had no conceivable relation to any interests of our own. The day was indeed a black one on which we found that our mothers had had their cards reprinted and that our names figured below theirs on the disgusting little white slips. But we, too, were drilled and disciplined.

Paying calls, for those who were assiduous about it, probably accounted for a couple of afternoons a week. It was really a two-way affair, for most of the ladies set aside an afternoon a week when they dressed up and produced extra cakes for tea and sat in their drawing-rooms awaiting the callers. Mother never did that, but then she was not assiduous - merely punctilious.

The technique, as I have said, was designed as a sieve whereby you could ensure that no impurities should slip into your society. In this connection, I remember mother's concern and bewilderment when one day she discovered the cards of a certain Mrs Smith decorating our hall table. Now Mrs Smith was relatively a new-comer and it had been agreed that, warm-hearted as she might be, she was not exactly 'one of us'. In the first place then, as a newcomer it had not been her business to begin the calling, and the fact that she had apparently done so was another black mark against her. Mother could not understand it, but having expended considerable thought on the matter she finally wrote to Mrs Smith suggesting as tactfully as she could that the cards must have been left under a misapprehension since she had made no advances. Mrs Smith replied, in fact I rather think she came in person to reply, in much confusion. Mother's cards had been found on her hall table and she was guiltless. The mystery deepened; finally it transpired, I forget how, that Mrs Smith's son had played a practical joke on his mother by subtracting mother's cards from some neighbour's tray and leaving them conspicuously on the hall table in his own home. The intriguing point, of course, was at what house the parallel paths of mother and Mrs Smith had, contrary to all social Euclid, in fact intersected. That we never discovered, but mother was now furious on Mrs Smith's behalf. She explained to me the invidious position in which poor Mrs Smith had been placed and the cruelty and ill-breeding of this deception. And in the circumstances, the joke was just plain cruel. But there the matter rested, mother's sympathy for Mrs Smith did not lead to an acquaintance; they never knew one another officially.

In this connection, too, I received the worst row that I ever had from mother. At the bottom of our dell there was a brick wall which divided the garden from our next-door neighbours down the hill. Now these neighbours, too, were comparative new-comers and for some reason which I never managed to discover, were suspect. In their case, the suspicion really was a grim commentary on our snobbery, our fear of being taken socially unawares, for in fact the Shaws, as I much later discovered for myself and to my own enrichment, were a far more liberally minded, generous and cultured family than half a dozen others with whom I had to be, willing or unwilling, on social terms. At the time of the catastrophe, it was my practice, along with a friend of mine who was always encouraging me into dubious adventures towards which I should not have had the imagination or the initiative to be tempted of my own accord, to climb the dividing wall and lynx-eyed rake the demesne on the other side for any novelties. The fun was increased because of the necessity for a lightning leap down if anyone appeared either in the home or the further garden. Unobserved, we had during holidays frequently noticed the younger son of the house, a boy a year or two older than ourselves, playing in his garden, and one day it occurred to us that it would be exciting fun to make his acquaintance on our own account, so we concocted a suitable note and on the first occasion that offered attracted his attention and passed it over to him. Disastrously for us, one of the Ferns gardeners came down the dell at the critical moment and saw what we were doing. He told mother. That evening I was on the carpet. I was even told to report to father in the morning, a measure of the extreme gravity of my offence. But the fantastic sociological point of the row was tipped on mother's words as she finally dismissed me to bed: 'And look at the difficulty you've put me in. I've never called and I don't want to call.'

Years after this boy was killed in France. But in the months before that happened, mother and Mrs Shaw had ceased to be strangers who passed each other on the hill without a greeting. My brother, too, was a soldier in France, and mother and Mrs Shaw had overdrawn together on a common account of anxiety. Now they tramped up the hill in company as neighbours should having worked all morning to make surgical dressings for other people's sons. If Mrs Shaw bethought her that it needed a holocaust of thousands of lives to bring about their new spontaneous and natural relation, she kept her reflections to herself; she was a generous woman.

Snobbery was also geographical; it was almost an axiom for instance that, socially speaking, no good thing would be likely to come out of Wilmslow, the neighbouring village nearer Manchester. On the other hand, Peover, a village deeper in Cheshire than Alderley Edge, where the manager of the Manchester branch of the Bank of England lived in semi-county state, was regarded by most of our ladies with equal though different scorn as the preserve of people who liked to be 'in with' the county. The people who lived round about Peover reciprocated, of course, and suspected a good many of us as we suspected the Wilmslow families.

The complications were endless. Mother and Mrs Schill, for instance, both got on admirably with 'the lower classes' because these they could meet without any fear of being drawn in or needing to draw them in to their own entourage. It was the people immediately below and immediately above that caused the trouble. The 'aboves' were as troublesome as the 'belows' for mother and Mrs Schill had twisted their sturdy self-respect into a ridiculous pattern of inverted snobbery. Some of our ladies 'sucked up' to the county. Mother and Mrs Schill would never have employed an expression of such dubious pedigree, but once roused they might have used an even stronger word whose good old English lineage carried a more biting tradition of disdain. Poor Mrs A or Mrs B who had received, perhaps quite innocently, an invitation to lunch or tennis at Peover or some other county centre would be dismissed nem. con. as toadying. I recall mother's positive annoyance when Lady Sheffield of Alderley Park called upon her as a preliminary to an invitation to lunch. The invitation was given, I don't doubt, largely because Lord Sheffield, who had been a Liberal minister and had a razor-like intelligence, wanted to meet father on easier ground than the Macclesfield to London rail compartment so as to pick his brains on some topic in regard to which he admitted father's superior expertise. And mother was annoyed, partly because she recognized this and partly because she had too much pride to become mixed up with a set which might single individuals out from the society into which she had married, but would certainly never welcome or accept it collectively. Father, on the other hand, was always keen to meet anyone who had lived a forceful, interesting and individualized life, and I think considered on the whole that you were more likely to find such people among those who had been endowed by birth with the freedom of a ruling position. And the social path was always a good deal wider on both sides for men than for women.

Wives with the views of mother and Mrs Schill had to walk on a social tight-rope. The social path was also, I think, a good deal wider in Didsbury or Withington, those suburbs so much nearer in to Manchester where many of the residents were the younger professional men and their wives, teachers at the university, members of the Manchester Bar, doctors. It was a less local and a more intellectual society than ours and consequently freer. And I think that some of its younger members such as my cousins the Hursts, who were planning an eventual move from the Manchester Bar to London, found the tight-rope not a little amusing.

The younger and more energetic of our women played games not as an occasional means of getting exercise and relaxation, but as a regular occupation. Often they would put in a couple of rounds of golf on one day and in summer, all afternoon, the tennis club courts would be dotted with white long-skirted figures hitting balls with a serious zeal which was certainly not applied to most of the other possible interests of life. They had a standard about games; not so necessarily a standard of performance as a standard of attitude. Still, it is as well to have a standard of attitude towards something; a standard of attitude is a saving grace even when it only derives from something so intrinsically unimportant as a game of tennis.

And, of course, they danced. When a girl came home for good from school, then God help her if it were found that she could neither play games adequately nor dance nicely. Hagar-like, she would have to go forth into a social wilderness.

For the older ladies there was bridge. But I do not think the bridge disease had ravaged Alderley Edge with the same insidious ferocity with which it had rotted one or two neighbouring residential villages. We were saved because we had the reputation for excellence in outdoor games. Mother and Mrs Pilkington, for instance, did not play bridge at all and no one thought the worse of them, and quite a few of our ladies honourably felt that it was wrong to spend the whole afternoon, several times a week, clamped to a card table.

'Sewing for charity' filled in a little more time. Always there were sales of work for some good cause in the offing. And their final result would be, on the one hand, certainly, a good dollop of money for the charity or religious mission involved, but on the other hand, at home, a drawer full of miscellaneous garments and knick-knacks which mother would bring under review about Christmas time. Then useful garments would be sorted out and parcelled up and sent away to needy individuals or distributing committees, and the rest would be regretfully put back to clutter up the drawer and mother would consider whether perhaps she couldn't pass some of them into circulation again at a forthcoming sale of work.

Just a few ladies, Mrs Pilkington, for instance, really could cut out, sew and finish a major garment with almost professional competence. Their contribution towards clothing 'the needy' was serious and they saw to it that their work was not wasted.

For a good number of them, more active sorts of philanthropy occupied more or less of the week according to individual tastes and talents. Mother would 'go visiting' in Manchester. That did not mean paying and returning social calls. It meant looking up the housewives of Ancoats from an accredited list, in her case provided by Aunt Mary, listening to the tale of their difficulties, giving sympathy and advice and arranging for material help. It meant getting to know how they really lived and how they could really be helped within the compass of their circumstances (nobody thought of altering the compass). It meant bridging the gulf between Alderley Edge and Ancoats with that bridging stuff which is the hardest of all to handle, the thin silken strands of human sympathy. If it were done sensibly and sensitively, and mother did it that way, then I think Ancoats accepted it with gladness, but if it were done in a prying and patronizing spirit, and sometimes it was, then it became the most revolting insult, taking into account the difference between the two sides of the gulf and the reasons for it, that one woman could offer to another. But then, I forget that one was a lady and the other a working-woman, so there couldn't really be any question of insult any more than there could have been the question of a duel between a gentleman and his servant. However, insult or no insult, Ancoats needed the help and if it were given decently, received the material part with dignity and the human sympathy gratefully, but if it were given in the bad way, Ancoats avoided the sympathy and accepted the rest with scornful cynicism. For Ancoats was not witless and insensitive; Ancoats understood and where necessary knew how to hate.

Ladies who did not have a taste for direct human contacts sat on one or another of the innumerable committees which administered the charities and charitable institutions, or if the men reserved the right of direction to themselves, they sat on advisory committees which proffered discreet and humble advice to the main committee on points where it might be thought that just possibly a wife might have a more experienced view than her husband. The more energetic often combined committee work with the personal linking up. Mrs Schill made the two almost a wholetime occupation, and was looked at a little askance by some because it was felt that she did not spend enough time in her home or on the fiddling social occasions of Alderley Edge. But then Mrs Schill had a big heart and an energy of mind which needed to come to grips with life more in a man's way. Mother sat on one or two committees in addition to her visiting and I remember how proud she was when, years later, she was invited to join the Board of Salford Hospital as its first woman member. But she wasn't going to let her pleasure disguise the fact that she considered it very right and proper and normal that a woman should sit on that Board. She had not much use for the advisory committees:

'If they (meaning the men) don't want us as equals then they had better not have us at all,' she would say. 'I wouldn't sit on that kind of committee. It's undignified and lacking in self-respect.'

And yet mother was anything but a feminist. Indeed, very few of our ladies were. The suffrage movement did not have much support in Alderley Edge; the violence and even the heroic self-sacrifices of some of the suffragettes evoked disgust rather than sympathy.

I have said that there was very little which they really had to do whether they wanted to or not. That was perfectly true; their time was their own to fill, but as I look back, I see they were always busying themselves about something, futile or useful as the case might be. Any odd remaining gaps in time were plugged by exhibitions of arts and crafts and Oxford Extension lectures.

The arts and crafts provided some sort of opening into a world where creative values counted. Indeed, I think it was the only opening; the homely ways of entering that world were denied to them. They did not have to be cooks, for instance, so they could not enjoy the creative pleasure and satisfaction of preparing a meal with tastes and textures nicely chosen and balanced. They could not enjoy that deep pleasure in carrying on an essential craft for the sake of the people you love. At the exhibitions they showed knitting and crochet and embroideries and watercolour sketches, and won prizes and diplomas. The embroideries were typical. They turned out beautiful stitchery and workmanship quite often, but almost invariably wasted it and their own creative faculty on the most lamentable mass-produced designs ironed on from transfers. To make something is not the same thing as to create it; making may be merely imitative. So, when all was said and done our ladies' creative talents really got only the most perfunctory encouragement and expansion from the art and crafts, not much beyond the choosing of a group of colours.

It is very amusing but also a little pathetic to look back upon the extension lectures and the place which they held in our community life. So far as I know, father was the only one among the older men who had been to Oxford or Cambridge. Even though a good few sent their sons there, those seats of ancient learning - that would be where they subconsciously placed the adjective - were objects of faint and ill-defined suspicions. Those who did not send their sons to one of them took the definite line that they made a thoroughly bad preparation for a merchant's or industrialist's career. The workpeople did not like 'Varsity manners, and the young men who had them would not knuckle under to the discipline of business life. So they said. But father stood up uncompromisingly for the products of the Isis and the Cam. He was always anxious for the bright lads from the Engineering School at Cambridge to come to Mather & Platt. And not only because he believed that they would make the best engineers. I think that he would have endorsed a wider verdict:

'For a well-to-do Englishman it is a great thing to have been at a university. However reactionary he may become in later life there will always be something about him that will distinguish him from those members of his class who never went to a university. The fact that for one short period of his life he was compelled to think, that he was once part of a community in which every known point of view was represented and hotly discussed, in which everyone had tremendous enthusiasms and in which everyone had his mind and body working at full pressure all the time, must inevitably have left its mark upon him.'

That verdict was certainly true of father himself - not that he was particularly reactionary or had ever stopped thinking. And it was the root cause why a good many of the others did not trust Oxford and Cambridge and hence why, when the extension lectures were announced, husbands and fathers were apt to treat the announcement with a mixture of mild contempt mixed with suspicion lest something slightly subversive should be afoot. Of course, they never came to the lectures themselves; only the ladies attended, and these sat at the feet of J.A.R. Marriott or another, and for one short hour during the winter weeks lived with the personalities and through the processes of the French Revolution or caught in a prim Alderley Edge meeting-hall some flashed reflection of the glory that was Greece.

After the lecture it was the custom for one or other student to transform herself into a hostess and take the lecturer home for dinner and the night. That custom focused the vague suspicions of husbands and fathers and objectivized them in a live human being - a don. And dons were a priori theorists, and danger was always to be apprehended from theorists. 'Putting ideas into people's heads'; that was the comment when something had been said publicly which it was thought might seduce the lower classes from their allegiance to capital. And I am quite sure that several of the hosts felt the same about the extension lecturers and approached the dinner table at which the lecturer would sit down with them convinced that they were being made into intellectual cuckolds. Because, of course, they considered, as I have indicated, that they had exclusive rights in regard to their wives' minds. The cream of it all was that so often, before the end of dinner, the lecturer had become a social success. J.A.R. Marriott, for example, was always successful. He broke down suspicion at once and all the men liked him and paid him the compliment of commenting after his departure that he looked at life like a practical man.

By midday on a Saturday our ladies were preparing themselves to bask in the sunshine of masculine society. For the men arrived home from Manchester in time for a latish lunch, and by three o'clock had changed out of their business suits and were accoutred for the golf club in tweeds which smelt faintly of hillsides and the damp fleeces of mountain sheep, or for the tennis club in white flannels and impeccably blancoed shoes. The ladies were also accoutred; their golfing tweeds were authentic, too, and their tennis shoes dazzled like driven snow. As for their tennis dresses, the starch and the absurdly long skirts produced an illusion of white-garmented marionettes. But withal they were dutiful and humble. If it was the question of a round of golf and three or four ladies were not paired off in mixed foursomes, it would never occur to them to challenge the rule that on Saturday afternoons no ladies might take up space on the course by playing together. If the menfolk had decided on tennis and preferred to play men's doubles, no girl demurred because she was thereby prevented from getting a game since men's singles and men's doubles took precedence on the courts. It was all accepted as part of the right pattern of life. The ladies could play any afternoon or any morning (save the mark!), but the breadwinners had only Saturday afternoon. Sunday was ruled out. We were pseudo-sabbatarians in those days and had, I believe, after some argument decided against opening the tennis club on Sundays lest it should give scandal in the village and set a bad example to the village people. Besides, quite a few of the members whose counsel carried most weight had courts of their own and a little discreet Sunday tennis in the privacy of the home could do no harm. It was hard luck on the numerous young men who 'lodged' in the village, boys who had come from the length and breadth of England to make their careers in Manchester, but they had to put up with it just as the girls had to make the best of the unwritten ukase that they must do nothing during a weekend that could interfere with masculine pleasures or masculine freedom. The men had a pleasantly subtle method for ensuring that this ukase should be enforced. Those who drew up the rules for the golf and tennis clubs had seen to it that the women s subscriptions in each case should be lower than the men's. And since in Alderley Edge the tag that he who pays the piper calls the tune was an article of faith, so it followed that she who paid the piper less was entitled to call for fewer tunes.

In summer, the cricket and tennis club was the main centre of social activity. It had been laid out on flat fields at the northern foot of the Edge.

There were tennis courts and croquet lawns and a couple of cricket pitches with ample space for the fielders. The pavilion with its changing-rooms and lockers and friendly tea-room and makeshift bar was a wonderful place to me in my early teens, largely, I suppose, because it was dominated by the heroes of cricket and tennis and also by the groundsman who had known most of them since they were small boys and referred to them always by their Christian names with surname casually attached, but never a 'mister'. He chased off children whenever they were likely to get in the way of their elders, and he watched us lynx-eyed if we had a court lest we should damage his precious turf. We were inordinately proud if Tomlinson for once treated one of us as a grown-up and actually passed the time of day as he would with Miss Crewdson or the young Swinsides.

About three o'clock people began to saunter into the cricket club and distribute themselves for their various activities. Everybody knew each other and the atmosphere was agreeably like a large informal garden-party. Elderly ladies and gentlemen played croquet in dignified clothes and with serious demeanours. The young men contorted themselves on the baseline of tennis courts trying out the new American service. The less lucky younger women wandered around swinging hopeful tennis racquets on the chance of being asked to make up a four. A row of matrons occupied garden chairs to watch the cricket. But the cricket was not English village cricket. The teams were all composed of Manchester business men, our lot playing Bowdon or Hale or Didsbury or some other residential suburb. So even if I had the gift of description I could paint no picture of our cricket to sort with the classic accounts of village matches from Dickens's Muggletonians at Dingley Dell to the contests from which Siegfried Sassoon's Fox-hunting Man carried off his bat on those golden summer evenings which made an ideal but illusioning background for the pre-war English country scene. We lacked the cheerful spontaneous mixing of social ingredients. On a village pitch the squire's son and the doctor's son and the young groom and the son of the shopkeeper who kept the omnibus store where flies buzzed happily all the summer through could meet as equals distinguished only by their handling of bat and ball. But with us there was no squire's son and the shopkeeper's sons and the grooms had to get their cricket at secondhand by watching between the slats of the tall fence which shielded the club from the road. It was a pity, the social pattern of English village cricket was, I know, only a small part of the great complex pattern which made up the England of my childhood, but it was a good small part, a tiny gem of pattern repeating again and again up and down the English counties and I am sorry we did not weave one of those repeats at Alderley Edge.

Mother played no games except mild croquet on the home lawn

with father or me, and she was not in the least interested in watching her neighbours disport themselves, so she could seldom be induced to visit the tennis club on Saturday afternoons. Father seldom went there either because he preferred tennis at home. In my teens I'm afraid this was a secret cause of disappointment to me. It seemed to keep us rather out of the social swim and I was beginning to realize that if life at Alderley Edge was to be agreeable for me after I left school I should have to conform more or less successfully to the social imperatives of my neighbours. Besides, I wanted to conform. I had few dearer ambitions than to be asked to enter for the mixed doubles of the July tennis tournament with one of those Olympian youths who could pull off an American service. I realized well enough that at Alderley Edge it was not women who bestowed favours on men, and I knew with what feelings of envy and admiration my older contemporaries regarded those girls who were never at a loss for tennis or golf or dancing partners. Everyone likes to be liked; there is no simpler or more harmless balm for self-respect. The trouble with us was that you wouldn't get liked except in the most offhand and useless way unless you could do the right things and do them relatively well.

All my older friends, whatever their private interests, struggled to fit themselves for this set-up, all that is except the two Pilkington girls, Margaret and Dorothy. Margaret flatly would not play games at all and Dorothy merely toyed fitfully with a tennis racquet after a dutiful and lack-interest fashion. I found their unorthodoxy very odd and even damning and could not imagine what they did with their Saturday afternoons. When I was small I had not been much bothered by the promptings of herd psychology and had indeed tended to sheer off on my own, but I succumbed in my teens, partly I suppose from an instinct of self-preservation. One result was that I looked askance at Margaret and Dorothy which was my considerable loss for thereby I retarded the growth of a close friendship which eventually took me far from the atmosphere of Alderley Edge into a world where art and letters really mattered and acquaintances' holidays did not mostly consist of transferring their golf clubs from the local course to Llandudno or Seacale, but had to do with splendid names like Venice or Florence or Rome.

When they first came home from school, Margaret and Dorothy had both made spasmodic efforts to conform in one or another direction, but their resolution did not last long. Dorothy struggled along half-heartedly until the war released her and she sloped off to become a hospital orderly among congenial companions in London. Margaret had shaken herself free with a final 'to hell with all that' even before the war had helped to loosen up the social framework for all of us. She went away to study painting at the Slade. This was an outrageous happening. Even for girls it didn't do to take art too seriously. You could have sketching lessons, and a series of Miss So-and-so's came and taught classes of our ladies genteel methods of washing watercolour paint on to Whatman blocks, but you could not adopt a professional attitude or aspire to a professional standard. Margaret's action was all the more outrageous because she took it with her parents' consent. People were amazed. Think of all the dubious characters, both male and female, with whom Margaret would be mixing in that suspect world of art. But then the Pilkingtons always had a subtly different outlook; everybody sensed that. And it was perhaps only to be expected that their latent vein of nonconformity would break out somewhere. They made up for the Slade by an excessive burst of conventionality in other directions every now and then.

On one occasion Campbell was home on leave and having nothing particular to do one afternoon telephoned Margaret to suggest a walk on the Edge. Margaret was mildly pleased; subalterns were not three a penny at Alderley Edge, and anyway it was always fun to be asked out if only for a walk over the Edge, so she arranged to meet him. But at lunch she apprised her mother of the invitation and was firmly told that her acceptance must be withdrawn. 'People will talk if you and Campbell go for a walk together.' So Margaret had to ring up and explain that she had developed a sudden and racking headache.

I think that if I were asked to sum up the relations of the males and females in our society I should have to say that from one rather obtrusive aspect they were based on a pathetic distortion, even a somewhat disagreeable guying of the fine old principle of chivalry. In the days of chivalry, though the lord protected his lady and wore her favour when he went to the wars, in return she had to work with vigour and intelligence to keep her side of a tacit bargain. She was the chatelaine on whom depended the complicated and exacting economy of the manor house or castle. She had to command both men and women. She had a status of her own and a serious position. But most of our poor ladies had neither. They were jealously protected from the jostles of the outside world, yet a mechanical age had seen to it that servicing a home was no longer work urgently requiring fine character and intelligence and full-time application.

Food factories, clothes factories, electric-lighting plants and the rest had filched most of the business from them. And although a home like Ferns to which visitors from the big world were constantly coming required considerable organization, mostly the homes could be run efficiently enough with very little expenditure of energy or leadership or brain. This was not their fault and it was hardly their fault that they had, as yet, found no substitute to absorb their energies. They were displaced like the hand-workers of the overlap into the Industrial Revolution who had to adjust themselves as best they could to the dominion of the machines.

Yet once again I think of Ferns and of Firwood and indeed of half a dozen other homes I knew, and I realize that this summing-up of the Alderley Edge women through the eyes of my own harassed generation is too sweeping. It is too easy for us for whom servicing a home has become once again a full-time and essential occupation to look back and see only the futilities of Edwardian feminine leisure, to remember it only as an expensive decoration to which self-respecting individuals should not lend themselves and which a self-respecting community should not tolerate. It is too easy to forget that a leisured life can create good values as well as bad ones, values so delicate and illusive that they are almost impossible to define. But hardly knowing what I was doing I found that I had conjured up these values from the past one evening not long ago when I took out a box of lace which had belonged to my mother in order to choose something for a friend. As we turned over the veils and scarves of Limerick and Honiton still neatly wrapped in blue tissue-paper it occurred to me that things can be, as it were, natural sacraments, tangible and visible signs conveying from past to present by something more than association the values of another way of life. And what was conveyed to me as I handled the lace as gently as I could because it was beautiful was not a sense of futility or of leisure like an ostentatious decoration, but rather a pervading sense of life as a trust given to us to handle as gently and graciously as we can. I think that, safeguarded as it were by their exasperating and seemingly absurd conventions, mother and Mrs Pilkington and Mrs Schill and others, too, did handle it that way.

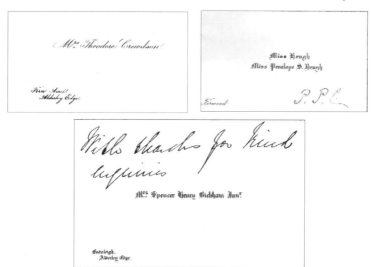

Visiting cards of the period
courtesy the Alderley Edge Association

Chapter Ten
SUNDAYS

Sunday was a good day at Ferns, a temperate day marked off from other days by an atmosphere of serenity and quiet relaxation. It was mother, of course, who made this atmosphere; father could never have produced it on his own account for his energies were too dynamic and he was always pressed for time, but on Sundays some part of mother's controlled calm influenced and quietened him.

We began with breakfast at half-past eight instead of at seven-forty-five and we ate kidneys and bacon. If I had come down to Sunday breakfast and found some other dish warming on the hotplate I should have known at once that a major disaster had overtaken the household. Father ate more leisurely than on weekdays because there was no train to catch, but whereas it was permitted to me to be late for breakfast sometimes on other days, on Sundays I must never be late because that interfered with the maids getting their work done in time to go to church.

Mother and I both appeared in Sunday dresses and about half-past ten we set off down the hill for church. Every now and then father came with us. Going down the hill and along the flat road past the station we would meet a little stream of parents shepherding their young. There was a fair proportion of fathers; I think a good many of the fathers were more assiduous churchgoers than mine, but I would not like to say how many were assiduous because church-going was still a normal and mannerly activity of society and how many for more relevant reasons. Stepping out with that purposeful walk of hers, mother always raced to church because she hated to pick up our neighbours on the way and so need to gear her mind on to small talk when she wanted it quiet and contained. Those she did overtake she dodged quite ruthlessly, not caring in the least on these occasions whether she was being discourteous. But usually we started so early that we were almost the first in church which meant a boring wait for me. I flicked the pages of a hymn book whilst mother went far away from me into a region of the spirit where I could not penetrate. Not that I really minded going to church, in fact, it was so much a part of the normal procedure of life that it would never have occurred to me to ask myself at that stage whether I did mind. And I certainly liked singing hymns, at the top of my voice and very much out of tune, a performance that was torture to mother's sensitive ear, and she would sometimes lean towards me and whisper: 'Kathie, dear, you must not sing this verse so loud; it's marked

A Sunday outing in the motor c1912.

Off to skate on Alderley Mere on a wintry Sunday c1912.

piano', whereupon I would restrain myself with difficulty, particularly on Christmas Day, since, in my opinion, the one marked piano was the best verse of 'Hark the Herald Angels Sing' and therefore, I felt, really demanded fortissimo treatment. I think, too, that any child with an ear for the beauty of words, and I did have that kind of ear, could not fail to derive some deep satisfaction from the English liturgy - more perhaps from its form than from its content, for the noble presentation of the vicissitudes of human life and the relations between God and man were beyond my limited experience.

None the less, though I did not mind going to church, I did welcome, with a gratitude which I am sure must have touched the grown-up who was responsible, those rare Sunday mornings when I was invited and allowed to play truant. Campbell was never expected to go to church when he was at home and sometimes he got me off and occasionally father did. In winter when the ice was bearing I was always allowed off to go to skate with father, and the sense of truancy added a spice of pleasure to those expeditions across the frozen fields to Alderley mere. The iron ground held no mark of our footprints, either of my light ones or father's heavier tread. The cold still air seemed to enclose and hold our voices when we spoke. Squatting on the bank of the mere, father would help me screw on and tighten up my skates and then we would slide off on the black springy ice towards the unfrozen pool in the middle where the water birds from miles around would congregate to drink. Towards the pool we went, but not too near; keeping a gingerly distance we would by-pass it and make for the opposite shore where the woodland came down to the water, tangled bare trees with interweaving branches whose glossy chocolate-hued twigs were veiled by haze. I have skated on many finer sheets of water since then, on lakes and tarns set among frost-bound fells, but I have never quite recaptured the delight of those truant Sunday mornings with my father.

We - that is the residents on the hill - hardly ever went to church on Sunday evening. There was a social distinction between morning and evening service. The village people went in the evening and the various maids who were not free on Sunday morning. It was felt that the evening service was their preserve and that they would prefer to have it to themselves. Later on, when I was older, I used occasionally to go in the evening of my own accord, and then I had a pleasant titillation of doing something that was just slightly socially outrageous. It was in almost the same category of unsuitability as visiting your doctor during his consulting hours instead of having him visit you at home.

There was, of course, another social distinction between church and chapel. As mother and I went to church we would pass a second string of people going off at right angles from our line to the Wesleyan chapel. Mother never had any difficulty in avoiding them because she knew very few of them socially. The chapel people were well aware of the distinction and all over the north there had been a continuous drift from chapel to church. As one or other chapel family came to mix in freer and wider circles they tended to find the ways and personnel of dissent narrow and socially distasteful and the chapel service and surroundings aesthetically jarring, so they transferred their allegiance to the Establishment, but with a casual ease and so far as appearances went a complete absence of heart-searching. Mrs Schill, for instance, had been born and bred 'chapel' and had continued to attend chapel for years after she married in the town below the Derbyshire hills where she had lived before moving to Alderley Edge. But gradually she came to compare church and chapel congregations and the grave and noble dignity of the Book of Common Prayer with chapel methods, and at last she came to feel that she could bear her chapel surroundings at Sunday service no longer, so she forsook chapel for church. She admitted quite frankly that these were her reasons. Yet Mrs Schill believed her religion and did not practise it because it was socially desirable to do so. And where 'works' were concerned, I would not give up to any criticism my admiration for her applied Christianity. 'All women labouring of child, all sick persons and young children ... all prisoners and captives' - she did not spare herself to help those categories of needy human beings, particularly the last, which are appealed for in the Litany of the church which she had entered so casually. What is more, she was adept in a rare art of charity; she contrived to give help in a way that would never damage the recipient's self-respect.

One way or another the same went for all the other Nonconformists who came over to swell the ranks of the church as by law established. My father's brothers and sisters were among them, having deserted one by one the Congregationalist chapels of their upbringing. As I have pointed out, their Nonconformity would have withstood any number of penal laws, yet ever since I can remember my uncles and aunts mostly went to church and with complete private sincerity. And they did so for the most part, I am sure, because they were drawn by the alluring beauty and majesty of the Liturgy. The Church of England has been cemented by Cranmer's prose. The general result was certainly a softening of the picture of north-country religion; the hard definite lineaments became more vague and gentle and the braced and tense Nonconformist way of life relaxed.

I should add that the Unitarians with us were not troubled by any social difficulty. There was no loss of caste in attending the Unitarian chapel, I suppose because some of the leading Manchester families happened to be Unitarians. So when a Unitarian went over to the Church of England, as sometimes happened, it was presumably from conviction, though I suspect that the lure of Cranmer's prose may occasionally have had something to do with the conviction.

After mother and I returned from church there would be a half-hour's ritual walk round the garden before 'dinner', 'lunch' being reserved for weekdays. I did not enjoy these tours, 'Capability Brown' discussions were not much in my line and the flowers seemed more remote than usual as if they, too, were constricted by Sunday dresses, a circumstance that was chafing in my own case since it prevented me from swinging up on to the big cedar tree or plunging into the shrubberies. Dinner was at one o'clock, roast mutton because father preferred mutton to beef, apple-pie and Stilton cheese. Mother was on tenterhooks for five minutes before the meal to ensure that everyone and father, in particular, should be punctual. Punctuality was invariably a struggle for father because he always assumed that it would take him several minutes less to complete whatever he was doing than would actually prove to be the case. Yet he never missed a train. Notwithstanding that, his habit of leaving his compartment and going for a stroll during two-minute stops on foreign railway journeys caused mother, who would have hated to be left alone in a continental train, acute anxiety. Before Sunday dinner, of course, her anxiety was once more for the benefit of the maids, this time so that they might be able to get through their washing up in good time and so be free to go out early in the afternoon. Not that they could all go out every Sunday. One always had to stay behind for it was unthinkable that the house should be left without a maid in it. Mother was adamant about what she considered to be the just rights of her dependents. Never, for instance, would she allow the carriage, or later the car, to be taken out on Sunday, because she held that the coachman or the chauffeur had the right to spend the day in the bosom of their families.

Thus I remember Sunday a good deal as a day on which I had rather specially to consider other people - which was not so bad for me. In fact, one way or another there was a good deal of such salutary discipline at home. In carriage days, for instance, if I were going to a children's party and the waggonette was to call for me, mother would say before I set off: 'Now remember, you are to come away as soon as Godfrey comes. You must not keep the horses waiting.'

Queerly enough it was always the comfort of the horses that was stressed in this case; it was they that must not stand about in the wet or the cold - incidentally, there was only one, but he was always generalized as a plural, a hangover perhaps in mother's mind from the more spacious days of her Irish youth. I never remember being told that I must not keep Godfrey waiting. And if by any chance I succumbed to temptation and stayed to the end of some exciting game, Godfrey himself would look at me reproachfully as I emerged, not for his own sake but for the sake of Bobs or Paddy.

After dinner I would get myself a book until it was time to go for a walk on the Edge with father. There was no set Sunday reading, but it was tacitly understood, at least when I was small, that Sunday was the day for such literary fare as Jessica's First Prayer or Little Meg and her Children or Teddy's Button or A Peep Behind the Scenes. They were thin paper-bound volumes and very uplifting, and I wish I had them now so that I could recapture with a suitable quotation the aroma of sentimental Victorian piety which they exhaled from every page. But they all seemed good stories with plenty of dramatic interest centring, for example, on the efforts of the hero or the heroine to withstand the gay temptations offered by their unconverted and wicked school mates, or conversely and indeed concurrently on the efforts of the aforesaid hero and heroine to convert their more dashing companions. The plots were varied; I forget about 'Jessica', but 'Little Meg', so far as I remember, brought up her motherless brothers and sisters in evangelical rectitude, and 'Teddy' converted an old man, and the hero of A Peep survived the environment of a circus. One or two of these books, one called Pilgrim Street, for instance, gave me some insight into the life of a Manchester slum. I'm afraid I read them all with avidity, but being a normal child with a sufficient dose of original sin was happily prevented from becoming a prig.

Meanwhile, mother had settled down with the Spectator and the Life of Faith. The latter was an evangelical religious weekly. Mother never talked about religion, nor do I remember that she ever taught me formally the scheme of Christian beliefs. Until I went away to school I seem to have picked up the major ones in a haphazard way, probably from the Prayer Book and Hymns Ancient and Modern. The result was an assortment rather than a construction. But perhaps I am wrong, perhaps she taught me when I was too young to recall having lessons. I have no idea what father really believed. The intense Nonconformist Christianity of his home, unlightened by any saving sense of humour, any of that saving humour which helps to hold a religion in balance, had been, I think, diffused and softened for him into a gentler yet ennobling sentiment rather than an intellectual belief, but a sentiment which mattered to him and mapped some kind of path through the storms of post-Darwinian controversy which must surely have assailed his alert intelligence at some point or another of his life, though we never heard very much about them at Ferns. It was mother who said grace before meals: 'For what we are about to receive, the Lord make us truly thankful', and mother who read prayers after breakfast, a rite attended only by the maids and me, and perhaps a visitor. Father would already have gone to Manchester and Campbell if he was at home was exempted from attendance. The males were never expected to perform religious duties unless they wanted to, a differentiation that I might well have regarded as unfair unless I had been conditioned from babyhood to accept that boys could enjoy all sorts of freedoms that were denied to girls.

But though mother never talked about her beliefs, the force and beauty of them were clear, a plain fact of our household apprehensible by the same process of discernment that made me aware as a small child of her love and protection of my father. Only once do I remember a religious discussion in which she had to join. Somehow or another Satan came into the conversation and mother affirmed her belief in an objective spirit of evil. Father began gently to rag her and mother was called upon to testify to her conviction. I remember only too well her discomfiture because she hated so to lay bare her convictions. She could not stand the rough and tumble of the market-place when her private and deep feelings were concerned, and in any case disliked argument about religion. How she would have loathed what is known as Christian Apologetics. I think she would much sooner have died for her faith than apologize for it.

I do not know what mother believed about hell; it did not come into this conversation and I do not remember ever receiving from her any specific teaching on the subject. I believe that some of my contemporaries still lay awake at night torturing themselves with the thought that some trivial series of offences might be avenged by eternal damnation. Nurses more often than not were responsible, I think, for purveying savage and distorted beliefs to their recalcitrant charges for whom no distinction was made between mortal and venial sins and who had no means of relief in confession and a direct and spoken absolution, but had to make do as well as they could with the uneasy and conditional absolution they might extend to themselves during their midnight communings with conscience. Meme's sweet nature would never have allowed her to handle for a second this devilish disciplinary weapon. So my own sleep was untroubled. Nor, for that matter, was I very much interested in heaven, my inadequate conception of which derived from such pictures as I had received from those Hymns Ancient and Modern. I was bursting with physical energy and life lay ahead an unexplored dream country. The idea of a finale where

> Every little pilgrim
> Shall rest eternally

was not attractive. So the sanction of reward and punishment did not affect me very much, and if I made spasmodic efforts to behave decently or felt occasional remorse when I had behaved badly, I did so out of childish loyalty to a Person who had suffered terrible things in order to help me and expected my allegiance in return. That was about the sum total of my working theology. But I am grateful that the first view of Christianity I had was not spoilt by fear.

I never remember father sitting down to read a book on a Sunday afternoon, indeed he hardly ever read a book through to the end. I doubt if he had really studied any subject from books since he left the university. A good part of the book-space in the drawing-room was filled with volumes which he had acquired as prizes at Owens College in Manchester and later at Cambridge, or with books he had bought as a young man with money donated by engineering societies for some scientific work. Most of these books were editions of the poets, but there was also a complete Ruskin bound in blue calf with the Emmanuel College crest, the set which contains Ruskin's own lovely and delicate drawings. I think he must have dipped a good bit into Ruskin; his ideal of womanhood - a little unfortunately for me as I grew older - was obviously founded on Sesame and Lilies. Then there were Lecky's History of England and De Quincey's Essays and Macaulay's History and Essays bought with the Tellford Premium in 1893. I have them now. And there was a great leather-bound dozen volume Milton complete even to the Latin works. I don't remember where that came from, but father read to me the Areopagitica out of it, and how he enjoyed Milton's august rhetoric, particularly the passage which ends: *'Methinks I see in my mind a noble and puissant nation rousing herself like a strong man after sleep, and shaking her invincible locks; methinks I see her as an eagle muing her mighty youth, and kindling her undazzled eyes at the full midday beam ....'* I know what he cared for because he would choose his favourites for our reading time on Sunday evening. They were mostly poems, Tennyson, Wordsworth, Coleridge, a bit of Matthew Arnold, a bit of Byron, Milton for his sonorous rhythms and splendid words. Every New Year's Eve we read Tennyson's 'Ring out wild bells' and every Christmas Milton's Ode to the Nativity. I associate Milton with him most. One spring when he was in bed with a threatening of duodenal ulcer we read through Paradise Lost, or rather on this occasion I read it to him. I was sixteen and quite incapable of reading Milton as he ought to be read, but father seemed to enjoy it, though in the end he usually went to sleep in the middle of a canto! When I was much younger he had read to me the sonnets, 'Avenge O Lord Thy slaughtered Saints' and 'When I consider how my light is spent'. He had read to me Lycidas and the Odes to Pleasure and to Melancholy. A good deal of these was beyond me and sometimes I found it difficult to concentrate, but I do not forget that early half- comprehended introduction to Milton, and I think that I have to thank father for putting me in the way to fall in love with the English language on those long-ago Sunday evenings. Curiously enough he never read Shakespeare to me. He liked his prose in the rhetorical tradition. The quieter tempo and lucid chiselled exposition of Addison and Lamb and Hazlitt did not rouse him; I found out their beauties later. But it was from father and the rhetoricians that I learned how a great English sentence builds up to its climax with each complicated subordinate clause dropping into place as into a specially prepared slot and holding the next one firmly on its shoulders. Years after he died I found in his Byron a marked verse from Childe Harold. I have often wondered whether it was the key to his cosmogony.

> Not vainly did the early Persian make
> His altar the high places and the peak
> Of earth o'er-gazing mountains, and thus take
> Afit and unwall'd temple, there to seek
> The Spirit in whose honour shrines are weak,
> Upreared of human hands.

And so my reading with father brought to an end a sensible, happy and civilized Sunday, one I think that some of my cousins who were still under a strict sabbatarian regime must have envied, for as I grew older I was free to choose my own reading, free to play games so long as I did so quietly, free even to lark about with Campbell on the lawn. I am rather glad that I did not have to hate Sunday.

As I look back on Sunday at Ferns I see very clearly that I must distinguish between a materialist philosophy of life and a belief in the economics of capitalism as a basis for one's activities in the world. Father and mother believed, as I have pointed out perhaps ad nauseam, in the capitalist system, and the outer setting of their lives was framed on its harsh and impersonal economic assumptions, but they and most of their friends were not materialists. For them the inward personal life of a human being was directed to values sanctioned by some authority more august and compelling even than the inexorable law of the market. Although she might never talk about it, mother I know lived with the sense of a last reckoning, a final judgment in the course of which men's motives and actions would be assessed and explained on a standard of absolute and unshakeable values and by an Authority whose verdict admitted of no appeal. In short, most of them believed in absolute and objective values and were immune from the rotting miasma of subjectivism which has soaked into the vision of their successors. We, their successors, have been pleased to regard absolute values as out of date because we have cheapened and made superficial the speculations of thinkers whose researches we have only half understood and half understanding have erected into laws of life. And so, encouraged by the determinists who set us off thinking that we really could not help ourselves since circumstances and environment and heredity shaped our characters and controlled our actions numbers of which were reflex anyway, and by the psycho-analysts who told us that what we are derives from recondite happenings of our remote childhood, we have substituted a sentimental subjectivism for the virile and uncompromising conviction of personal responsibility to which our parents subscribed. And further enlightened by the creative evolutionists who explained to us that conscience and ethics are simply varying products of the experience of countless generations of human beings striving to bond themselves into societies in order to live, we have obliterated the distinction between social morality and personal sin. My generation makes mistakes but it does not commit sins.

Perhaps it was easier for our parents since they were protected by a civilization to all appearances secure and permanent whereas we are insecure and anxious. We have seen through their economic assumptions and found them cruel and unjust and fallacious. We have, or so we think, traced out a design of our own for a finer social and economic life. Yet the fog of subjectivism has so seeped into our minds that we are no longer able properly to distinguish a means from an end, a process from a purpose. We have condemned the economics of capitalism because they enslaved men for the sake of a material gain. But a condemnation is not an affirmation, a condemnation is only half the mental battle. We are too fogged and uncertain to make an affirmation. So the quantitative economic means is confused with the qualitative end, the material process with the purposes of the human spirit. Our fathers and grandfathers permitted men's bodies to be broken and their minds stunted in the interests of an economic machine, but we are in a fair way to extinguishing men's souls because we have not been able to see ahead to lead beyond the process of more this and more that, more radios, more speed, more houses, more efficiency, more children, more education, more entertainment, more leisure, even more work, abstract and concrete, serious and trivial all mixed up together - we cannot see ahead to any goal and purpose for it all that has an absolute and therefore a satisfying value. Cui bono?

In 1851 my engineer grandfather, then a young man in his late twenties, visited the Great Exhibition at the Crystal Palace. This is what he wrote about it to his wife: *'We reached the Crystal Palace at 12 o'clock and found our largest conceptions of its wondrous extent and magnificence more than realized. There was not the same feeling of vanity about this great show which sometimes one feels on the occurrence of a great pageant. I felt that it was a place to worship in, not intellect, not industry, but the God who has made men so much better than the brutes. Endless as are the productions of human ingenuity and skill which abound on every side, it is not a place for self-glorification. Of its varied wonders I can attempt no description - Eastern romance is fact here. Every country under heaven is present. The mind and the affections are expanded and a brotherly feeling to other nations rises in one's heart. You feel, on seeing some of the beautiful productions, I wish the workman who designed or executed this beautiful fabric were here that I might shake hands with him and thank him for the pleasure I had in witnessing his handiwork and congratulate him on his skill and ask him if he was not grateful to God for having given him his intellect and his hands ....'* Allowing for the stiff importance of Victorian epistolary style, I think it might be said that grandfather, at any rate, tinctured though he might be by the philosophy of capitalism and the Protestant ethic, and absorbed though he was in all his working life in the application of inventions of his own to further the process of material progress, nevertheless kept his head cool and clear and did not confuse a process with a purpose. Nor did grandfather fall a victim to that other sin of hubris, the swelling up of conceit in our own capacities to dominate life and get along entirely by ourselves, the sin of hubris which the old Greeks defined and which is born afresh in every age which forgets the duty of humility, in our time as the bastard offspring of the religion of progressive evolution.

Two thousand years ago a Roman poet wrote a great Ode which was half a prayer and half a hope that his friend, a greater poet even than he, might make a safe passage over the difficult sea. In that poem Horace used the idea of hubris, the death bringing pride of men in their own sovereignty, not as a literary conceit but as the very stuff of his thinking. *'God',* he says, *'severed the seas, but our ships recking nothing plunge through that sacred barrier ..... Prometheus stole fire from heaven, but once he had done so fever and decay spread over the corrupted earth. Daedalus conquered the air on wings not given to man ..... Nil mortalibus arduist;* he concludes, *caelum ipsum petimus stultitia ....*

The whip-cut of Horace's sarcasm is not directed to the deeds but to the spirit in which they are done. He might have been writing for the world of the twentieth-century intelligentsia between the wars, a world which built for itself a lopsided and insecure monument out of fine and generous social ideals and often a personal libertarianism derived in no small measure from a distorted application of an ideal of generosity. Its monument is lopsided and unstable because the common denominator of its thinking has been suspicion of the past rationalized into a boundless self-confidence and confidence in its own capacity to restate the terms of human life. For long enough it never occurred to me that 'modernism' - the worship of our own discoveries and our own modes of thought and our own empirical values - leads not only to the sin of hubris, but also as often as not to the atrophying entanglement of Narcissus about which psycho-analysts have had a good deal to tell us and which is likely to prove all the more frustrating when it is the abnormality not of individuals but of a whole social group. It never occurred to me either that in relation to the long march of history modernism in this sense becomes only too easily the outlook of a provincial in time.

Father and mother would not have been taken in by modernism and in spite of their setting at the apex of Victorian progress they did not fall victims to hubris any more than my grandfather had, and when I look back to Ferns the contemporary fog lifts and I see the answer that was given there. The values of my home were kept sane and clear first and foremost because it was a Christian home. Mother made it so, not primarily because she tried to practise Christian ethics in her personal life, though she certainly did that with more success than most people I have known, but because she held wholeheartedly and unreservedly that the great beliefs of Christianity are true. It was the beliefs, as I have tried to show, that irradiated her personality and gave purpose to her life. And I am the more sure of this just because she never talked about them directly, so that the mere fact that in spite of this one knew so well that they were there showed unmistakably that they were the mainspring of her being. She would have been far too clear-headed to entertain for a moment that modern view that the ethics of Christianity can be detached from the beliefs and used independently for the benefit and instruction of mankind. It is a persuasive view conveniently designed to meet the objections of the disillusioned and worried idealists who regard the beliefs as a myth but recoil in horror from the moral chaos of our world. But Christianity cannot claim to have made a corner in moral teaching. Almost any ethical precept of the Gospels, cut out of its context and shorn of the quickening insight and authority of him who spoke it, can be well matched in the sayings of the great Jewish and pagan and Chinese moralists. There is really no reason for the disillusioned idealists to bother about retaining the detached ethics of Christianity since a nicely chosen anthology from half a dozen of the great non-Christian moral teachers would give them almost exactly the same results. 'Thou shalt love thy neighbour as thyself'; there is nothing exclusively Christian in that. Christian ethics begin only when you remember that that commandment was linked as the corollary to a greater one: 'Thou shalt love the Lord thy God.' Well, we shall see, indeed we are seeing, how the ethics fare released from the dynamic tension between those two commandments and presented to us as philosophers' precepts, dry and devitalized.

Even the old pagan poets saw more clearly than we do by the flickering light they had the inefficacy of that dichotomy, just as by their light they understood hubris. 'Fear the Gods, Achilles, and pity an old man like your own father,' said old humbled Priam in the Trojan epic when he came to the Greek lines to beg the body of his son from the man who had dragged Hector's corpse at his chariot wheels round the circumference of Troy. He had to dispel the red mist of battle and vengeance and anger from Achilles' mind and he said: 'Honour the Gods and BECAUSE you honour the Gods, take pity on me.

Cecil Welland, Rector of Alderley Edge

Pigtails

Taking tea in the school garden

Chapter Eleven
EDUCATING A DAUGHTER

Father's and mother's view of a woman's function in life was naturally reflected in the education which they designed for me. My schooling should lead up to a few years of life at home before, if all went well, I got suitably married, my days being filled by golf and tennis with other social activities, some philanthropy - that was important - and some reading and perhaps a little art. Music had been abandoned after the occasion when I accused mother to her face of deliberately making trouble about notes I was playing, allegedly wrong, when she could not see the keyboard or music. Years later she told me of her utter bewilderment at this accusation and then how suddenly it had come to her that the only reasonable explanation could be that I had no ear whatsoever and genuinely believed that you could not tell whether a note was right unless you could correlate it with the written symbols in front of you. Her solution, I regret to say, was quite correct. I shall have more to say later about the mental conflict which this plan of life for post-school years thrust upon me since it was carried over without basic modifications into the altered world of 1919. Meanwhile, I must be educated and they very much disliked any sort of day school which approximated to the high school type. In their opinion, education at an establishment of this kind involved a 'roughening' process, a physical and intellectual scramble combined with contacts whose suitability they would not be able to control. In short, they affirmed the ideals for young women set out in Ruskin's Sesame and Lilies and felt that these were not likely to be nourished in a high school. Hence, placed as we were, when the régime of Meme was brought to an end, a governess had to be found for me.

But of Meme I must speak again. I was eight years old at the time of Meme's departure and heartbroken as I have already indicated. I have tried to sketch in her portrait in its place in the Ferns garden which is the setting which I associate with her most continuously, but there were other settings, too, the nursery, early holidays, Rathfern. All these settings were lifted by Meme into a realm of the imagination where she and I dwelled together. It was a realm furnished and populated indiscriminately with the objects and personnel of fairy stories and romances and of anecdotes of everyday life and history. Meme's birth during that storm at sea in the trooper, a full-rigged sailing ship, bound for South Africa, the scenery of Ardnamurchan where Meme spent the happiest part of her youth, Meme's father as the Indian Mutiny veteran (there was a faded photograph of him with a beard and a low shako, a frogged jacket, tight trousers and a cavalry sabre), Bonnie Prince Charlie, the characters of Feats on the Fjords or Coral Island, Snow White and the Sleeping Beauty, Androcles and the Lion, the friendly owl who dropped me notes (written, of course, by Meme in a laboriously disguised hand) down the bedroom chimney which I would read when I awoke in the morning, David and Goliath, the Three Wise Men and the shepherds who watched their flocks by night; each and all as they passed through the lens of Meme's mind and shone on to the slender unfolding strip of apprehension that was mine acquired a quality of enchantment and an equal value of reality. It was the same with objects you could see and handle yourself. My wooden horse, Florink, mounted as a tricycle, was as much alive as Dot, the pony or Major, our collie dog, the predecessor of the gamin mongrel Patou; indeed, perhaps Florink seemed more alive than Major because Meme and I could control him and fashion his character to our own liking. And the secret of the wicker chaise-longue which I had endowed with all the attributes of a ship and which could actually be made to move over the shiny linoleum of the nursery floor by a sort of rowing motion of the body was one which I could share with her without any access of self-consciousness.

Meme and I shared a bedroom both at home and when each summer she took me over to stay at Rathfern, but though I was always alone until she came to bed I never remember, during those years, being troubled by the terrifying populace of the dark except for one night of uncanny fear after I had been taken round the museum of Manchester University and had glimpsed an exhibit of mummies en passant. I am sure that I owed this immunity to the influence of her imagination which was always clear and wholesome as a mountain pool.

At Rathfern we awoke in the big airy bedroom filled always, so it seems to me now, with gentle morning sunshine; we awoke early and Meme would employ the time before we had to get up in teaching me a poem or a hymn:

> Up the airy mountain
> Down the rushy glen
> We daren't go a-hunting
> For fear of little men,

was a favourite, varied by 'My heart's in the highlands' or 'Once in royal David's city' or 'We plough the fields and scatter the good seed on the land'. It was an idyllic existence, and one in which a miracle, for instance, could scarcely happen, not because science had declared any interference with the routine processes of nature to be impossible, but because there was no definition and separation of normality and abnormality, so that an interference would have seemed just as normal as anything else and a part of the common form of life.

It was then hardly surprising that the wrenching apart of Meme's life from mine left me stark and lonely and that I was scarcely in the mood to welcome her successor. This was to be a foreigner since mother held the sensible view that to know a foreign language well is a great asset and that it can best be acquired young and as nearly as possible after the manner in which you learn your own tongue. So Meme was replaced by Miss Margharetti, a stocky Italian from Trieste, with oiled black hair and a pasty face. I disliked her immediately, adopted a wary and resentful attitude, and I am afraid took it out of her in any way I could think of in order to recoup myself for my sorrow at the loss of Meme. Miss Margharetti had not the first idea of how to cope with and win over a non-co-operative English urchin and her régime was brought to an end after six weeks by mother. Apparently I had fixed Miss Margharetti one day with a sulky and resentful stare and told her that I could easily murder her with my new pocket-knife if I wished and that in certain circumstances I might be prepared to do so. She complained in due form to mother and, so mother told me years afterwards, with a seriousness which betokened genuine alarm. Mother had a sense of humour and proportion; after this episode it did not take her long to decide that Miss Margharetti was not a suitable mentor.

Then Mademoiselle Dupuy came on the scene and for six years I was disciplined mentally, morally and physically in a way for which I cannot ever sufficiently say 'thank you'. I grew to love Mademoiselle, but my affection was always tinged by a healthy fear and respect. She was a Frenchwoman in her middle twenties from the old province of Guienne and in almost every way the antithesis to Meme. Her black hair was wiry like a mane and piled on the top of her head whereas Meme's hair, as I have said, was fine as silk, parted in the middle and done up at the nape of her neck in a glossy plait. Her brown eyes were alert and watchful whereas Meme's were gently dark like water held in a basin of peat. Her smooth skin with its overall olive hue on face and hands made her seem physically rather remote, whereas I had known so familiarly the touch of Meme's hands, bony and yet soft, and the feel of her cheeks when she had drawn mine against hers at bedtime or in comfort for some fleeting misery.

Mademoiselle had a clear mind free from cant and with a cutting edge to it which she could and frequently did use with some effect against the little and large hypocrisies as she saw them of English life. I used sometimes to overhear conversations between herself and her sister who taught at a school in Manchester and sometimes her comments were made directly to me. She was a critic of the real world where Meme had been the creator of an imaginative one, a debunker where Meme had been a romantic. As a result I lost a good deal of my unquestioning trustfulness, but it was time for me to do so. Her influence was an astringent and under it I began to separate the actual world from the world of my imagination as again it was time for me to do. All sorts of sprouting centres of emollient thought were cauterized for me by Mademoiselle.

Mademoiselle taught me everything except mathematics and English poetry which father supervised and scripture which I learned from mother. She was very strict and kept a mark book which I had to show to my parents every Sunday evening. There were marks not only for lessons, but also for tenue and conduite, and many were the Sunday afternoons clouded by apprehension when I knew that I had only a 3/10 or a 4/10 for tenue and perhaps at best a 5/10 for conduite to show up. Lost marks for conduite were chronically the result of having disputé avec sa mère. Mademoiselle had little mercy for the young who argue with their elders. She was an admirable teacher, but it was not only from her teaching gift that I profited; what I learned of most value came from the impact of an outlook at variance with almost all the cherished assumptions on which most English children are brought up. I was saved, for instance, from an uncritical admiration for English history and from the superior and patronizing attitude towards Latin countries which Anglo-Saxons so often seem to think it clever to adopt. By the time that I was fourteen I knew as much of French history as I did of English and from a French point of view. French historical stories were as much a part of my childish mental equipment as English. Bayard, the knight 'sans peur et sans reproche', was a figure as rounded and well lighted by anecdote as Drake or Raleigh. Francis the First, lying in prison after the battle of Pavia, excited my sympathy quite as deeply as Richard the Lionheart languishing in his Austrian castle. I knew more about St Louis of France than I did about St Edward the Confessor or his pious namesake the sixth of the Edwardian series. And as for the activities of the English in France during the Hundred Years' War, I was taught to regard them from a point of view very different from the story of glorious pageantry which my English history book unfolded. I can remember to this day Mademoiselle's contempt when I trotted out the tale of the Burghers of Calais and under her searing criticism I soon ceased to regard the Black Prince and Henry V as nobly heroic figures. In this way I lost a good many of the national heroes who were the historical stock in trade of my contemporaries, but I gained an inestimable advantage whose value I came to understand far later when I began to read history seriously for myself. Then I found that I had acquired unconsciously a Latin as well as an Anglo-Saxon angle of vision and, in general, a sceptical approach to writers of history, a realization that always an enormous allowance must be made for the writer's personal outlook on life and his country of origin.

There were other jolts, too, for an insular outlook; differences in manners which appeared during our French readings - an absence of primness, for instance - or differences which appeared suddenly as a comment on our daily life and which Mademoiselle was apt to analyse very persuasively to the disadvantage of the island race. She was a Catholic and it was an understood thing that she took no hand in my religious upbringing which was reserved exclusively to mother's care. She had great loyalty about this, a loyalty which was indeed rather remarkable when contrasted with her general debunking proclivities, for she certainly took the shine off several aspects of English life which, I am sure, mother would have preferred left for me lighted by their pristine sentimental glow.

Mademoiselle was said to come of a 'good' family (the adjective had no moral significance), consequently she had the highly developed sense of social caste to which the French of 'good' family cling so tenaciously, no doubt as an offset to the slogan of Liberté, Egalité, Fraternité, which they read ad nauseam inscribed on all their public buildings. She was not impervious to the prestige of material possessions, but she judged by birth and breeding and manners rather than the success of one's immediate forebears in the economic scramble. Thus the values she set upon our various neighbours did not by any means always coincide with the values they set upon themselves. Moreover, she knew more about formal manners and courtesy than some of them did or appeared to do and, forgetting that the English are often brusque and ungallant in these matters out of sheer absent-mindedness and indolence, she was apt to accuse people unfairly of deliberate ungraciousness. I recollect a trivial lapse of my brother's when we were all in London at the time of King Edward VII's funeral. Campbell came to our hotel in full regimentals, helmet, scarlet tunic, crimson sash and gleaming sword scabbard, after his battalion had been lining the streets for the funeral procession and he cheerfully shook hands with her without having first removed his white gauntleted glove. Mademoiselle was scandalized by such behaviour on the part of 'an officer and a gentleman'. She was careful to tell me all about Campbell's lapse for the sake of education.

I think this preoccupation with formal manners, which incidentally certainly was a useful education for me, made her feel her own position in the house in a way that Meme, who was personally rather insensitive, never appeared to do. At any rate Mademoiselle did feel it in some way as socially difficult and rather invidious and when she used the word snob, or when her sister did, it was almost always in reference to an attitude or a manner which someone had adopted towards themselves. When guests were present she held aloof and would sit silent and often rather sulky-looking at table. I sensed this atmosphere and felt irritated and uncomfortable, and used to make absurd efforts to drag her into a conversation, a conversation into which obviously I had no call to enter myself, with shall we say, Sir John Wormald or Sir William Mather. Only when Miss Hall came to stay did Mademoiselle unbend and become part of the family. I suspect that Miss Hall thought she might be finding it a little difficult to keep braced as a practising Catholic and so made a definite effort to seek her out and be friendly. Probably being thus quite definitely sought out gave her a feeling of personal standing which she lacked with our other guests. Moreover, Mademoiselle sang in a pleasant alto voice and during Miss Hall's visits she was always persuaded to join her and mother at the piano. I think this was why I enjoyed Miss Hall's visits so much myself; the slight sense of social tension which troubled me with other guests was relaxed. None the less, the sense of tension served quite usefully to emphasize the critical quality of Mademoiselle's makeup and to increase the share of it which she imparted to me. I began to be able to detach myself from my entourage and to see it from an outside point of view.

There was, for instance, the Bradshaw family. The Bradshaws lived a few miles away farther out on the plain at a fine old Cheshire hall with half-timbered gables, sandstone walls, and inside a warren of rooms to chase through. Phyllis Bradshaw was a great friend of mine; we learned German together from her governess and she used often to come over to play with me or alternatively I would go over in the pony-trap to play with her. I liked Phyllis a lot, and she was good at loosening up my prim morals. I think it was in her company that I first filched a couple of father's cigarettes having learned to do that at her house. And on one bank holiday we made gallons of nettle beer and did a brisk trade selling it to the crowds out from Manchester who were enjoying the country lane at the bottom of the Bradshaw garden. But I did not like Phyllis's family whom I might meet in force when I was at her home for lunch. I did not get on with her elder sister or her good-looking and well-dressed mother with the chill voice, or her dashing brother who was in the Hussars whereas Campbell was a foot-slogging infantryman, or her lean, dark, sallow-faced father, whose cultural use of his riches seemed to have stopped abruptly with the acquisition of an old Cheshire hall. Somehow his personality did not consort with the gracious old dining-room with its view out on to an eighteenth-century garden with cropped yews and formal borders. And the meals were a challenge to me with their pretentious formality. To be served by a butler and footman in livery instead of by the smiling Louisa at home aroused to fighting pitch the vague sense of social criticism which Mademoiselle had somehow or another engendered - but which later, I am afraid, developed along lines which she would have found rather shocking. I could not have formulated my reaction to the Bradshaw régime, but I knew in my bones that a son in a smart cavalry regiment and any number of butlers and footmen did not make a culture and that merely to live in an old house with a long tradition did not make a Cheshire family with its pride of soil and its feudal sense of service. I knew that we had never tried to do that, but that none the less we had an authentic culture and I felt proud of my own family. On one occasion, I regret to say, I was really rude. The conversation was on shopping and the various smart and expensive shops in Manchester were being reviewed. Suddenly I burst out that I thought all those shops were nonsense. 'Oldham Street is much the best place to shop,' I announced didactically.

Now only those who know the social nuances of Manchester in the first decade of the century can understand properly the enormity of this remark. For Oldham Street was where the maids made their purchases and you did not invade their preserves. It was like going to church on Sunday evening or visiting your doctor during his consulting hours instead of having him attend on you. There was a chilly silence and I felt that perhaps I had gone rather far in abandon. But Mademoiselle would have enjoyed and appreciated my contribution to that conversation. She had all a Frenchwoman's sense of laying out money to the best advantage regardless of other considerations. For that matter, I expect it was she who had told me about the possibilities of Oldham Street.

Looking back, it seems to me that the six years with Mademoiselle gave an unorthodox twist to my education, although I am quite sure that this was very far from any effect intended by her and mother. For one thing, she did not come with us on holidays so that I was then thrown into a company of elders drawn from a much wider circle than Alderley Edge. For another thing, she spent the weekends in Manchester with her sister so that from Saturday to Monday I was relatively free and independent, and spent my time with father and mother or on ploys of my own. Sometimes this liberty developed into licence, or so mother thought. It was on such occasions that I slipped off to hobnob by the hour with Richardson at the carpenter's bench in an outhouse of the stable-yard. And one year when mother was ill for many weeks I was very much alone and took the opportunity to strike up a comradeship, quite unsentimental, with Bagnall, the stable boy. He was the son of a travelling showman who each year brought his merry-go-round to a field opposite the Wizard Inn on top of the Edge, and he had a smattering of gipsyish lore. He taught me how to cut and splice two lengths of wood and lash them with waxed thread so that everything was finished neat and smooth and strong. He taught me how to make a fishing-rod in three sections which would fit cleanly into each other. He understood horses and showed me how to groom the pony and feed her and how to drive the trap, sitting straight-spined with gathered reins and a jauntily slanted whip in the bumping rear corner seat. Unfortunately, mother became aware of the hours I was spending in Bagnall's company while he worked or when I had lured him away from his work to do jobs for me. Quietly but firmly I was prevented from having anything more to do with Bagnall except in the most distant way. I felt sore and rather ashamed. It seemed so unnecessary to spoil what had been such a pleasant and instructive relation and I thought Bagnall would find it very odd. Probably he never gave the matter a thought; no doubt I was merely a less tedious method than normal of spending his working time.

When Mademoiselle left I was just fourteen; it was the beginning of the Christmas holidays of 1911 and in January I was due to go away to boarding-school. I can still feel the bleak and secret atmosphere which suddenly seemed to attach itself to all the intimate familiar objects of the schoolroom and our bedroom on the afternoon when she said good-bye. Campbell was at home for Christmas leave, full of animal spirits, and he had arranged a bicycle hockey match in a neighbouring field. He had invited me to play and I longed to do so, but mother had vetoed this because she said it was too rough a game when all the other players were grown-up boys and girls. So I sat disconsolately at my bedroom window looking out on to the dun damp lawn and the stark trees, weighed down by a loneliness which was only emphasized when I thought of the unknown prospect of school.

The school, at Folkestone, had been carefully selected. It was an offshoot of a school, rather famous of its kind, in a northern suburb of London the head mistress of which, Miss Soulsby, had given years of work and thought to evolving an educational technique guaranteed to mould suitable female material to her chosen pattern. When I say suitable female material I mean socially suitable; parental standing was carefully inquired into before any girl was accepted. As for the chosen pattern, it can be summed up very shortly. Miss Soulsby aimed to turn out high-minded and cultured home-makers. Ruskin again! And I am quite sure that had Ruskin been active during the heyday of her school he would have made himself at home there as he so oddly did for weeks on end at Winnington Hall in Cheshire, a school which the Manor House must have resembled in many ways, for he enjoyed romanticizing from time to time, not only on paper, about adolescent girls of the leisured classes, and he would have found Miss Soulsby's ideals for her flock altogether to his taste. She herself was a remarkable woman, deeply read, prolific and

Dot and Bagnall, the stableboy

Katharine and Dot

exuberant in ideas which she was always noting down in writing or translating into action in the management of her school, Christian with an informed and serious but rather emotional faith, embellished with various personal glosses which occasionally, I think, committed her to some rather surprising positions, definite in her conclusions about life, one of which, that the male is superior to the female in intellect and judgment whereas women are more sensitive than men to the things of the spirit, was for better or worse a main base for her theory of education. Her girls carried the Manor House mark into their adult lives and you would always find that intellectual men who liked nice manners and a measure of cultivated attainment and intelligent poise in their womenfolk approved them. But let her speak for herself as she did in a book which she wrote for her old girls when she retired from the school and handed it over to my head mistress who amalgamated it with her own: *'What was my ambition for you? That you should realize your mother's love all the better for leaving her. That you should gain a certain flair for books and ideas. That you should keep Lady Elizabeth's'* (I forget who Lady Elizabeth was; a sort of amateur patron saint of the school, I think) *'standards of ways and manners and deference to elders. That you should be marked by ... common sense, deediness and organization in daily life! ...*

'The school was based on recognition of the inherited capacities for spirituality, cultivation and ruling power which belonged to the race of Lady Elizabeths, which sent them back to their homes sympathetic, not superior, and also to introduce them to the wider modern ideas and social service which would rightly fill their future life. I expected you to live a life of responsibility - the responsibility of right ruling of yourself and your fellows.

'Perhaps you are feeling I have left out religion. To my thinking all this involves religion .... You are of royal birth and to be a great and gracious woman, a fellow worker with God, is the only thing a royal natured woman can wish to be!'

As for the final suggestion, one cannot avoid a fancy that the Almighty must have been faintly amused by this offer of a bevy of fellow-workers of royal birth and may even have raised a metaphorical eyebrow over the bland assurance of such an interpretation of a creature's relations with its Creator. 'Education', Miss Soulsby wrote, 'happens to be the channel through which I carry out my life's interest, yet my interest is not primarily in education, but in making you as grateful to your mother as I am to mine.' Compare the spirit of her interpretation with that of Villon's noble Ballad of Intercession to Our Lady, written at the request of his mother:

Dame du ciel, regente terrienne,

Emperiere des infernaux palus,
Recevez moi, vostre humble chrestienne,
Que comprinse soye entre vos eleus,
Ce non obstant qu'oncques rien ne valus.
Les biens de vous, Ma Dame et Ma Maîtresse,
Sont trop plus grans que ne suis pecheresse,
Sans lesquelz biens ame ne peut merir
N'avoir les cieulx, je ne'en suis jangleresse,
En ceste foy je veuil vivre et mourir.

A vostre Filz dictes que je suis sienne;
De lui soyent mes pechiez abolus ....

But then Villon and his mother lived among the lights and shadows of the mediaeval Church and had no comfortable illusions about their relations with their Maker, and she was an obscure old woman with a heart riven by the lawless doings of her son, the frequenter of wild taverns, the gaol-bird and candidate for the gallows, whose motto might have been the pagan poet's baffled and poignant cry: *Video meliora, proboque, deteriora sequor,* that cry that the Church might explain by her doctrine of the fall of man but could never render obsolete. Whereas God's co-workers from the Manor House were the daughters of English gentlewomen nourished on five centuries of progressive enlightenment.

Miss Soulsby's educational ideals were pursued at my school at Folkestone, but in a simplified and less intense way. My head mistress, Miss Abbott, had been trained under her and, as I have said, took over the Manor House when she retired. But she had a quieter temperament and she kept her mind which was a good one, sane and shrewd and sensitive, well pruned emotionally. She was short and neat and rather plump in figure and she had crisp dark hair and brown eyes. She was scarcely middle-aged when I came to school, but in the evenings she always wore a long dress of stiff black brocade with a fichu of old lace. When she came into a room you were aware that her dignity and authority were personal to her and not only the attributes of her office.

Having got over the first term or two at Folkestone during which I felt strange and lonely and rather friendless, I was very happy during my four years at school. None the less, a few years after I left I rose in revolt against the whole conception of life on which the school was based. I could not see that the underlying ideals were permanent and valid, and the Ruskinian sentiment and the arrogant leisured class assumptions only an adventitious dress. I could only see the glaring lacunae and the circumscriptions in my own education as a result of the latter. Continuous red lights had blinked at us, so it seemed to me, from every direction, and

Miss Abbott was always on point duty regulating each detail of our existence so that it should tend towards the chosen goal.

Church twice a day on Sunday was compulsory and after the morning service we marched up and down the Leas winding in a decorous crocodile with a mistress at the tail among the strolling weekend visitors from London who, it seemed to us, so palpably belonged to a world of glamorous freedom. We returned to roast beef, apple pie and custard and a change of places at the long trestle tables. A place next to Miss Abbott meant that the ensuing mealtimes for a week would be spent in shy and desperate efforts to learn the conversational art of opening gambits. Miss Abbott, purposely, I think, did not help us out much, nor did she encourage a real discussion about anything or attempts on our part to be expansive on any subject which she could see absorbed our interest. The point, presumably, was how to keep a courteous conversation going on the thinnest nourishment, how to give airy nothings the local habitation and the name that would make them look presentable, how to talk without ever giving away that you are a human being with passions and aspirations and prejudices and compelling interests. Useful accomplishments, but I could never learn them. Yet I looked forward to my turn next to Miss Abbott because I knew that she could talk about all sorts of interesting things if only she would, and I always hoped that one day I should succeed in making her do so. Perhaps if I had been a better natural conversationalist I should have done, but it is a high art to draw out your guarded partner and I was not capable of that.

At some point during Sunday Miss Abbott heard us say our 'Christian Year'. We had to learn two or three verses from the appropriate section of Keble's poem in our own time, but this was no great imposition since you could always mug them up in the lavatory or at other odd moments, and though it hardly made for intelligence it could be done without reading any but the verses allotted to you. If the 'Christian Year' had taken up more than a minute or two it would have been a real imposition because we had scarcely any 'own time' - merely an hour or two on Saturday and Sunday when we could read a self-chosen book. Every time beat of the day was allotted to some activity whose pursuit at that particular moment was imposed from above. Nevertheless, we healthily found a good many uncovenanted opportunities to let off animal spirits. There was the term when a selected few of us brought back to school some very fine water-pistols and organized a pitched battle in the cloakroom. We had had our crowded hour of glorious life before the havoc we were making was discovered, and it was worth the rest of the term - which was spent by the water-pistols locked away in Miss Abbott's confiscation drawer. Nor were we without a rudimentary capacity for wit.

That was the term when we had a craze for wearing our sailor ties in the colours of schools and colleges and clubs which had been patronized by our fathers and brothers - a comic expression of old school-tie snobbism - and I sported an Emm. College Cambridge blue and salmon. During the water-pistol battle my chief friend was captured and held by the other side. I do not doubt that it was the sudden rising strains of

> Oh come Oh come Emmanuel
> And ransom captive Israel
> that brought Authority on to our scene of action.

Games, too, were an outlet for animal spirits and we took very seriously the rare matches against other schools. The matches were rare since among the schools whose crocs trailed up and down the Leas after church on Sunday only three were considered suitable for us to play. The necessary accomplishment of refusing invitations politely on secret grounds of social ineligibility was thus taught us early. The Games Captain knew exactly what she had to reply when a challenge was received from this or that establishment whose pupils were 'not quite like ourselves'. She sat down at her desk with a sheet of best note-paper and indited an answer to the effect that all Saturdays were regrettably filled until the end of term.

Twice a week, on Wednesday and Sunday, time was given us for writing letters, but we were not allowed to write to anyone except our parents unless we left the envelopes open for inspection or enclosed our correspondence in our letter home. It would have been quite impossible to by-pass this rule since we were never permitted outside the school garden by ourselves so could have made no opportunity to find a post-box. Even brothers were regarded with epistolary suspicion, and elder brothers were regarded with suspicion all round. I could sense that it was not really welcome when mine came to Folkestone and offered to take me out, particularly on the one or two occasions when he came there as a subaltern doing a course of instruction at Shorncliffe Camp. Once, permission was actually refused me to go out with him, but I think Miss Abbott was away on that occasion. I did not see Campbell very often and my anger and resentment smouldered for a long time. No doubt all these restrictions were due to Miss Abbott's twin aversions: silly schoolgirl friendships and an interest in young men; but since the main purpose of our school life was to train us for suitable matrimony it did seem an odd method to begin by making us self-conscious about any personable male.

Miss Abbott set great store by social reserve and also by courtesy, and I think she believed that these are best inculcated by learning so well to submit to a convention of manners that their use becomes instinctive. I am grateful for that discipline though amused by some of the enduring results of her indoctrination. For instance, it requires the greatest effort on my part to remember that having attained middle-age I do not need invariably to leap to my feet when another person enters the room, nor to fall modestly behind my companion when passing out of the door. She was less successful in her efforts to teach me how to enter or retire from a room with a degree of elegance and assurance.

I think our lessons were chosen so as to provide a soil into which we could strike cultural roots for ourselves, but too often, or so it seems to me, they provided us only with a top-dressing, a sprinkling of soil in which an appreciation of the arts and intellectual matters might flourish without raising any dynamic issues in our minds.

Music and art were taught by visiting masters, heavily chaperoned, dancing and elocution by women. For elocution we sat at the feet of an underling of the celebrated Miss Foggarty, but Miss Foggarty herself - large, dark, frighteningly expansive, with loose silk ruffling at her throat and flashes of gold about her person, such is my recollection - descended upon us about twice a term to check up on her lieutenant and subjected us to an hour of what was for me unmitigated dread. I could not produce the rich and rounded diphthongs, the full vowel sounds which Miss Foggarty very properly demanded. In particular, those diphthongs in the sentence I have just written emerged from my mouth, to her energetically expressed disgust, clipped into the noise one instinctively makes when someone treads suddenly upon one's sensitive little toe. As for the long 'O's', we learned them by repeating over and over that stanza from Tom Hood's 'Miss Kilmansegg and Her Golden Leg', which begins

> *Gold, gold, gold, gold,*
> *Bright and yellow, hard and cold.*

I used to hope that my voice would be drowned in the general mooing from the class, but I seldom managed to avoid the crack of Miss Foggarty's tongue. She alleged that I had a Lancashire accent and one day, in front of the whole school, she informed me: *'If you continue to speak like this you will find in your future life that many doors you would like to pass through will be closed to you.'*

I cannot reproduce in print the peculiar overtone of sarcasm that made this possibly quite correct statement hurt like a whip-cut. Sarcasm is legitimate among equals, but it is a sadist's weapon when you use it on the defenceless young.

We were taught no science, not even botany or physical geography although these two subjects were generally considered sufficiently lady-like to receive some attention from the female young. As a result I left school with only the haziest notions of the most elementary laws descriptive of the working of the physical universe and no conception at all of scientific method or the history of scientific thought. Of course, a school like mine could never, in any case, have afforded a laboratory, but a flash of imaginative teaching from the mistress's desk might have illuminated for us the secret of mental discipline, the fascinating devoted processes of thought - experiment, formulation of the hypothesis and final verification or rejection - by which the great men of science had arrived at their discoveries. Why those branches of the sciences of which we might have learned something whilst sitting in our classroom were considered irrelevant or even inimical to our proper development I cannot tell, and I am even more baffled to know why father who was, after all, a scientist himself should have acquiesced in this judgment.

We learned history from Miss Abbott and from Oxford Extension lecturers for whom we wrote essays. I spent hours over these essays, stealing time wherever I could from my other preps., and they were the happiest hours that I passed in school. But we were taught no 'civics'. We knew about the development of English institutions under the Plantagenets and could have given a sensible account of the principles of government at stake during the Parliamentary Wars, but if anyone had asked us to discuss not the days of long ago but the government of our country as it was organized on the day which we had just crossed off on our private calendars as bringing us twenty-four hours nearer the holidays except for a vague reference to parliament and general elections we should have cheerfully shown up a blank piece of paper. We knew nothing of the interlocking, counter-checking, complementary functions of local and central institutions, and we had no notion of the simplest principles of English law nor of the processes of justice. Except that we believed that trade unions promoted strikes and the British Medical Association prevented quacks, we had no idea of the functions of the great corporations and professional bodies nor of the pulls they exerted inside our national life. We knew more about mediaeval guilds and the struggle of a rising central government to break the pull of feudal privilege and prerogative; which was all very interesting and important, and I can only suppose that it was not important and interesting that we should understand the machinery of the car in which we were going to ride ourselves. Indeed, perhaps it was wiser that we should not know how the brake and the accelerator worked in case we took up with the idea of interfering with their application. I don't think Miss Abbott approved of feminists. A few years after I left I read C.F.G. Masterman's admirable little book, *How England is Governed*. I was fascinated, as one always is when bewildering bits and pieces of unrelated information suddenly fit themselves together into a coherent structure. I think we might have tackled Masterman without undue danger to our Ruskinian bloom.

A current affairs period with free discussion such as is common form in any self-respecting school to-day would have been bluntly deemed subversive. We were discouraged from discussing politics at all and no newspapers were allowed to us. After midday dinner, when we had to lie flat on our backs on the floor for ten minutes, a penitentiary performance intended to straighten and strengthen our spines so that we should hold ourselves well, the mistress in charge read to us from the Daily Telegraph or the Morning Post. She never appeared to be in the least interested herself in what was going on in the great world outside; as a result neither were we.

Our private reading was strictly censored in the interests largely of a lowest common denominator of supposed parental approval. Miss Abbott took the view that it was not her business to raise any issues in our minds which our parents might prefer to let lie like sleeping dogs. Since, naturally, we came from homes of varying intelligence and freedom this common denominator bore rather hardly on some of us. It was a custom for parents to present a book to the school library every now and then, and one holiday I suggested that father should give Kipling's *Kim* which I had just been reading. There were several Kiplings in the library and I brought it back to school in all innocence and happily presented it to Miss Abbott. To my disgust she refused to accept it and locked it away in her drawer. I can make no comment on this because I still have not the vaguest idea where Kim had produced a factor which would not go into the lowest common denominator.

Certain subjects, by their discipline, should teach you to use your mind under severe control as an athlete uses his body. You can't leap just anyhow to conclusions in a problem of algebra or Latin prose. If you do you will almost certainly fall into the ditch. So far as they went, and they went quite far enough for me, mathematics were very well taught by a strange neurotic little woman whose double set of ill-fitting dentures which were always apt to come adrift relieved the tedium attaching to strings of quadratic equations whose point I could never see. Other people got much further than I did; after an attack of typhoid fever, picked up out of school in my last year and whose onset coincided with a couple of zeros for two consecutive preps which I was sent to show up to Miss Abbott (I can still see the angry flourish of the mistress's pen), I was excused any more mathematics when I returned to work. But I longed to learn Latin although I found it very difficult, and all we did was to wade slowly through a couple of books of Caesar and a few hundred lines of Virgil.

French was considered important and we were fortunate in our teacher. Miss Abbott gave her the time and the freedom and she supplied a personal talent for teaching and an educated mind that set her far above any of the other mistresses, except Miss Abbott herself As a result the firm groundwork which I had got from Mademoiselle Dupuy was built on so solidly and yet so lightly that I have never lost my pleasure in the French tongue nor my sympathetic admiration for almost every facet of French civilization. It is years since I heard news of Mademoiselle Couchoud, but among the people who influenced me she is another to whom it would be a pleasure to say 'thank you'. It was not so with the pedestrian frauleins who dealt with German; they could evoke no such response. One term a German book was read aloud to us while we did our sewing; the hero was a certain Lieutenant Malthen, but I got through the best part of that term in the firm conviction that we were hearing about the adventures of a couple of twins named Leuthen und Malthen.

Most, but not all of the English literature lessons were dulled. I remember poems and essays that lighted one's mind, but I never read a Shakespeare play for pleasure until I had left school long enough to recover from those we 'did' in class. Perhaps it was my own fault but it seems to me that the great humanity, the poetry had been sapped out by the reams of notes which one had to learn by heart and the action straggled and lagged through week after week behind these serried ranks of notes. Similarly with the Bible. We 'did' the historical books of the Old Testament in a red reader and I have never been able to bring myself to read them since. And we 'did' the 'Acts of the Apostles' in another reader even more heavily weighted with notes than the Shakespeares so that by the time we had finished with him St Paul, the most vivid figure in history, was as dead as a door-post. Years later I read the 'Acts' through to one of my children; I think it was the first time I had read them from end to end since my schooldays, I had forgotten long since all the notes and, as I read, trying haltingly and hopelessly to make the great speeches break as crested waves break and as they would have done on the Acropolis under the hard Greek sky or in the judgment hall of Festus, I thought I knew what Keats had felt when he wrote the sonnet on his discovery of a supreme book. The Gospels went better, since even a semi-bored schoolgirl ruling pencil lines along key passages of a Revised Version could hardly contrive to escape from them with an imagination quite unlit.

I find it difficult to recall what we actually learned during these lessons. It seems to me that no attempt was made in class to give us an intellectual support for our religion. We knew nothing of the vast labours of scholars to establish or refute, as the case might be, the authenticity and historical truth of the books of the New Testament, and could not have cited a single example of the kind of evidence they adduced in order to maintain their rival claims. The books were never properly fixed for us in their setting of Jewish and Roman history. For me they were simply sui generis, a sort of true fiction tenuously attached to the normal historical world by the names of one or two Roman emperors whom I had met in other connections. It would have been news to me to hear that St Paul could quote a proverb used by the rakish poet Menander (not that I had been introduced to such a one as Menander by Miss Abbott!) and that the Roman pro-Consul before whom he was haled at Corinth was a brother of Seneca. It would have been news to hear that Pilate had probably seen active service with his legion in a country so near at hand as Germany. Yet little vivid facts like these build solid links with normal history, bridges on which one may stand and consider. I think, too, that it would have done our minds good if we could have discussed some of the Christian 'Evidences', for example, some of the numerous ingenious theories which scholars have propounded in their straits to account naturally for what happened after the crucifixion, following them out till we had tracked down the conclusions inherent in them as remorselessly as we had to follow out those exercises of Euclid which ended with a whooping 'Which is absurd'. But no; - ours not to reason why, at any rate not in class. It was almost as if apologetics were regarded as an indecent subject - like sex biology.

Yet Miss Abbott certainly thought it more important that, when we emerged into the big world, we should remain Christians even than that we should preside at our future husbands' dinner-tables with grace and reasonable intelligence. With quiet seriousness, she taught us something of the devotional side of religion, and she taught us our Christian doctrines, based I think on Bishop Gore's exposition. And she was always ready if you came to her alone to discuss sympathetically and calmly any difficulties you might have about religion. She expected us to keep them to ourselves and discouraged us from discussing religion between ourselves as she discouraged us from discussing politics, but she did not expect inquiring adolescents to forgo altogether the use of their budding reasons or to stifle their speculations provided they kept the results for the privacy of her study after bedtime, an hour when she would see those of us who needed advice about this or that in circumstances which made for easy confidences. And if you showed her that you needed reasoned arguments she would tell you where to go to find some. I remember that on one such occasion - I must have been in my last term - she recommended me to read a two-volume book of Giffard Lectures by Caird on Natural Theology! I am afraid she had taken my intellectual measure too generously. The hardheaded Scot was altogether too tough for me and I found it much simpler to entertain the difficulties, whatever they were, than to brace my mind in an effort to resolve them.

How far my school was closely typical of the kind of school to which girls of our sort were sent at the start of this twentieth century, I am not sure. Indeed, I doubt whether any private school can be closely typical since its quality is always determined by the individual personality of its head. And as I re-read what I have just written I feel that somehow I have got the picture unfairly distorted and I am sorry. Looking at the pattern bit by bit I have got the whole out of balance. I have left out something which I find very hard to describe in words, something which was given us by Miss Abbott as an individual soul and not as the protagonist of a certain kind of society. She gave us a supporting affection which was quietly demonstrated in all sorts of ways but never forced demands on us emotionally, a sense of discipline and courteous and comely living, a feeling for form in life, not in the sense meant by the second mistress (whom, incidentally, I liked very much) when she commented as she so frequently did: 'That's awf'lly bad form', but in the sense of form as it is used in a Chinese vase or a sonnet or a Bach prelude to imply a limiting, a sort of voluntary renunciation of the grand extravagances latent in the medium - in our case it was in the medium of life. Perhaps, after all, she did not encourage us to jostle each other with our sprouting ideas not because she was afraid of intellectual adventuring for the mature, but because she disliked cocksure and immature judgments and believed that intellectual manners are as important as any other sort and that it is best not to bandy about too many opinions until you have learned this courtesy. Fortitudo et decor indumentum eius et ridebit in die novissimo was the motto she chose for her school.

And so, filtering through all the jarring limitations and restrictions, there shone the silver clarity of Miss Abbott's spirit. It was like the beam of a fixed light playing along its own path, but never ranging to probe the unexplored tracts on either hand. And where the light fell freely and naturally its illumination was nearly perfect. Out of class, for instance, Miss Abbott could be a wonderfully infectious and persuasive teacher. One term we spent an occasional Saturday afternoon rubbing brasses in old Kentish churches. I think that awoke my appreciation for incisive line. Another term we passed a long day in Canterbury Cathedral. And sometimes in the evening she would read to us from Wordsworth or Browning. She read in a clear-toned voice with a perfect balance and emphasis so that every shade of meaning became lucid and the actual words took on each its true value of beauty. Then she would give us a list of quotations and leave us to browse through the volumes of poems until we had found the contexts. By these means I learned to know and love Wordsworth and Browning for myself and was led on to browse for myself among other English poets, watching out for the striking phrase, the music of sequent words, the apt and lovely simile. This was real education and made up for not a few of those wasted hours in class. And from Browning, too, we learned to recognize a noble philosophy of life. Because when Miss Abbott read Browning to us she stripped off the exasperating accretions on her outlook and let the poet mould her mind. The other day I turned up a series of comments which she had written on an essay I had done for her on A Death in the Desert. It was only then perhaps that I realized how fine was her insight into life when she set it free, and how much I owe to her.

Miss Hordern   Miss Abbott

School group at Canterbury

Chapter Twelve
HOLIDAYS

The best companionship I had with father when I was a child drew its nourishment from active holiday pursuits. He had leisure on holidays to be a companion. He was not good at games though he played golf and tennis and enjoyed them, and he had no hobbies except that he sometimes made watercolour sketches of views he liked. But he had been a fine swimmer and mountaineer and he loved travel. Travel appealed to the restless streak in him. Also, I think his feeling for the beauty of nature and the beauty of the work of men s hands set in nature - a Gothic Abbey or an Italian town - satisfied his aesthetic side through emotions which, in themselves, are not really aesthetic. He had, too, a sense of the past encouraged by mother who cared a good deal about history.

When he was a young man with surplus physical energy to expend and a desire for adventure to satisfy, father had spent almost all his holidays in the Alps or the Lake District. He was a mountaineer in the classical age of mountaineering. His name is associated with more than one first ascent of a Lake District rock-climb and in the Alps with the first descent of the north-east ridge of the Nesthorn. But he was not in the least interested in mountaineering records. Years after his death I found in an old diary the most casual entry regarding this magnificent climb which he and his brothers, with Wm. Cecil Slingsby, had done without guides. He must have known it was a virgin ridge, but apparently he derived no special satisfaction or exhilaration from that. At any rate, he did not bother to record the fact in his diary. He climbed because he enjoyed climbing and because mountain scenery appealed to him. And he climbed difficult climbs because his spirit rose to danger. The Nesthorn ridge was repeated as an ascent fourteen years later, in 1911, by Mr Geoffrey Winthrop Young. And then father had his tribute from the pen of one of the great writers of mountain literature:

'The muscular output was tremendous; for the continuity of the ridge, neither rising nor falling, nor growing harder nor easing off, was so persistent that we had never a reason for varying the pace or for slackening in our steady pursuit of the clock. I have not often traversed a ridge that put such a premium upon good combined climbing, or developed so much consciousness of a real rhythm of the rope. It was a delight to picture the passage of the Hopkinsons along it in the reverse direction, after their first descent of the Nesthorn ridge, with Cecil

Postcard from Ullswater, 1917.

Slingsby, fourteen years before. I had heard so often from eye-witnesses that the combination of the famous brothers was a model of what team-work might be made.'

The mountaineering career came to an abrupt and tragic close. In 1898, father's eldest brother, John Hopkinson, was killed with three of his children on the Petite Dent de Veisivi. That tragedy shadowed all our mountaineering lives, even those of my generation. I longed to climb, but got no encouragement at home, though secretly I think father sympathized with my aspirations. Long after I was grown up and free to go my own way, whenever I got into any real difficulty upon a mountain I felt that I was committing a kind of hubris. As for father, he never climbed seriously again. I think he would have liked to, but felt he had no right to put such a burden of anxiety upon mother. She had never enjoyed physical adventure for the fun of it. Life, she argued, had too many inevitable hazards and problems without creating artificial ones. And the catastrophe on the Petite Dent de Veisivi, when a great scientist's life and three promising young lives were thrown away, seemed to her, I think, like gambling with God's trust of existence. I think, too, that the wide and deep personal suffering which it occasioned wounded her permanently.

Of course the proper cure for all of us who were mountaineers would have been to go back to Arolla and climb the Petit Dent. Not quite forty years after the accident I had the opportunity to do this. The mountain is a good rock peak and the natural opening climb from Arolla. We duly planned the expedition, but the evening before I felt rather unfit and went to bed in two minds whether to stay behind next day or force my body in order to carry through the exorcism which I had privately decided to perform on myself. The alarum clock went before dawn, and in that hour of guttering vitality when mountaineers curse the strange urgency of desire which drives them to forgo rest and comfort, I made an excuse of my lassitude, genuine though it was, turned over in bed and allowed the others to go out into the greying light and chilled air without me. Hours later I walked leisurely up the valley to meet them on their return and watched the sunlight playing over the tawny precipices of the Petite Dent. But there was no exhilaration for me in the sight of those lean feline sweeps of cliff, for I had evaded their challenge. I have since realized that I ought to have felt frightened as well as secretly ashamed, for the evasion of one challenge only makes it harder the next time that life throws down a gauntlet to stoop fearlessly and pick it up. And next time you cannot tell ahead, it may be the challenge that will stretch you to the uttermost.

After father's health began to collapse after the 1914-18 war I was thrown on my own resources for holidays. My body was grown and strong, I could trust my muscles and endure long days on the hills; my sinews braced and slacked to the rhythm of physical endeavour and rest as once his had done when, with the whole of my small fist comfortably enclosed in his palm and my slips of legs striving to measure up to his stride, he had taught me to understand the ways of wind and rain and mist and sun upon a mountain. Sometimes, when I had been to the Lake District or to Wales for a particularly good weekend, the stirred sap of youth seemed to well up so as to burst through physical limits and issue in a kind of mental elation so that I could hardly forbear singing at the top of my voice as I walked across Manchester from one station to the other to catch the train for home. When I got in I would go up to father's room to tell him of my doings. I wonder if he guessed how sharp the pain was when I recalled with a sudden flash of remembrance some day from the past which now would never be repeated. I do not suppose he did guess; the gaucherie of youthful expression and the inhibition of youthful reserve result in an appearance of callousness more often than not. Anyway, privately, I remembered the sanded lip and rocky jaws of an Anglesey bay where he had begun to teach me to swim by making me cling to an oar, well out of my depth, a cutting of humanity tensely kicking in fathoms of clear green water. I remembered our descent with my Uncle Alfred of the Fox's Path on Cader Idris when I was about seven or eight years old. It was my first scree-shoot, and we took it as scree-shoots ought to be taken, not gingerly and procrastinating but at a glorious run. Secure in the familiar grasp of father's hand, I committed myself with wholehearted trust to the movement of the scree as our weight set the stone avalanches going. Cader is a sizable mountain, and in any case I had yet to learn that slack rather than taut leg muscles are best on a scree-shoot; I was very tired when we came to the level run out at the foot of the lower slopes. Then Uncle Alfred took me astride his shoulders and so we marched back to the railway through the twilight.

I remembered the row home down Caragh lake in Co. Kerry against a rising angry wind. Uncle Alfred was with us on that occasion, too. Father and he had both rowed at their universities and on the outward voyage they had been teaching me - to flick my wrists back for feathering, to pull with the weight of my body, such as it was, on the stroke and not with the muscles of my arms, to pull slowly and sweep the sculls through the water instead of dipping them with a jerk. But with the rising wind I had been stowed in the stern and, wetted every now and then by the slap of the water hustled against the gunwale, I watched with fascination the rhythmic co-ordination of their effort and listened for the measured creak of the stretchers as they pulled and the clink of the rowlocks.

I had a number of great days to remember. There was the blizzard day on the Styhead Pass in Cumberland one Easter, when I had actually swallowed my pride at the shelter-stone on the summit and opted to go home because the ordeal was too severe for my eleven-years-old endurance. There was the day on the little glacier above the Romsdal in Norway to which we had climbed from Aak, the long low house in the valley which belonged to a great-uncle who had house-parties there each summer for the salmon-fishing. That was my first glacier and we had not, I think, really intended to cross it, but father and Uncle Alfred, like hounds which sniff scent on the wind, could not resist when they were confronted by the queer quiet stirrings of air and the queer scarcely sensible smell which are peculiar to glaciers. At one point the way was barred by a crevasse half filled with snow. Father and Uncle Alfred jumped and told me to follow. It looked an intimidating leap for my much shorter legs and, hesitating, I jumped short, floundered, might have disappeared but for the hands, father's and Uncle Alfred's, which in a second had caught mine and dragged me back on to the firm ice. As I collected myself I noticed blood on the ice and the trickle of it streaking Uncle Alfred's hand which he had scored against the rough lip of the crevasse.

But the most hoarded memory of all was that of my first Alpine day, just before I was fourteen, when father had included me in a party to go to the Théodule Pass, the classic route to Italy from Zermatt. It was an easy glacier and snow expedition, but for the first time in my life I was on a climbing rope with father ahead probing in proper style for hidden crevasses. That day, too, I, a child of the north, looked from the great mountain barrier which I had broken over deep into an Italian valley whose streamlets, merging with a host of others, would eventually send the River Po heavy laden across Lombardy to empty its burden into the Adriatic.

Standing on that wall which divides the northern from the southern lands, I have saluted Italy a number of times since then; once again from the Théodule Pass, once from the Neu Weissthor down a clearing between mists which had been parted for a moment like drawn curtains, once from the summit of an Austrian glacier through the swirling of a March snowstorm, once in sunshine from a peak of the Tarentaise Alps whose slim crest of rock and snow was tipped by an iron statue of the Madonna or perhaps the Sainte Vierge, for I forget whether Italian or French hands had carried it there. To secure it against storms, they had bonded it to the mountain by a tripod bedded in the rock, and this base had been twisted awry so that it stood, with its surfaces scored by ice and seared by lightning, ungainly against the lovely snow curve of the summit ridge. But the face was turned towards Italy. So much that we Northerners prize, or ought to prize, comes to us passed through that mighty prism of Italy. Thus it is that aloft on the rampart of the Alps, the understanding may come to us, charged with wonder and more sharply than in any other surroundings, of the debt we owe to that civilization of the Mediterranean basin which through so many centuries and by so many varying paths has brought sweetness and light to us and to Europe.

I cannot say whether this thought was articulate in father's mind on the top of the Théodule, but I know that he regarded holidays as a good foundation for a liberal education. Altogether, we Hopkinsons rather fancied ourselves in regard to the holidays we took. Uncle Alfred, for example, was a born wanderer and used his holidays not so much as a respite or escape from the problems of thought and action which life sets up as a withdrawal, a fallow time during which solutions might germinate of their own accord. Solvitur ambulando should have been his motto. Hitching on a rucksack he would disappear for days on end into the hills of Greece, into the Black Forest, into the heart of his favourite Tyrol, and emerge again with a scorched face decorated with strips of peeling skin, incongruous enough when, a day or two later perhaps, it was contrasted against full evening dress or his vice-chancellor's robes.

He looked very fine in evening dress and quite magnificent in his robes. The ermine tippet set off his silky white hair which curled up from the nape of his neck like father's, only more profusely. The upper part of his forehead arched back to join the crown of his head, he had bushy eyebrows and roomy deep eye-sockets which held his big grey eyes firm but a little withdrawn. The straight nose, the thin lips and bossed finish to the chin, the well-built cheekbones, all seemed to lead up to those eye-sockets and eyes. If Aunt Mary's spirit and mood expressed themselves in the sensitive changes of her mouth and father's in the play of light or shadowed gloom over his whole face, Uncle Alfred's was manifest in his eyes which were always a little unhappy, sometimes smouldering with obstinacy or anger - his obstinacy was in his personal affairs, but not his anger which flared up for others against any attitude or action which he thought canting or unjust - but sometimes luminous like pools which clear as the stirred sediment of their beds begins to settle so that they can take the beauty of sunlight into their depths. He had a rather troubled spirit, partly because his temperament was restless and ambitious and the setting of his personal affairs not always easy, partly, I suspect, on account of an unresolved philosophy of life. His deep Christian ideals and emotional veneration for the Christian faith of his forebears were not articulated in a scheme of the universe which properly satisfied his intellect, so I doubt whether his many problems really yielded to solvitur ambulando. I think the ambulando was more a catharsis than a solution.

However that may be, he always reappeared from a Wanderung with a very well articulated and dogmatically expressed holiday philosophy. The exposition of it, accompanied by numerous illustrations taken from his adventures, kept me entranced. The basic principle was that you can never win full value from a holiday unless you set out unencumbered by preconceived notions as to where you should go and what you should see. Give yourself to the mood of the country and its people and they will give themselves to you. And, above all things, 'Get off the beaten track'. Uncle Alfred had an almost pathological distrust of the beaten track as the broad way which leadeth to holiday destruction. At Oxford, with a touch of the mediaeval student spirit, he had nourished himself on bread and cheese, Ruskin, Byron, Shelley and the classics, and somehow aspects of all these had got themselves woven into his holiday point of view. He never minded where he slept or what he ate, he liked the large panoramic background and the sentimental or romantic foreground. He liked the casual encounters of the road, the monk with whom he trudged over some Tyrolean pass discoursing the while in Latin as they might have done six hundred years before had they met as wandering scholars trudging over the same mountain track from one university to another. Not that Uncle Alfred would have been content with the scholarly part of that life for long. Like father, he needed to express himself in the world of affairs and he seldom appeared to read. Yet he had a great literature at his tongue's end. In this he was Greek. A man of action whose action is fed from a noble tradition of letters and philosophy, a man of thought whose thinking is touched to life by practical affairs. He loathed 'theories' and most sorts of modernist thought, and could be arrogant and deliberately dense where his sympathies were alienated. He hated Shaw and psycho-analysis and any educational experiment which he was pleased to regard as high-falutin'. He hated Epstein and Vers Libre and any painting which did not portray landscape or the human form in terms which squared with his own vision. He was vaguely attracted by Roman Catholicism (he liked sometimes to slip in to Mass on Sunday) and got on famously, so he said, with the old Nonconformist type of trade union M.P. But he disliked Anglo-Catholicism and detested left-wing intellectuals. It was a heterogeneous assortment of antipathies and yet one master key fitted them all. Uncle Alfred believed that life should be saluted with reverence, and in his mind all these antipathies attacked his principle of reverence either because they were shams or because they undermined his chivalric conception of human nature. He considered himself a realist, and in regard to the sins of the flesh he was far more understanding and compassionate than most of his generation, but where, in his view, he discerned sins of the intellect he became as unmanageable in argument as a shying horse. He was, of course, in fact an incurable romantic, but his romanticism demanded respect for it was fed from fine springs. In sum, he combined humility before the mystery of life with a deliberate intolerance towards any seeker after truth who was trying to sink a shaft into the mine of mystery, in order to bring up samples for experiment and analysis, at some point where he, Uncle Alfred, shrank from a disturbance.

For years he and I had a lovely and intimate relationship which spanned completely the forty-five years which separated us. He took father's place as a holiday mentor for, until he was well over seventy, he had astonishing physical vitality. Together we tramped over Welsh mountains and through Yorkshire dales, wandered across Sussex downland and nosed our boat between stretches of pink-flowered water weed on the Isis. With my cousins Gertrude and Mary Anson, we went to Normandy and Brittany for a first holiday abroad after the 1914-18 war and drifted in and out of French cathedral towns and French fishing villages in the manner of Uncle Alfred's engaging interpretation of the instruction to take no thought for the morrow. Father, as he grew older, had wanted comfort and security on his holidays; he was not luxurious but he did like a well-appointed life. With Uncle Alfred, however, I learned to welcome the vicissitudes of the road whatever they might be, to eat and sleep where luck greeted us at the end of a roving day, to find out the beauty which has no asterisk in a guide-book, but glances like a sword-thrust when clouds drift apart on a mountain, or lies tranquil where water meadows are patterned with the shadow of trees by a dipping sun and run back to a church whose gnarled walls seem to wear a fitted garment of transparent gold. Before scenes like these Uncle Alfred's spirit made the frank response which communicates itself at once to other people, and he was happily untroubled by sophisticated misgivings about the sentimental lure of the gilded water meadows and church.

Sometimes we met in London and after a lunch in Soho would go to the National Gallery: Uncle Alfred wandered from one picture to another, but sooner or later he always came to anchor before the Bellinis and the Raphaels. I surmise that Raphael's Madonnas pleased him more for their sentiment than for their sublime beauty of line and form. But perhaps I misrepresent him, perhaps it was the graciousness and serenity which were conveyed by that line and form that appealed to him, cooling the conflict of ambition and bitterness with humility and sympathy in his own nature, a nature whose sensitive strings I knew had sometimes been roughly plucked and hurt.

I accepted him uncritically; his charm and comprehension of the young, his obstinacy and prejudices, his sensitivity and essential tolerance, his maddening indecisions about the small affairs of practical life. And so long as I did accept uncritically I held his sympathy and comradeship, and was able to extract the golden ore from a vein of wisdom which twisted in and out among all these idiosyncrasies. Once he said to me: 'If you are not sure of the right course to take in any choice of action, think of the best person you have ever known in life or in a book and what they would have done.' I wonder if Uncle Alfred realized that he was almost quoting a part of the method proposed by St Ignatius Loyola for coming to right decisions.

It was not his fault that later we drifted rather apart. When one is young the impact on one's own of other minds is a heady thing and I began to find other mentors whose minds appealed to developing sides of mine for which Uncle Alfred had little sympathy or understanding. Moreover, as he grew old his prejudices set harder and I found them baffling and exasperating and difficult to fit into the scheme of my life, for by then I was married. I had not the insight to see that human beings who love each other are, in fact, sharing an ideal which goes deeper than any specific difference of view. I had not the patience to be always gentle and receptive, and often I must have hurt him - a poor return for the long evenings at Ferns when he led me along every pathway of his mind, for the rainswept and sunlit days on hill or river when he taught me the art of making holiday.

The close intimacy with Uncle Alfred flowered after I was grown up during the holidays which we took à deux. When I was a child he was just one among a dazzling group of uncles and aunts. The social basis of almost all our holidays then was a group of relatives held in ballast by one or two outside friends; and on game-playing holidays, Uncle Charlie and Auntie May took the centre of the picture and Uncle Alfred faded off to the margins for he was no good at games.

Uncle Charlie and Auntie May, on the other hand, were born games players and my childish memories of them are almost all connected with games which they played with far greater seriousness and more skill than any other members of our family. Indeed, we young ones almost had a cult of Uncle Charlie and Auntie May as games players. They lived at Didsbury which was only four miles outside Manchester and hardly ranked as a country suburb. The society there merged with that of Victoria Park and was, as I have said, more intellectual than at Alderley Edge. A few business men of the old Manchester culture still lived in Didsbury, along with the barristers at the Manchester bar, the medical specialists, and the professors from the university. There was also a contingent of the ex-Germans who added considerably to its more intellectual and cultivated atmosphere. Uncle Charlie and Auntie May lived in a square, early Victorian house with large windows set with blank-looking panes of glass. It was a good-sized dignified house, but oddly enough semi-detached, and it was built of red brick long since grimed to grey and purple hues. But the doorsteps were always stoned immaculately with an apricot colour which I have never seen elsewhere and the brass furniture of the front door shone with a flashing dazzle which the midday sun itself never achieved through the Manchester sky. Auntie May almost made a religion of her domestic appointments and arrangements, and perhaps because she had no children to create untidiness her practice seldom fell short of her ideal. She and Uncle Charlie were eminently sociable; they attended the Manchester Assemblies with a troop of young people under their wings and themselves danced enthusiastically. They gave numerous dinner-parties often, I think, followed by bridge, or if the company was youthful by less brain-demanding games. Their dinner-table was always covered by a snow-white cloth of the finest Irish damask, for Auntie May, like mother, would never have demeaned herself to buy linen outside her native Belfast, and this made a pleasant variation, in my view, on the polished mahogany of Ferns. The dishes were brought round by 'Emily', the plump house-parlourmaid with the charming smile and the soft brown hair and soft red cheeks, and had been chosen and cooked with the nicest discrimination.

Their 'young people's dinner-parties' were famous, and the evening when I was first bidden to come with Campbell and Olive and Melland Schill and my cousins, Uncle Albert's sons, from Withington, was a landmark in my annals. I had only my school white silk frock, but I sat between two young men in immaculate black and white and was drawn into the ping-pong of chaff which passed up and down the table, almost dizzily gay so it seemed to me, but always bounded, so the young males had to remember, by our hosts' sensitive sense of decorum. After dinner that evening we played shovette, a game which belonged exclusively to 'The Limes'. You flipped wooden counters so that they slid across concentric rings on a polished board; the inmost ring was guarded by tiny rubber posts and inside that there was a slot the size of a penny and you got a score of twenty if you could slide your counter into it. The fun was in cannoning your opponents so as to shoot them off the board and into the minus-five ditch which surrounded it. All the cousins who frequented 'The Limes', had been brought up on shovette almost from babyhood. When I stayed at 'The Limes' as a small child Auntie May would sit down with me the minute breakfast was finished, even before she went through to the kitchen to 'order the dinner,' and give me a lesson in shovette playing. She always had very definite ideas as to how you should play any game, indeed her ideas as to how you should conduct yourself in all the circumstances of life were definite and she made no bones about expressing them. Sometimes this characteristic seemed to make her rather censorious and to overlay her natural kindliness and warmth of heart, and as we grew older and began to have our own notions we did not always find it easy to manage our affairs with Auntie May. Campbell and Olive did best by gently taking their own line to a judicious accompaniment of teasing. She liked being teased if it was done in the right way.

Nothing ever seemed to alter at 'The Limes'. They maintained gas lighting with candles on their dinner-table long after everyone else had gone on to electric light. The little doors of the cuckoo clock in the hall flew open day after day and year after year without a failure as the cuckoo emerged to tell us the hours. When I was very small I used to sit on the stairs and wait for him spellbound. The tea-table always carried a sponge cake of delicious and incredible sponginess and ginger biscuits very thin and very hot, baked at home. The walls of the study, a cosy room upstairs which I much preferred to the long-shaped and more formal drawing-room, were covered with scarce an inch of paper to show between them by watercolours in gold frames, some of them done by Uncle Charlie on holidays, others by masters like David Cox. They must have been acquired one by one, yet in my recollection there were never spaces of wall-paper.

Uncle Charlie and Auntie May both had another life besides the sociable one of their home. Uncle Charlie was a consulting engineer by profession, but like the other Manchester men with public spirit he gave much of his time to philanthropic pursuits; his work as chairman of the building committee of the great new infirmary would have given many men sufficient occupation without a profession to pursue into the bargain. And Auntie May was lavish of her time and interest in helping to run a college for training children's nurses and took a leading part in an undertaking called the Gentlewomen's Employment Association - or more ribaldly the 'Gentle Asses'. The admirable purpose of the 'Gentle Asses' was to assist elderly and needy gentlewomen to earn money for themselves by needlework and dress-making which the Association sold for them and further, and perhaps more important, to help young and needy gentlewomen to acquire training for real jobs. The whole thing had an amusingly Victorian flavour owing to the insistence that recipients of help must measure up to the required social standard. And many were the heart-searchings to arrive at a satisfactory general working definition or to gauge the particular social antecedents of some young woman who had written applying for a loan without making her parents' position crystal clear. When in doubt Auntie May was apt to examine the applicant's brand of note-paper. The Association became rich with the passage of years thanks to the generosity of various donors who left it fairly large sums of money. And the numbers of young women requiring help grew as more and more needed expensive training to fit them for jobs. The work went a good way towards fulfilling a really serious need, and in the end Auntie

May had quite a vast correspondence to conduct. She never stinted her time on this, but took endless personal trouble with each applicant.

However, to return to our holidays. On game-playing holidays my activities were mainly directed towards 'caddying' and generally getting in the way on the golf links of St Ives or Windermere. I tried to hit a golf ball clean and hard, but without success. And the Windermere links I found very tantalizing because from almost every hole there was a view of the 'delectable mountains' which I longed above everything to climb. Even Uncle Charlie's gift for companionship with the young and my admiration for him as a golfer could not make up to me for those withdrawn fells dim and blue in the distance and whose nearer flanks, dappled by the shadows of clouds, held secrets half revealed. Uncle Charlie had been a magnificent rock- climber as a young man, the finest rock-climber of the family, but when I knew him it seemed that he preferred days on the links to days on the hills, a strange aberration of taste in my opinion. So I would bend all my ingenuity and persuasions to detach father from the golf-playing party and induce him to take me up a mountain. Twice, we had Easter parties in the Lake District when the golf-clubs were left behind and the whole party gave itself up to a weekend of adolescent joie de vivre. I was always the youngest, but I tagged along in a mist of happiness behind Campbell and Olive and Melland Schill and the various friends and cousins, Campbell's contemporaries, who were present. We dammed a stream on Armboth Fell, we plunged absurdly down the precipitous face of Castle Crag in father's wake, we climbed the rafters of the barn at Seathwaite because it was too wet to climb Scafell Pike, we held a regatta on the Derwent, whose star event was a wild bumping race. We played hockey in the hotel hall with walking-sticks and oranges, and in the billiard-room a riotous billiard fives which entailed a considerable bill for broken picture glass. In the evening, the pièce de résistance might be a mock trial, or there would be Racing Demon and Poker Patience, General Knowledge, Clumps, Proverbs, Capping Verses, one or another of an innumerable assortment of games which lent themselves to a mixture of chaff and verbal rapier-play. Father and Uncle Alfred, Uncle Charlie and Melland could manage wit; the rest of us had to be content with the cruder standard of repartee.

Mother was always quiet and contained and a little aloof on these occasions, but she would play any game with enjoyment except cards which she hated. And she gave me more rein than, as the youngest, I had any right to expect.

Uncle Alfred, Uncle Charlie, Auntie May, these were the relations whom I associate chiefly with holidays; but there was also Aunt Evelyn. Aunt Evelyn was the widow of my Uncle John and the most courageous and one of the most remarkable women I have ever known. Her vitality and courage carried her through a life whose tragedy would have capsized and overwhelmed any ordinary spirit. In 1898 she had lost her husband and three of her children in that accident on the Petite Dent de Veisivi. There remained to her a daughter and two sons. When the 1914 war broke out the elder was holding the chair of engineering at Cambridge and the younger was about to embark on an engineering career of promise. Bertie was killed in an aeroplane crash whilst testing out experiments he was making for the R.F.C. Cecil came back from France with a severe head wound, lingered ill at home and then died after many months of ebb and flow of hope. Yet Aunt Evelyn still kept her own ship afloat, and not only afloat but in full proud sail, a feat all the more magnificent, since her philosophy of life threw her on to her own resources and offered her neither comfort nor explanation. She did without and, unarmed, threw back the challenge of suffering with a gallant 'No Surrender'.

She thought in large-scale terms and her energy was rather like a head of steam; canalize it and it will provide the power to drive any undertaking. She used it to found and run various philanthropic undertakings which she served with a zeal that never flagged. Not only did she serve them herself, she enlisted the services of her friends, occasionally, so they found, by methods not far removed from a press-gang persuasion.

To look at she was short and stocky and stout, without graces, yet she entered any room like a queen and lent it dignity by her presence. And she welcomed guests whom she had chosen with a courtesy that went deeper than the good manners of her period, for those she did not trouble very assiduously to cultivate. I came to know her well and to understand her stature after I was grown up and married. She liked young men who were trying to make careers for themselves, always provided she thought the careers had a chance of success. I am afraid she had no use for human mice. Her people must have a label of attainment attached to them, or if they were young she must see in them the possibility of a future Lord Chancellor or Cabinet Minister or Regius Professor. So long as Aunt Evelyn saw the possibility - and in a circle of her young men friends she almost always did and, what is more, infected them with her own enthusiasm for their careers - it was all right because there was plenty of time in which to cement a warm and genuine relationship before it would be necessary for those with offices to dispense to see or fail to see with her eyes. She and my husband took to each other immediately. We would go down from London to stay with her in the big pleasant Cambridge house which still retained an authentic flavour of Edwardian amplitude. We would breakfast in the sun parlour which snared all the warmth of

March sunshine, silver on the table, coffee, leisure, conversation and a sense of physical and mental well-being which was partly due to the warming sun and partly to the overspill of Aunt Evelyn's personality. We would dress for the evening dinner-party Edwardian fashion and await the guests in the big music-room, a room made up with Persian rugs and tables of books and distinguished furniture. 'Distinguished' was a word that Aunt Evelyn liked very much to use. Her conversation was strewn with references to 'that distinguished man So-and-so', and no dinner-party was complete without one or more distinguished guests. As we awaited them, she would run over their points rather as if we were discussing form in race-horses. She always had the right descriptive phrase to clip on to each guest. A tall thin friend of ours from the university library, blue-eyed, fair-skinned, golden-haired and of Danish origin, was always known as 'that attenuated young Viking'. It was more than an outward descriptive epithet; Aunt Evelyn had realized in five minutes that the rude vitality which is supposed to go with Viking blood had been refined in him by poor health and his own innate sensitivity.

Aunt Evelyn liked men better than women, perhaps because her own mind had a virile quality which went with strong emotions. And the lions, as they arrived, greeted her with a respect and pleasant deference which was always a tribute to her own interior substance, never to the accidents of her surroundings and accoutrements. Indeed, these last, so far as personal accessories went, were sometimes rather disastrous. Her hands, for instance, which she decorated with too many fine but unkempt rings, were themselves apt to be hastily washed and imperfectly manicured. This worried father not a little. He did like the women of his circle to look as well as to be unspotted by the world. Mother was very particular about her hands, partly on his account. The gloves which encased them in sunny weather even on holidays were designed to prevent the freckles which father disliked (the freckles on Aunt Evelyn's hands were legion, she would never have constricted her holiday freedom by wearing gloves in such a cause) and she wore, as a rule, just one fine ring, her diamond engagement ring which glistened from regular scrubbing with, if I remember right, ammonia and water which was her de fide recipe for cleaning diamonds.

When I was a child and Aunt Evelyn was of the holiday party I saw her mostly from the amusing if less heroic angle of her foibles. We laughed at her partiality for distinguished people and her habit of referring to them by their surnames, without any prefix of rank or quality, was considered rather unfeminine. Even her son-in-law she always referred to as 'Ewing'. He was a scientist whom she had known well for many years before he married my cousin. Later he became principal of Edinburgh

University and was a president of the British Association. So he fulfilled all the conditions of distinction demanded by Aunt Evelyn; there was nothing distant or grudging in her continued use of his surname, it was just that she was accustomed to call him Ewing, and for the little matter of a marriage saw no reason to give her attention to altering this habit in favour of his Christian name. Mother and the other relations were never quite sure whether to be shocked or amused by the constant references to 'Ewing'. Mother herself was very particular about the division of surnames and Christian names, and she never failed to put in the proper prefix when speaking of any of father's friends, and even Campbell's friends were always accorded a 'Mr' both to their faces and behind their backs, unless they had grown up with us and were therefore eligible for a Christian name. The Christian names which she bestowed were few and far between; she would have hated as an encroachment on decent reserve the agreeable modern convention of dropping into Christian names so soon as an easy and equal relationship is established.

Aunt Evelyn had a whole collection of foibles which caused a mixture of amusement and embarrassment. Her method of conversation at a hotel dinner-table was one of them. She always talked rather loudly because she was slightly deaf, and she would insist on discussing the intimate affairs and assessing the characters of her relatives and distinguished acquaintance in a voice which echoed from table to table. In the privacy of the dining-room at home this added a welcome and amusing spice to the conversation, but in an hotel it was highly embarrassing; you could see the other guests pricking up their ears. Father and mother would try desperately to damp her down, but we younger members of the party found it all very good fun and gleefully egged her on from revelation to revelation. She had yet another troublesome hotel habit. During walks on a warm day she would get very hot owing to her stout heavy figure and sweat profusely. That was her own private affair, but she made the results public when she came in by hanging to dry from her bedroom window a collection of voluminous Aertex underwear. As she always insisted on having that bedroom which gave the best view, the other hotel guests would turn from the contemplation of a sunset over mountains or the sea to a vista of strange but unmistakable garments gently stirring in the evening zephyr above their heads.

Yet these awkward characteristics were so much a part of the Aunt Evelyn whom we all loved and admired that I think no one except in moments of peculiarly exasperated embarrassment would really have had her otherwise. The tang of her personality was inseparable from her foibles. No one would have wished to miss that squat gallant figure sweating up a hillside because her endeavours would later be proclaimed from the beflagged windowsill. No one would have exchanged the overflow of her big humanity for any number of conventional graces and reserves. And here I would like to say that Aunt Evelyn was of German origin. Her father was an Oldenburg, a member of a family whose fine south German culture had led them towards publishing. But he, like so many others, had come over to the north of England during the first half of the nineteenth century and had been naturalized. He had married a Yorkshire wife, but Aunt Evelyn always kept up closely with her German relations, and as a girl had spent months on end with them in Dresden and Munich. I think that environment of south German culture, so much softer and sunnier and more expansive than the stern discipline and armoured morals of the English north which made the other half of her setting, infused into her outlook the richness and the freedom which raised her mentally a head and shoulders above almost all the women I knew when I was young. Dear Aunt Evelyn! I can see your quality emerge so plainly as I try to picture you now; your respect for splendid things and your carelessness of convention in the rich but rather neglected dresses with lace at the neck and lavish jewellery which you wore; your gallant courage, your masculine energy of mind, your large unplanned affections in your hastily dressed grey hair and ravaged but unbeaten face. The flesh of it was heavy on cheekbones and jowl and mouth, battered into shape by the blows on your spirit which you had withstood for half a lifetime, and withstood not through the refining strength of a principle of redemption by suffering, but Prometheus fashion from the strength and largesse of your own indomitable soul.

Looking back in order to decipher the pattern of those holiday parties of ours before the 1914-18 war, I realize with gratitude my own good fortune. I did not get left behind or relegated to a seaside lodging-house, and although I missed the simple fun proper to children of building sand castles and splashing in the surf I gained, so I believe, incalculably more than I had lost. In the scenes of beauty, the episodes and situations of strange surroundings, I gained material with which my imagination could build as I grew older; in the disciplines of holiday endeavour I gained a knowledge of man's age-long struggle to subdue and manage untamed nature. I was shown how to row a boat on a squally lake, how to sail a boat in the open sea, how to cross a glacier in safety, how to put out my strength on a mountain in any weather. I was taught to endure discomfort for some finer end and to meet physical danger naturally and intelligently. In addition, I was taken clean away from the atmosphere of Alderley Edge into a wider world where men and women of parts met in a mood of freedom and personalities played one upon another untrammelled by the narrower vision of our home society. People came out in the round, they moved more freely, there was a kind of mental sunlight which flashed on the facets of their characters. Being always the youngest must have been an unconscious strain, and since I was thus perpetually on the stretch I suspect that I was not a pleasant child. It was as if I were being brought up not on the children's books proper to my understanding and imagination but on a great literature which I could only half comprehend. But though I acquired material from which I could later construct a vision of the world which went far beyond the confines of Alderley Edge somewhat at the expense of the elders who had to put up with me I can only be grateful to father and mother who gave me the chance.

William Cecil Slingsby

At the top of Sparrhorn, 1895. A rare photograph taken just three years before the tragic accident of 1898 which claimed the lives of John Hopkinson and two of his children, showing John Hopkinson, left, his wife Evelyn, centre with alpenstock and my father Edward Hopkinson, right

A contemporary of Cecil Slingsby, Haskett Smith is widely regarded as the father of modern rock-climbing

Norway 1908. Aak, home of H O Wills of the tobacco family

Norwegian picnic during a holiday at Aak, Romsdal 1908

Zermatt, descending to the Gorner glacier, 1911

The 'Cricket Field' at the Riffel, with the Matterhorn in the background. Father can be seen in the centre of the picture, seated. 1911

Aak 1908.
Hopkinson and Wills
families on the steps of
the veranda

Below:
Salmon fishing. On the
right can be seen
Katharine's parents,
Edward and Minnie

Chamois in the Alps, Summer 1911

Staffel Alp, Zermatt, 1911

Katharine at Lake
Thun, Switzerland
1911.

The Alps, 1911

Gratcap 1914, with dogs

Campbell and Katharine,
Mürren 1911

Alfred Hopkinson, Katharine, ?, ?, .far right RST Chorley, whom Katharine later married

Chapter Thirteen
POLITICS

The Hopkinsons were Liberals by tradition largely because, as my Uncle Alfred wrote in his book Penultima half a century later, 'It was impossible for us to be Conservatives' ('us' meaning the north-country Nonconformists) 'to be content with existing conditions at a time when Nonconformists were excluded from the public schools and from the universities; when contribution to church rates was compulsory and when even the graveyards by the churches, which were called national, were closed to almost half of the nation.'

This basis was not perhaps a very solid one on which to build stable loyalty to the Liberal Party, since the disabilities were removed one by one, and as time went on Uncle Alfred and father were always quarrelling with the Liberals about one thing or another. But they remained lifelong free-traders, and as boys and young men they shared the Liberal sympathy for the struggles of oppressed peoples for freedom, all except sympathy for the struggles for freedom of the people of Ireland; this, very emphatically, they did not share. There were plenty of peoples struggling for freedom in the years that the older children could remember. A portrait of Kossuth hung in their home. Below it was printed his tribute to England: 'Ah, now I am free, I feel I am free, I am free when I touch your shores.' My grandfather had heard him speak at the Free Trade Hall when he visited Manchester. They followed the fortunes of Garibaldi with enthusiasm, and throughout the American Civil War their sympathies lay with the North, because they believed that victory for the Union meant freedom for the slaves. All the generosity of Lancashire men and women of every class was mobilized in support of the North and that in spite of the misery caused throughout the county by the Northern blockade of the Southern ports which stopped the supply of cotton to Lancashire mills.

The books they read helped to nourish a Liberal rather than a Radical attitude of mind. They read Motley's Rise of the Dutch Republic and rose in sympathetic imagination with the Protestants of Holland against their Spanish masters. They read Macaulay's History and steeped themselves in the ideology of the 'Glorious Revolution'. They read John Halifax Gentleman and noted the hero's public spirit in the famous episode where he ostentatiously pays his money into a breaking bank in order to stop the run which must ruin a community of small middle-class people. They read The Idylls of the King. The sentimental chivalry of

Tennyson may seem an ersatz substitute for Malory's masculine and business-like romance, and I cannot imagine my own children willing to exchange Malory for Tennyson. Yet Tennyson did infuse something of that generous overspill of the Victorian Liberal spirit into his Idylls, because his emphasis was always on the rescue of the weak and the overthrow of the strong oppressor. Odd that so few, relatively speaking, of those Victorian Liberals whose blood surged when they read about Neapolitan prisoners or negro slaves, thought to include in the sweep of their generous indignation the economic serfdom on their own doorsteps. Selective indignation spoilt their claim to champion the weak, and men like Sir William Mather, whose indignation was not selective but all-inclusive, towered above their ruck.

My Uncle Alfred stood for Parliament several times and sat in the House of Commons of 1895 as a Liberal Unionist, and again nearly thirty years later in that of 1926 for the Combined Universities. This time he was returned on the nomination of the Conservatives and, in fact, he had become by now a Conservative with an unorthodox twist on a few secondary matters. He would not have been Uncle Alfred if he had failed to contrive an endearing twist of unorthodoxy somewhere. Father had usually voted Liberal except during Home Rule crises. Since all of these fell within his manhood it could hardly be said that his support of the Liberal Party was very continuous, nor was it ever very enthusiastic except when Free Trade was directly threatened. It ended for good when Lloyd George produced his Radical budget of 1909, while Conservative street boys were trotting around singing a comic song whose chorus ran, so far as I remember:

> Move up a bit higher
> Away from the fire
> And make room for the blighter from Wales.

But which politicians of previous eras were being thus exhorted to vacate their front bench seats in hell, I forget.

The first general election that I remember personally was the great Free Trade and Chinese Labour fight of 1906. Father came out uncompromisingly on the Liberal side and spoke for our local candidate, Mr Alfred King, who was an old friend of his and a fine-minded and cultivated Quaker Radical. I tied red ribbons to the electric light switches at home (why the switches, I don't know), chalked 'Vote for King' laboriously along our garden wall and went about with a vermilion rosette. But during the period between 1906 and the two quickly succeeding elections of 1910, my budding liberalism was killed, nipped not so much by the talk at home of the perils attendant on radical budgeting, Home Rule and interference with the House of Lords as cynically deserted in order to pursue the lure of other gods. This was thanks to the insidious influence of Richardson our sailor chauffeur. Richardson was a fast friend of mine and I used to spend every moment that I could in his company whilst he altered for me the hulk of an old miniature yacht and refitted it as a full-rigged ship. The refitting was never finished because father and mother decided that too much of Richardson's time was being subtracted from the car and perhaps also that too much of mine was being spent metaphorically sitting at Richardson's feet. I learned a lot of nautical and other lore in the process and could speak with authority of blocks and yards and t'gallant sails and the rest. And, personally, I have never seen cause to regret a moment of the hours I spent with Richardson. But he was, of course, a true blue Tory and because I admired him I naturally found his politics captivating. Toryism in the dining-room was a grudging necessity, but Toryism in the stable yard was a romantic and colourful faith. So in the 1910 campaign I shamelessly deserted my old hero Mr King.

Father had been in London during the last days of the campaign and was due home on polling day. Richardson and I went in the car to meet him at the station. We both knew that father was going to vote Conservative this time. So, spurred on by Richardson, and unknown to mother, I bought up all the blue ribbon that I could afford and Richardson and I decorated the car with tasteful blue streamers and Richardson sported a blue rosette on his livery coat. Thus caparisoned, we proceeded to the station. Father emerged from the train a little abstracted and we were already halfway along the village street before he observed the party label; I had not been able to afford a very lavish display. His face darkened. He ordered Richardson to stop. He ordered us both to get out and untwine the beautiful damning blue ribbon. I don't doubt that his cross was put that evening against the name of Mr King's Conservative opponent, but he did not propose to identify himself with the Tory Party. I have seldom been made to feel more conspicuously and more completely a fool, but as I look back I am glad that father did that.

He carried his practical acceptance and his theoretical dislike of Conservatism to quite comic lengths, and he must have been a standing exasperation to the party managers on both sides. The Liberals were always losing his vote and the Conservatives could never land a very promising and useful fish; until the Coupon Election of 1918 when, for all practical purposes, they did land him. The Conservative Association asked him to stand for the Clayton division which lay close to Park Works and contained a good proportion of the Mather & Platt workpeople. He accepted the invitation and the backing of the divisional Conservative organization, but all through the campaign he insisted that his supporters should describe him as the Coalition and not as the Conservative candidate.

It was the mad rollicking election of a people drunk with victory who had yet to experience the bitter hangover from war. And it was quite a family party for us, since one of my cousins, Austin Hopkinson, was standing for Mossley and another, Gerald Hurst, was contesting Moss Side. Both had just returned from the war. I rushed about from father's meetings to Gerald's and enjoyed myself enormously and irresponsibly, but below the surface I was beginning to have political misgivings.

Father, however, was not drunk with victory. He was prescient about many of the difficulties which were going to confront the post-war industrial world and he would have scorned to hand out the wordy dope with which stupid or unscrupulous candidates drugged their electors into believing that Utopia could be bought by a Coalition Government with easy money. Just twenty-five years after the Coupon Election, I found myself sitting once more in a Lancashire hall listening to a political speech. And once again it was a speech on 'Reconstruction', but this time a forecast for the second World War was still on, and it was delivered by Mr Herbert Morrison. Sitting in the body of the hall with intent faces of Lancashire men and women all around me, my youth came flooding back in memories of that mad 1918 election campaign. There had been the same cautious toil-lined faces of the workers in search of leaders who would show them the way to a better world. But myself, twenty-one, with a heartful of slogans about 'a world safe for democracy' and 'homes fit for heroes' and a head as void of critical judgment as an empty peascod. And father on the platform, troubled a bit with his voice which was not strong, and completely concentrated on what he wanted to say, so concentrated that he never knew when he had got hold of a chair and was speaking with one hand on the back and a leg raised with the foot planted firmly on the seat. He would be expounding his picture of the post-war set-up of industry. 'War to work' was his slogan, and he believed that capitalists should lead and show by the worth of their service that they were fit to be leaders. It did not appear to occur to him that the motives of service to shareholders' profit and service to the community are not often easy bed-fellows, and that an industry which loyally serves the one will have to be differently conducted in order that it may as loyally serve the other. Private profit can be a by-product of service to the community, or service to the community can be a by-product of private profit, but they can never exist as equals. Yet father regarded service and profit as twin pillars on which the structure of industry could be firmly raised. For he still lived in the mental climate of the 'entrepreneur' to whom profit is the natural reward for the risks he takes and competition the guarantee of efficiency and volume of production. Those were still the days when capital was likened to the 'goose which lays the golden eggs'; if you kill the goose you get no golden eggs. I have often wondered how his thought would have developed had he lived through the inter-war years and witnessed the internecine struggles of the great firms to maintain themselves by cartels and combines and monopolies and the squeezing out of lesser firms by financial manipulation and the limiting of production in a world crying out for the good things of material life. I am quite sure that no motive of personal gain would have held him back from becoming a Socialist had he ever reached the conviction that the community would be better served by socialized industries. He remained a free-trader, as I have said, to the end of his days, although in his opinion protection would have benefited his own firm. But I am almost equally sure that his mental training would never have allowed him to reach a Socialist conviction. He always referred rather scornfully to writers like Tawney and G.D.H. Cole as theorists who would not think and plan the way they did if they had ever had the practical handling of an industry. Yet he was not unsympathetic to the emotional reactions of working-class Socialists. After glancing through the Hammonds' books on the Industrial Revolution he admitted frankly that the attitude of the workers towards the capitalist order was hardly surprising - with that heredity. But that was not the point. The point was that if you killed the goose which laid the golden eggs - and, in his view, Socialism was bound to kill it - the whole community would suffer and contract and the workers would be the first to feel the suffering and contraction.

I cannot sum up his outlook as an engineering employer better and more compactly than by quoting a part of the Address which he gave as president to the Institution of Mechanical Engineers in 1919.

'Our increasing supremacy in mechanical engineering, established as the war proceeded, was indeed an essential factor in victory. Do we and does the nation grasp with equal conviction that if that supremacy is impaired, we cannot hope to solve the problems of reconstruction? We are entering upon a new decade which may well prove as difficult and critical as that we have left behind. We can achieve success only by years of patient and strenuous work, whose keynote must be the national unity of effort in war translated into our industrial life. Industry must be reorganized with methods, personnel and plant more efficient, more productive and more perfectly adapted to their purpose. As Mechanical Engineers, we ought to realize that both the direction and the execution of this reconstruction lie largely with us. It is fitting, therefore, that we should leave no stone unturned in seeking out and eliminating the causes of our past failures and in finding means whereby we can best satisfy the present and future industrial needs of the country ......

'Though the more far-sighted leaders of public opinion, both among employers and employed, now realize that only by increased production can we recover from the losses and damage of war, recent events too clearly prove that this truth has not yet permeated all classes of the nation. It has been thrust into the background by the demand for a higher plane of living for the working classes without consideration of the means whereby it can be obtained. It would be unsuitable for me to discuss here this demand in its ethical and social and still less in its political aspects, but we, as engineers, would do well to realize that the problem has to be solved and that its solution lies largely with us. Unfortunately the real issue has been obscured by diversion of attention from the elementary physical facts to consideration of economic theories which lead into many side-tracks and involve side issues which only serve to distract the mind from the fundamental facts. The working classes of this country must be better fed, better housed, better clothed, and be able to enjoy the amenities of life in fuller measure than in the past; they must have more time for recreation of mind and body and ampler means for promoting physical and intellectual welfare. Surely it would appear obvious that these conditions can only be fulfilled by an increase in the productive power of English industries. This increase is ex hypothesi not to be obtained by longer hours of work, but is to be accompanied by shorter hours. Yet Labour has shown itself averse to the tapping of fresh sources of supply ....

'It must be remembered that increase in production must be far greater than is necessary to meet merely the added home consumption for, as a country, we produce only a fraction of the raw material we require for our own sustenance and the feeding of our industries, and the deficit must be made up out of imports which we pay for out of our manufactured products.

'Thus it follows that every step in increasing consumption can only be achieved by increasing production in a much larger ratio. It is too often popularly assumed that the higher remuneration of Labour will by itself secure an industrial Utopia, and that Labour, if it has more to spend, will be able to satisfy its desires. Experience has shown that the very contrary is the fact. Mere increase in wages, mere changes in the distribution of wealth, have the effect in themselves, divorced from other influences, of providing less rather than more of the good things of the earth. It has been proved again and again from actual figures of most of our staple industries that a redistribution of the profits of industry, however desirable on other grounds, cannot in itself add materially to the welfare of Labour unless it directly conduces to increased production.

'If, as a nation, we are to realize what we all desire, a fuller and happier life for all classes of Labour, every proposal for increase or change in the remuneration of Labour, every proposal for sharing or redistribution of profits, every proposal for change in control or in the management of industry ought to be subjected before adoption to crucial examination as to whether it will increase production per worker or can be accompanied by other changes in the conduct of the industry which will in their combined effect achieve the same object. Unless they satisfy this test we shall fail in attaining our end. Instead of promoting the welfare of the industry and of those engaged in it, we shall doom it to decay and ultimate extinction. I do not state the problem in this way in any spirit of pessimism. It is rather the reverse - because I believe it can be successfully solved and that its solution lies largely with the Mechanical Engineer .... The application of the forces of nature to the benefit of man, the avoidance of waste, the efficient use of physical and human energy, the replacement wherever possible of human effort by mechanical contrivance are his particular sphere, and it is by these things that our material prosperity in the future will be assured.'

So, in 1918, father wasted no breath on word-painting imaginary Utopias, but fought his Labour opponent, a colliery checkweighman, cleanly and ruthlessly on the applied principles of industrial reconstruction. I think the evening he enjoyed best was the one on which he met and argued with a batch of lean-faced, bitter and desperately earnest shop-stewards. He expected a scrap, but he got no scrap, for he held them even though he did not convince them by the force and sincerity of his reasoned arguments.

Father did not live to see the submerging tide of industrial depression mounting over Lancashire as the inter-war years advanced. I remembered that as I listened to Mr Morrison twenty-five years almost to the day after the opening of that 1918 campaign of glowing promises. Exactly a generation in the life of a community. And I was back once more in Lancashire among my own people, but this time with a heart empty of splendid slogans and a head perhaps too full of disillusion and criticism. For under the hard electric light there were the same work-worn and tense faces of men and women still in search of a better world, and what had been the tally of those twenty-five years? A generation of racking uncertainties, of unemployment, of broken hopes and corroding disappointment. The business men of Lancashire who had led her to greatness while time and expanding markets were on their side had failed to lead her safely and adventurously in the years of jostle and contraction. Mr Morrison spoke of the cotton industry and recalled how much of the disaster that had maimed that industry could be laid at the door of the rash and irresponsible paper over-capitalization into which so many of the cotton employers had launched their companies during the short immediate post-war boom. I could have told him that father had forecast on more than one occasion that if they went on like that catastrophe would follow. Father would have been a better pilot than most because he had foresight and courage and imagination. And he would have stuck to the tiller. He would never have pulled out on the proceeds of the post-war boom as so many of his compatriots did and made for the sunny south leaving Lancashire to fend for herself. 'The epitaph of Lancashire is written on the tombstones of Bournemouth.' There is more than a streak of truth in that bitter epigram. But father escapes the indictment with a clean record, for he had made no rosy promises and indulged in no selfish advantages, and he had died in Lancashire harness.

Gerald and Margaret Hurst with their children
Molly, Peggy, Quentin and Eve
Courtesy Richard Seebohm

Chapter Fourteen
A DAUGHTER AT HOME

Father was only sixty-two when he died, and the last two or three years of his life he had spent as a semi-invalid. Frequently he had to direct his many activities as best he could from bed, but he never gave up. It was not in his nature to cut himself off from affairs and remake a life from books, the conversation of friends, and the smaller interests of home.

It is a regret to me that these were the years when I had just entered adult life and would have been able to share so much with him. He had the kind of personality which can be known most easily through shared action, and the action was now so very much restricted. The parliamentary career, for instance, was almost stillborn. He was able to attend the House only a few dozen times and he made but one speech. Even granted good health he would never have become a parliamentarian because he could never have found the patience to sit through long debates. The talking shop aspect of the House was completely alien to his make-up. But in that parliament of 'hard-faced men' he would have made some contribution of value through his combination of practical knowledge with a clear ideal of industrial reconstruction. Politics were a developing interest of mine, and though we did not always by any means see eye to eye, yet I think the pleasure and interest of working for him would have kept me in my place, at any rate for some time. I do not know what his attitude was to his subordinates in business, but so far as I was concerned he had the rare and inspiring gift of making any work one did for him appear a shared enterprise. After the war I became his secretary and he made me conversant with all his affairs and, contracted though they had to be, they were certainly still quite various enough to stretch my wits and interest. His was a forthcoming nature and he was ready to discuss all sorts of points with me and to consider my opinion if I had one, for though he wanted his womenfolk to be home-makers he did not take the line that women have no intelligence to use except in the home. Perhaps this was partly his technique for getting willing work, but I think it was even more his plan to widen my mind and his own pleasure in working with an enthusiastic and admiring subaltern.

At the same time his death, when I was just twenty-four, released a tension that was beginning to tighten and might in the end have driven me into a psychological mess. I was a late developer and his personality still held and dazzled me, and even frightened me a bit. I had neither the self-

Father in his later years

Richardson the chauffeur, Easter 1913

Afternoon tea in the garden at Ferns, September 1914

reliance nor the courage to risk collisions. Yet by the end of the war I had already gone some way to formulate my own reactions to life, to the books I read and to the people I met, to the problems of reconstruction, political and social, which everybody was discussing and with which many people I knew were experimenting. And my reactions certainly were not always his reactions. After a fashion and confusedly, I realized that the pattern of society into which I had expected to grow up, when I lay in bed at school in 1913 and looked ahead to the sort of life I wanted to lead when I came home for good, no longer had relevance. It might survive, the young people of Alderley Edge might go on weaving their lives to that pattern, but it was no longer alive; it was a pattern in a museum. I did not reason it out, but I knew that the scheme which, in 1913, had seemed natural and desirable was now unattractive and unrealistic, even repugnant. How could I settle down to the life of a daughter at home without a sense of frustration and even of guilt; dependent for my interests and contacts with the big world on what I got secondhand through father, dissipating any creative capacity I might have in dilettante attempts at literature, dabbling here and there with odd charities in order to ease my social conscience, playing golf and tennis for hours on end with my equally unharnessed contemporaries, and for the rest waiting to get married and start the ball rolling all over again with a new generation. That was the scheme which had seemed natural and agreeable enough in bed at school, but since those days too many of my cousins and the young men with whom I should have grown up had been killed in France, my brother's health had been smashed in France, there were teeming new ideas in the air as to how society should be conducted; the continuity of the pattern was broken. The trouble was that father and mother did not see that as a live pattern it was broken; they thought that with minor modifications it could be rewoven by me, and that a daughter at home was still a proper and agreeable ideal. My difficulties were symbolized over my going to Cambridge. About the end of 1917 I had already decided that when the war was over I could not settle down to build a life out of those 1913 ingredients. I wanted something to bite on, a job, not perhaps a whole-time job - I was too lazy to want that - but something that would give me the self-respect of being a working hand and not a passenger in the ship of civilization. I wanted to do something about the minds of young people whose intellectual and cultural chances had been thinner than mine. I dare say there was a good deal of conceited and romantic idealism about this, but I don't think it was priggish or altogether contemptible. And I wanted desperately to have my three years at Cambridge for a start. No doubt I was inspired to some extent by the fact that two of my closest friends, Olive Schill and my cousin Gertrude Anson, were both going to the university for the same sort of reason. Another Alderley friend, Kathleen Chesney, who went to my school, was also proposing to go to Oxford to read French literature. But in Alderley Edge it had been unheard of that a girl should go to Oxford or Cambridge. Mrs Swinside had not even heard that there were women's colleges at Cambridge, and one day shattered Olive, who had made some remark about 'Girton', by asking her what place that was. Even those who had heard of Girton and Newnham thought them infected resorts whose products must emerge pitted for life by the intellectual smallpox they would be bound to contract, a disfigurement that would unfit them for the marriage market.

Olive, the two Pilkington girls and I were always steering clear of intellectual complications at Alderley Edge. People would ask for the sake of something to say what one had been reading lately. We knew that if we produced any literature more worthy than Ethel M. Dell, or perhaps Vachell or Benson, the comment would be: 'Oh, you're so clever.' A peculiar tone of voice was reserved for this, at once deprecating, shaming and completely damning. At the same time Olive and I very much enjoyed playing tennis and we wanted to be accepted by, and get on with, the game-playing crowd. Thus our intimate comradeship, a comradeship which has widened and deepened through thirty years, was largely begun on the coalition we made to win our spurs at the tennis club whilst at the same time we maintained a private intellectual life of our own. She was older than I, had been away in London during the war, and had had more opportunities to make friends outside Alderley Edge circles, so that her contribution to the coalition must have been far more valuable to me than mine could be to her. Without it I should have been often unendurably lonely. But this sense of having to win and hold a place in what seemed an essentially hostile community was not good for one, and so far as I am concerned, at any rate, its legacy has been an instinctive and permanent distrust of geographical contiguity as a field for friendships.

I think it came hardest on the one or two older women who really longed to live in a more intellectual climate. There was Mrs Roby, for instance, who always gave one the impression that she was frustrated and starved at Alderley Edge. She was a tall handsome woman with a magnificent bosom over which a lace jabot usually fell like a creamy waterfall setting off her beautifully cut suits or cloth dresses. She gave children's parties on All Hallows' E'en (she had no children of her own), and later tried to draw out any of us whom she suspected of intellectual interests. I think she genuinely liked young people, but the drawing-out process was also undertaken, I am sure, because she was so hungry for an intellectual life and tried to compensate this hunger by showing her young friends, not her own intellectual attainments for she was almost touchingly humble, but that she could produce an intellectual atmosphere in her home. Personally, I disliked the drawing-out process intensely and could never allow myself to advance on to any satisfactory footing with her and was, I am afraid, with the callousness of youth, quite pitiless in my refusal to allow her to come to intellectual terms with me. But some of my friends, Olive and the two Pilkington girls, for instance, had the insight to see that Mrs Roby really suffered and having come to terms with her got far below the outward rather conscious intellectual atmosphere which, I fear, I thought was merely a pose. Years after the war Mrs Roby moved to Oxford and ended her life, I am glad to say, in the congenial atmosphere of Boar's Hill. It really did not do to have Mrs Roby's tastes at Alderley Edge.

Neither Olive's parents nor mine would have been swayed in their opinions as to the propriety of women going to the university by the attitude of our more Philistine neighbours. I cannot recall whether Kathleen Chesney had difficulties with her parents, but I think probably not; for one thing her brain was so obviously of first-class university calibre. I think she had more difficulty in getting the necessary coaching at school for, as may be deduced from the picture of our school that I have given, preparation for Oxford or Cambridge was not among its standard activities. When it came to the point, Olive did not have much trouble with her parents either. She had already tasted Alderley Edge life in its full flavour before the war, her brother had been killed, she had been away doing a real job; it was easier for her to convince her parents than it was for me to convince mine that for us the pre-war social salt had lost its savour.

Her course was already settled when I proposed mine, and I think the fact that it was settled and that she spoke up for me and put the post-war generation's point of view with more weight and cogency than I could put it myself helped considerably. Anyway, father's response was typical of his innate generosity combined with his refusal to accept, as they emerged from the war, the altered lineaments of the society he had known. He was not at all anxious that I should go to Cambridge. For one thing he did not approve of women invading his own university. And he took a poor view of my announcement that I wanted to go to Cambridge in order to equip myself to do a proper job. Paid jobs, mother explained (it was almost always mother who did the explaining), when taken by girls who did not need the money were really a form of abstracting the bread from the mouths of girls who did need the money. I felt that this was noblesse oblige in a very dubious dress, and pointed out that the same argument might be applied to boys whose parents were sufficiently well off to keep them on merely voluntary work. This was a prickly argument, for I knew quite well that both father and mother had a very healthy contempt for the idle rich. But it was no use since no argument of analogy from a boy to a girl was ever admitted. The defence was then shifted to the unsuitability, the absurdity, the narrowing effect of a full-time job. I ought to be free for general social development and also, incidentally, I ought to be free for use at home. The latter part of this reasoning they had the grace not to formulate quite so baldly, nor did they formulate their subconscious and final objection which, I think, was very near snob prejudice. But I remembered Eileen MacElpatrick and the difficulty about the tennis tournament before the war. This trouble was the same for Olive, and when she came home from Cambridge she had to compromise by doing unpaid social work in Manchester. Neither set of parents could see that we wanted to win out of the amateur dilettante status which tradition had assigned to us and achieve a professional status which, in rough practice, we both realized could only be measured by economic terms. I compromised on the idea of getting a history degree in order that I might do W.E.A. work or something of that kind. This was quite a happy compromise since, as I have said, I was lazy and had no particular wish really to commit myself to a full-time job.

Father acquiesced, and having acquiesced he never even raised the question of money for Cambridge and later, when I was working for Littlego, used to help me with my mathematics. My brain has always gone numb before any mathematical problem and I should certainly never have passed the Littlego maths but for the partial thawings which father used to produce with patience and wonder at my stupidity. So by the Armistice all seemed setting fair and it looked as if it rested only on myself to fit my life into the emergent post-war pattern. I still had the Greek and Latin sections of the exam to do and was awaiting the result of the history entrance exam to Newnham. Then came the khaki election and father was sent to Westminster to shape and guarantee the new pattern. Within a week or two I was told that Cambridge was now 'off' because he would need me to help him with his parliamentary work. Mother, of course, told me and that was the reason she gave. But I think, too, that both of them believed quite genuinely that working with father would give me a far better education for life than reading history at Newnham. I dare say it might have done, but the point was that at twenty-one I had no effective free choice in the direction of my own affairs. There was no sudden withdrawal of generosity on their part; it was simply that in 1919 they were still firmly settled in the old conception that a daughter serves her home until she gets married and that in any case her parents know better than she does what is best for her development, in contrast to a son who is free to make his own career. When my brother, for instance, had wanted to go into the army three or four years before the war it was not a popular choice of profession - father would have preferred his son to go to 'The Works' - but he was determined and his decision once made, father supported it generously and loyally. But I was shackled still to Sesame and Lilies.

It never occurred to me to fight, indeed how could I have fought since I was totally dependent economically. I just felt dumb about the whole thing and pushed my disappointment out of the way. When I heard that I had not won a high enough place in the post-war scramble to enter Newnham at once I was comforted rather than chagrined. That failure was my own fault and yet typical of the amateurish casual attitude towards women's education which had prevailed until the war. It had never been impressed upon me that I must take the Newnham exam seriously, and I had assumed that I could pass it if I read history by myself and had some pleasant but quite informal coaching from Olive who was, after all, not very much more qualified to coach me than I was to learn myself. I did not even know what books I ought to read on my period, and for the most part browsed contentedly on the rather hoary classics I found at home. I was driving a doctor's car during this later period of the war, and when he went out to visit a patient I used to fish Bryce's Holy Roman Empire or Macaulay's Essays from under the seat and replace the book hastily as he emerged lest I should be seen engaged with a 'heavy' book. Serious books were always 'heavy'.

I don't think I bore much conscious resentment about Cambridge. Incidentally, no one would have been more surprised than my parents if I had shown resentment. Indeed, I dare say I might have forgotten the episode had the better education for life materialized. It was not father's fault that this fizzled out, and that for the next three years a considerable part of my actual life was spent in taking down letters at his bedside and then spending long evenings alone by the fire in my own room whilst mother saw to father's needs and kept him company upstairs. Nor, indeed, was this perhaps such a bad education. I enjoyed the secretarial work because much of it stretched my interest and because of father's gift for making his subordinate feel a person and not a mere agent. And the long evenings taught me the useful lesson of looking after myself in my own company. Also the compensations that I was to have received in the way of a full political life might have worked well for some time, but I think that in the long run politics would have made a real cause of friction between us.

Father considered himself a non-party man yet he took the Conservative whip. But I had cropped the whole of Justin McCarthy's History of Our Own Times during a bout of measles, and from that lush Liberal pasturage was setting out to find new political fields on my own account. In this adventure I was encouraged by Gertrude Anson whose particular branch of the family really was Liberal, and not only Liberal but

Home Rule. Mother, of course, said that their Home Rule views were to be attributed to, if not condoned by, the fact that their knowledge of Irish affairs was purely academic. Views with which one disagreed were invariably academic. That was father's criticism, too, of intellectual Socialism. Gertrude and I used occasionally to go for short walking tours in the Lake District, and more than once we lost our physical bearings owing to the concentrated ardour of the discussions in which we had already long lost our mental bearings. And then Ronald Allen came home from the war and went up to Oxford. He was the son of an old acquaintance of father's and his relatives owned the *Manchester Evening News*, which was closely linked with the *Manchester Guardian*. Thus the Liberal tradition was incarnate in Ronald and somewhat enviously I used to listen to his and Gertrude's tales of young Oxford Liberalism, for by this time Gertrude was at Oxford, too.

Ronald was one of the few young men I knew to whom it was possible to talk reasonably and naturally and enthusiastically about the things that really interested one. Besides politics he was interested in poetry, and so was I. He was interested in writing and so was I. We showed each other our literary productions, discussed the brave new world endlessly and played a lot of tennis. Sometimes I would go to stay in Oxford while he and Gertrude were both up, meet their friends and blend the brave new world with tea-parties in their rooms or canoe parties on the river. Granted my own temper of mind, it was hardly surprising that after a year or two of this pleasant indoctrination I was accepting father's politics rather unhappily. I hated the Conservative label which attached to us because of Clayton, and comforted myself that since Lloyd George had been a great Radical once he might become one again, if only he could or would struggle loose from the stranglehold of the Conservative Central Office. And father, after all, had called himself a Coalition and not a Conservative candidate. So I suppressed my sprouting political conscience as best I could and for the rest tried not to take myself too seriously. But this was not easy since I was young. I had to keep my views on the Irish troubles which were, to say the least, heretical by the standards of home orthodoxy, to myself or trot them out feeling incredibly daring when I was in suitable company away from home. I was shocked when father kicked the League of Nations as he sometimes did with tongue or pen. He had no idealism to spare for the nascent international order which he thought unrealistic yet meddlesome, and for those reasons perhaps more likely in the end to bedevil world peace than to maintain it. But Ronald had fought for the new order and was determined to believe in it. So was Gertrude determined to believe in it, so was I, so was Olive Schill, although generally speaking her interest in politics was only lukewarm, an attitude which I found rather baffling. So would Olive's brother Melland have believed in it had he not been killed when 'K' battalion of the Manchester Regiment were wiped out on the Somme in 1916. Melland had gone up to Christ Church on a history scholarship a few years before the war. I do not think that he belonged in any way to the 'Grenfell group' whose lustre is remembered of the Oxford of those days, but of him it might have been written as I have read it written of them:

'It is effortless to say, as I have often heard said, that that heroic group loosely dubbed "the Grenfells" would have developed the weaknesses of every other generation. All we know is that they died young leaving a unique reputation for brilliance, high spirits, and grace, and that a rich, determining tradition in English life seems to have withered and died with them.'

His vivid temperament, his frank charm of manner, his keen mind were always present to Olive and through her to me, though I, too, had my own fresh sense of Melland's personality. But I was seven years younger, so before the war I could not know him as an equal; yet he had never treated me as a child and for long enough I had been admitted to his and Olive's friendship.

This disagreement about the League exemplified a difference between father's generation and ours which went deeper than the normal cleavage between the caution and conservatism of middle-age and the generous enthusiasm of youth. It is, of course, true that one section of the post-war youth, the section which later got all the publicity, was disillusioned and bedevilled by the callousing and uprooting effects of war, but another section rushed to the opposite extreme; it became apocalyptic-minded. And we belonged to that section. It had to be one extreme attitude or the other because we had all been bred in a society too easy for our new reality, a society in which we had been led to expect security and ordered progress, a society whose morals and ideals were personal and not communal, whose disciplines were imposed mostly by a convention of manners. And now we had to shoulder the burden of this shaken bourgeois society. We evaded that either by repudiating its values lock, stock and barrel and so escaping from it, or we escaped from it into a dream of the New Jerusalem. Along with Ronald and Gertrude and Olive I began at any rate with the New Jerusalem.

We could hardly formulate this underlying tension in our lives, and I do not think our parents had any conception of it because they were so completely identified with the old society that they could not sense that its illness was mortal, so that for them reconstruction simply meant nursing it back to a better and healthier life. It was hard for them to be patient with us, but it was equally hard for us to be patient with them. My own particular impatience was always exacerbated by mother's attitude that a disagreement with father was silly and presumptuous on my inexperienced part and due to an innate disposition towards argumentation and rebellion.

'Oh, Kathie, you're always agin the Government,' was her standard summing-up.

It is hard and strange to remember that I am now in the position which my parents occupied in 1920, but there is this difference. I have never lived as an adult in a secure and stable society which I respected, a society with a firm scheme of values into which one's personal life could be properly socketed. The golden visions which lent a glow of faith and enthusiasm to the early twenties flickered out because the post-war generation found itself impotent to translate them into realities. Perhaps they were untranslatable, perhaps we were only the gleanings of a generation whose harvest had been sacrificed in France. Their place was too often taken by a disillusioned sentimental realism of the gutter - the realism of Aldous Huxley's Point *Counterpoint* and Christopher Isherwood's *Mr Norris Changes Trains*. So as I look back it is with detachment, but also with understanding that the seeds of any withered society can only be awakened into new life by the dreams and enthusiasms of youth. And we have two such withered societies on our hands, the pre-1914 society in which we were nurtured and the post-1919 society which we tried to shape. It is not for an older generation to interfere with the dreams of the young. Our business surely is to sort the seeds of the withered societies, sifting by criticism as well as we can the wheat from the tares so that we can hand over to them a bag full of sound seed fit to be vivified by their dreams. There, surely, is the heart of the matter between youth and middle-age.

But to return to 1919 and 1920. In the main my political relations with father were fairly smooth because my adventurings were merely theoretical and involved no action on my part. But sooner or later I should have wanted to haul up my own flag and go into battle and then they would not have been so smooth. Then, I am pretty sure, we should have been all set for a showdown, and I might not have had the courage to stand out for my own things. I know that it was working up for that because only a few months after father's death I was confronted with a political choice which I could only make one way. My cousin, Gerald Hurst (he had married a daughter of my Uncle Alfred), asked me to work for him in the election campaign of 1922. In the misty and glamorous atmosphere of 1918 it had been easy enough to find reasons for supporting Gerald's Conservatism, but now I found it impossible. So I wrote him a long letter earnestly enumerating point by point the differences between us. Even that took a good deal of courage because I was very fond of Gerald and the standard view was that among women persons, and particularly relatives, came before political principles. Moreover, he had always been particularly kind and friendly to me and had given me my first chance of 'getting into print' by introducing me to the editor of the Nineteenth Century, who took several articles of mine on mountaineering subjects. So I would have liked to do what Gerald wanted, and apart from that I would have liked to avoid an open break-away. My brother, for instance, whose Conservatism was whole-hearted, had to be tackled, though why that should have been thought necessary I do not know, nor do I know why I submitted quite naturally to this idea that my political views were a concern of his. But I did, and stated my case all over again in another letter and received in return a very conditional absolution. It was, so far as I remember, just possible to fight under the Liberal flag without betraying one's own section of society, and so long as my flag was dyed no redder it was my own affair and he had nothing against me.

Incidentally, brothers were expected to carry a great deal of responsibility for their sisters, so I suppose it was only fair that they should demand a certain amount of conformity in return. A friend of mine, for example, had become engaged to a major in the Indian cavalry during a visit to friends in India. On his return to England, supposedly to claim a bride, he jilted her instead. Mother was very scornful because her brother did nothing at all about it. I think mother would have liked to see Jim go off armed at any rate with a metaphorical horsewhip, but whether in order to bring the major with the lash curling about him to the altar, or whether merely to teach him a lesson, I do not know. On other occasions when some brotherless girl had not been treated with correct gallantry, mother would say: 'Now this could never have happened if she had had a brother.' My political troubles were very youthful and I have no doubt that I was rather pompous about them. I was making much ado about nothing from the point of view of my elders, who thought it unreasonable and intransigent and lacking in proportion that I should have, at my age, political principles about which I really minded, particularly as it was axiomatic that I could not know anything seriously about politics. But to me it was not nothing for I was having to vindicate my own integrity for the first time in my life.

Another cousin by marriage, whose wife was Uncle Alfred's eldest daughter, was standing in West Leeds as some sort of Liberal. John Murray was then a don at Christ Church and he, too, asked me to come and work for him. This rather flattered my vanity, but I would not go until I had got his particular variety of Liberalism properly elucidated. I was rather wary of my relations politically since it seemed to me that sheep's clothing was a garb not unknown to them. And those were the days when the genus Liberal was branching into so many species that an expert sociologist would have been needed to disentangle them properly. I was attracted to Asquith's Wee Frees. A telegraphic correspondence ensued in the course of which I tried to find out John Murray's species. Mother was considerably irritated by this final exhibition of my obtrusive principles; I have no doubt that John Murray was equally amused. I was finally satisfied by a wire of four words 'without prefix or suffix'. And I went off to West Leeds where I found Gertrude already installed along with a quite unpolitical soldier friend of my cousin's, who put the candidate over in the pubs of an evening, and the present Conservative Member for the Combined Universities, who was an ex-pupil of John Murray's and did most of the speaking at meetings. We were a gay party; Bim Clarke kept us amused when he was not working the pubs, Harry Strauss was energetic and effervescent and sometimes provided Gertrude and myself with material for gloomy forebodings as to his future in the Liberal faith, the candidate and the candidate's wife treated us as if we were their weekend guests in a country house. It was a grand week and I came home having learned a little more how to act for myself. But by 1924 I should have found it very difficult to fight a Labour opponent. However, fortunately about that time marriage relieved me of the necessity of applying to my family for a nihil obstat every time that I wanted to embark on some political adventure.

In the early 1920's I was, of course, acting at home much the same part as would have been assigned to me in 1913 had I then been grown up. So that what I have written of my relations at home in the 1920's would be pretty much true of 1913, except that I probably should not have felt restless and sometimes rebellious because the objective incentives to restlessness and rebellion would have been absent. In 1913 I should not have felt that I was being tied to an obsolete social set-up. And this brings me, in order to complete the picture of a daughter at home, to the ideas about sex and marriage to which I was still expected to conform when the Armistice brought the remaining young men back and the Alderley Edge round of dances and tennis parties began once again. It was not always easy to conform. Father and mother seemed quite unaware that the war had turned the code of manners between the sexes upside down and inside out; they harked back to 1913, and if I describe the way it looked to me in the first years after the Armistice, I shall be presenting a picture of the way it had been for them in 1913, though a picture sketched in, I am afraid, with a certain amount of acerbity since I shall be seeing it through my own rather rebellious eyes.

Alderley Edge Surgical Requisite Guild

Brookdale, pressed into service by the British Red Cross for the duration of the First World War

Chapter Fifteen
YOUNG MEN AND MAIDENS

The basic purpose of the sex taboos and sex restrictions which were imposed on the middle-class young before 1914 was to maintain and enhance the prestige of marriage. I hesitate to say that it was designed to maintain the sanctity of marriage, though that aspect did come into it as well. I think the guardians of the social code, and all the people I knew were guardians of it, were very much confused in their minds between prestige and sanctity. Some of them, mother, for instance, really believed in both as it were along parallel lines, others paid lip service to sanctity, but their operative if unavowed belief was pure and simple prestige. Sanctity and prestige made an incongruous pair of bed-fellows, and young people fear and distrust the incongruous, mistaking it often for hypocrisy, a vice inevitably calculated to arouse their honourable indignation. It takes some time to learn that a sense of irony which can expend itself in amusement is a useful device through which one may come to terms with the incongruities of life. Moreover, the young are quite sure that they have no vested interest in their elders' social code; they are, therefore, in a position to see clearly behind it to the bare human relations which so often it strains and distorts into an untrue if serviceable pattern - another excuse for their charge of hypocrisy. It was therefore natural that I should dislike and feel a considerable contempt for my elders' view of sex relations culminating in their view of marriage. I could not, of course, sort out very clearly in my mind the various aspects which made up their view. For one thing it was never put to me as a coherent view related to a general consideration of life. Father's and mother's philosophy of life was never examined and discussed and defended against other standpoints. It was tacitly assumed; and it was also assumed that I would and could accept and understand it, without ever having had it set out for me as a reasoned and interlocking system. In fact, I am not quite sure how far father and mother did build up their detailed philosophy of life from reasoned deductions from their first principles, though I think mother did. At any rate, as I have said, they never discussed it with me as a coherent structure. It came across to me in unrelated bits and pieces, generally when some episode of practical life demanded a positive attitude, with which as often as not I disagreed because I could not see any underlying reason for it. A polarization on first principles was therefore something of which I had very little conception. And except that I had the concrete example of mother's own polarized life always before me, I was, like most of my contemporaries, ill-equipped to plunge into a post-war world of vertiginously changing ideas.

In matters which concerned sex the changing ideas of that post-war world were particularly difficult to harmonize with father's and mother's point of view, partly because they were so glaringly at variance with the parental pre-war code to which I must conform, partly because essentials were never sorted out from mere conventions and frankly discussed. I had to learn the code as my older contemporaries had done by bumping up against a restriction, by catching an impression from the reaction to some concrete instance, by being fed into the complicated mechanism designed to enable young men and maidens to meet and mate in circumstances which could be controlled by their elders, although, of course, by the time that I was being fed into the mechanism it was already breaking down.

At Alderley Edge the tennis club was part of this mechanism, dances were another part of it, and chief among the dances were the Manchester Assemblies. I forget how many Assemblies there were during the course of the winter, but it was they par excellence which put the Manchester débutante on to the marriageable map. The dancers were drawn from all the socially reputable suburbs. Alderley Edge, Knutsford, Bowdon, Didsbury, Eccles, sent their contingents made up of 'parties' carefully chaperoned by a couple of mammas or an aunt or two, ladies who in their day had danced and very probably met their husbands on the Assembly floor (and a lovely floor it was, swung on chains), but whose function now was to sit round in chairs and watch over the behaviour of their young whilst providing at the same time a temporary refuge for any girl who might be left for a dance without a partner. It was, of course, always a dreaded horror to be left for a dance partnerless, and it looked so much less obvious to sit out beside your own or someone else's chaperon than by yourself. You could at least hope that someone believed the fiction that you were doing it to keep the elders company for a little.

The chaperons watched the way a programme had been filled with eagle eyes. Three dances with any one young man was the maximum allowance for good taste. Anything above three caused talk and might easily merit a rebuke in the privacy of one's bedroom in the dawn hours after the return home. Prolonged disappearances for sitting out purposes were even more likely to call down rebukes, and any results arising from Assembly introductions and friendships were carefully checked. One of us, for instance, met a young man who was interested in books and keen to talk books, a fairly uncommon phenomenon. A few days later a parcel of new crisp-leaved volumes arrived for her at home. She was told to send them back with a polite note. The young man was not considered altogether suitable for ripening acquaintance, since ripening acquaintances were apt to lead to proposals, and it was unkind as well as bad form to 'encourage' young men from whom proposals would not be parentally welcome. Obediently she sent them back feeling thoroughly ashamed of the crudity and the gracelessness of the action she had been commanded to perform. That little episode, of course, took place before the 1914 war.

I was naturally too young to attend Assemblies during those pre-war winters, but after the war they were revived and I went in trepidation because I did not dance well, and for partners I had to rely on the three or four young men who appeared to like me for myself and on the other young men whose sense of manners made them feel that they owed me the courtesy of a dance or two because they came to tennis parties at Ferns.

I never had very much difficulty with partners for mixed tennis because I could play a reasonably hard game, and this saved my self-respect, and I looked forward to the July tennis tournament as the crown of our social year and enjoyed it to the full. For after the first post-war season or two my tennis had become good enough to secure me agreeable and fairly expert partners not only for the ladies' but also for the mixed doubles. And I enjoyed the dance at the finish of it for which we usually had a party staying in the house. It was a much freer affair than the Assemblies, touched by the new post-war atmosphere of liberty. There were no chaperons to check dances per young man and daring couples could retire to a parked motor-car for their sitting-out. But when we came home in the small hours we always found that a maid had been detailed by mother to sit up for us and see us to our rooms. Mother would have considered it quite indecorous that young men and women should sort themselves out at 3am without assistance and supervision by a neutral.

It took me years to conquer the shyness and self-consciousness generated by the various controls and caveats and prohibitions. I must not play golf on Sundays less, I think, on religious grounds than because the clubhouse was made mildly roisterous by some of the lads who spent their week-days in Manchester business houses. For some reason the tennis club, which had been thrown open on Sundays after the war, was less suspect, but I was discouraged from frequenting its pavilion where the same lads, along with our more daring womenfolk, drank long gins and ginger. I recall my first gin and ginger in company with our least reputable lady member. It was a fine adult moment, partly on account of her reputation, but also because she was a county player with whom I regarded it as an honour to be invited to have a drink. I could not meet X, who lived in digs near Manchester and was coming out to spend a Sunday at Ferns, at the station in the car because that would seem too forthcoming. I might have lunch tête-à-tête in London with Y, but I must not dine and dance with him unless there were a third, and of course that meant a fourth, present as well. And what a fool I felt when I had to admit this decision to Y who was a charming painter with a sardonic sense of humour. It made no difference that Y's parents had been old family friends.

The man who followed one of the fine arts as a profession was a specimen of humanity unknown to our circle and his natural habitat was assumed to be that untidy society known by those who are acquainted with it only at secondhand as Bohemia. I am not clear whether father and mother really thought that most artists lived the disorderly if engaging lives of Raoul, Mimi and their friends in Murger's Scènes de la vie de Bohême, or whether they thought that art was an unstable and insecure career or whether they thought it was slightly unmanly, but for one reason or another, probably for a mixture of all three reasons, I think that they were suspicious of artists. Art, as I have already remarked, could be taken seriously in our world as a complementary means to the good life, an enrichment of leisure hours, but by some strange contortion of reasoning the creator of art could not be taken seriously. The result so far as I was concerned was misleading. For I was driven to assume that there was something abnormal, however agreeable, in devoting one's life to the pursuit of art and that people who did so must be invested with a glamour denied to ordinary folk following humdrum occupations. In regard to this I was given an amusing if rude shock. The stage was, of course, regarded as the most suspect department of the arts and the one least likely to harbour respectable practitioners. But an old and very delightful business friend of father's actually had a daughter who was on the stage. On some occasion, about the time when I was just grown up, Esmé Hubbard was playing in Manchester and it was arranged that she should spend Sunday at Ferns. I awaited the visit with a good deal of anticipatory excitement, expecting a glamorous lady in whose presence I should feel at once shy and wickedly titivated. But I was introduced to a small dumpy woman, rather dully dressed, with plenty of kindliness and a general air of belonging quite naturally to the respectable world which I already knew. She was ensconced by the drawing-room fireside exactly as Mrs Russell, Miss Hall or any one of my aunts might have been. In short, she was like everyone else and my deflation was considerable.

After father died the strictness in regard to young men was very much relaxed. Perhaps mother realized that the liberty which my contemporaries had won could no longer be gainsaid, and realizing this felt that it was hardly fair to place me as a sort of barrier against the rising tide of changed manners. Perhaps her altered attitude was partly the insurance policy of timely concessions. Also it is only just to say that always my men friends, such as Ronald Allen, were welcome at home, and in surroundings which father and mother considered suitable I was allowed to spend as much time in their company as I liked. So far as I remember I never disobeyed any of the definite ad hoc prohibitions.

If I had put it baldly to mother that the restrictions and the prohibitions were all part of the great design to safeguard and exalt marriage she would, I feel sure, have been quite justly incensed. She would have taken the line that her ideal of decent and modest behaviour was a value in its own right. As for father, his ideal of wifehood and daughterhood was so whole-heartedly Ruskinian that any laxity of morals and manners must have wounded it at once. In his view a man's lot was cast in the rough outside world where he must take on the chin any battering of fortune and push his way as best he can through evil and defilement. But he came home for comfort and inspiration and cleansing and rest. The primary and exacting function of a wife, therefore, was to provide these.

'Whatever of best he can conceive, it is her part to be; whatever of highest he can hope, it is hers to promise; all that is dark in him she must purge into purity; all that is failing in him she must strengthen into truth; from her, through all the world's clamour, he must win his praise; in her through all the world's warfare, he must find his peace.' So Ruskin, I think, had expressed it, and obviously no ideal of this kind could be maintained for five minutes unless a very high value indeed was put on marriage. In brackets I might add that here it may be seen how the school they so carefully chose for me entered into the picture. Neither in practice could mother's ideal be maintained without putting a high value on marriage; thus, in fact, both of them were committed in all their views about sex problems to solutions which would defend and increase the prestige of marriage. Mother would have said 'the sanctity' of marriage, but then, as I have remarked, prestige and sanctity were inextricably mixed up even in the minds of the sensitive and thoughtful. As for the ruck, they deduced plain prestige from premises which were crudely social.

No doubt, in practice, prestige made a sort of framework for sanctity, but to the uncompromising vision of youth it looked very like a conspiracy of humbug, a conspiracy made all the more hateful by the cruelty which it entailed. For here, in the protection of the righteous, was to be found, I am afraid, the underlying reason for the complete social ostracism visited upon a transgressor, upon anyone who was known or believed to have a sex life outside marriage, upon anyone who had been even innocently through the divorce court. This was the explanation for the necessity of a demimonde. This was a major purpose of the terrific efforts made to gloss over unhappy marriages and to keep them going at any cost. Yet I do not want to simplify too much nor discount the finer strands of thought and feeling. In regard to unhappy marriages, for instance, I see now that they were held together as well by a more admirable cement. The relationship of husband and wife became something more than the sum of Mr X and Mrs X. Each, and in particular the woman, would have felt that a separation involved the loss of something more precious and personal than the prestige of the married state; each would have felt obscurely that a contraction of humanity was involved. And this subtle feeling was buttressed by a decent pride and a conscious sense of social and sometimes religious responsibility. You did not repudiate your responsibility simply because the cost was heavy.

I suppose that the maintenance of a marriage at almost any cost led to some very dishonest marital façades, but it did make for a disciplined and a dignified society, and I surmise that on balance it entailed less suffering for all and sundry concerned. And I think that there were fewer unhappy marriages, because couples, assuming a life contract, tried harder to arrange difficulties and accept limitations. They did not expect a Paradise. At any rate I, personally, only knew of three or four marriages that were really unhappy.

And before the war I knew only one couple who lived separated, none who were divorced and had remarried, and certainly none who 'lived together in sin'. Such relationships belonged only to the world of books and hushed hearsay. Free love - so called - was as remote from any contact with our lives as Mohammedan polygamy. The elders might read about it in the more daring novels of H.G. Wells. I remember vaguely snatches of discussion about a book called Ann Veronica. But I had no idea of the portent that book must have seemed, for were not Ann Veronica's parents assured members of the assured middle-class, until many years later I read it myself because I wanted to remove some of my ignorance of Wells's early novels. Mother certainly read Wells every now and then, but although she cared for distinguished prose I do not think she ever read George Moore, except perhaps Esther Waters, nor D. H. Lawrence. She would have been too deeply disgusted by the strain of lasciviousness in George Moore and by the glowing blood and brutality of Lawrence. I embarked on a course of George Moore in my early twenties - I loved his limpid writing - and had my eyes opened, not only in regard to matters of sex.

Looking back, I realize now how fantastically sheltered I was in the home environment. At the same time the shelter of home was disconcertingly uncertain, always liable to be suddenly pierced by conflicting points of view which I picked up from books or from people I met, and had to digest as well as I could unaided for I could never discuss such matters with father or mother. From time to time, the shelter was pierced by communications from mother about happenings which could not very well be 'kept from me'. I found these conversations terribly embarrassing, but my embarrassment was surpassed by mother's. I had been told, for instance, in the tone of voice specially reserved for information of this kind, about Miss X who had disappeared as quite a young woman into that forbidden world about which I wasn't supposed to know anything officially, even from books. But our society had expelled Miss X with ease and the puncture made by her ejection had closed at once. Only her immediate family ever gave a thought to Miss X or knew where and how she was conducting a flamboyant and/or miserable existence. It was a shame one did not talk about for Miss X's family's sake, and I think that I was only told in order to save Miss X's family the awkward questions which I might have asked.

Then during the war Major Y, unsettled by the lures of unaccustomed soldiering in the East, fell for a - presumed - siren, and at the end of hostilities refused to come home and shoulder once more his family responsibilities. He, too, was thrown out of our society with sorrow, anger and disgust.

A little later we were shaken by the behaviour of young A, one of the games stars from another of Manchester's residential villages who was often to be seen as a guest at our Club and who entangled himself with a girl from London. When it was found that she was going to bear his child, A's family and the girl's family exerted all the pressure they could to force a marriage, regardless of the fact that neither A nor the girl really loved each other or felt able to spend their lives together. So soon as A had 'made an honest woman of her' they would part for good. The vital point was to give the girl and her baby the sanction of a wedding-ring -

> For when I go out,
> The little boys shout:
> Did she never come back with a ring? —

as the comic song had it. It seemed a sinister and singular comment on the vaunted sanctity of marriage to me, but even mother appeared to think that it was the only course to take, since if they had not married the girl and her baby would have been forced out of any respectable society. I am afraid that had the girl belonged to a different walk of life this point of view would not have operated, and instead she would have been pensioned off with a money payment and I dare say would, in consequence, have lived more happily ever after. But she was a 'nice girl' and 'one of us', so she and A had to pay to the uttermost farthing for the breach they had made in the defences of marriage. Apparently it never occurred to any of the older generation that it might have been possible to stand by A's girl, support and warmly help her without giving up their own standards or prostituting an ideal of marriage by the farcical union undertaken in order to make it look as if the standards had been maintained all round. They were too panicky about the breach to consider an application of the conception of caritas, too panicky indeed to think clearly about the matter at all. And so, as I saw it, they forced A and his girl into committing a double wrong in order to save their own faces. Or rather, I should say that as I saw it, they forced the two into making a double mistake, for by the time that this had happened my generation was busy working out its own euphemistic hypocrisies.

If A and his girl had not married the latter would automatically have become a 'fallen woman' and would almost inevitably have disappeared into that mysterious demimonde which was an essential part of the structure needed to maintain the barrier between the soiled and the white-starched. The demi-monde was as remote as the planet Saturn from any world which mother had to do with. Not only was it a kind of oubliette into which offenders could be conveniently dropped, it was also the glittering and meretricious society in which young men 'sowed their wild oats'. But the sowing of wild oats was not regarded with any favour. Young men were expected to live up to an ideal of chastity before marriage, and those who put themselves into a position which suggested aggressively that they were not doing so, were looked on with mistrust. I should not have been allowed to be friendly, for instance, with the two or three young men who were known to frequent the dubious bars of the Midland Hotel. And a young man who was known to look for illicit pleasures in the fabulous demimonde, or who had notoriously 'got a girl into trouble', would have been cut off by the other males from the society of their womenfolk. None the less, male lapses could usually be kept quiet and secret so no one knew exactly how far the ideal of chastity was really maintained in practice. I think myself that it was maintained to a far greater extent than the succeeding generation would have thought possible, and not merely through fear of consequences, but frankly because it was an ideal and an accepted responsibility of decent living.

Moral standards loosen as a rule from above down, and well before the war, it was sufficiently notorious to have reached the ears which I used to cock to catch muffled comments on such subjects (if the comments had not been so discreetly muffled I probably should not have bothered to listen) that the loosening process was well under weigh in some aristocratic ranks. Our strict middle and professional class regarded the 'fast' aristocrats with acute disfavour, a disfavour all the sharper because they still really looked to the old aristocracy for a national lead. They held on to their Victorian code long after the loosening process had percolated downwards from the aristocracy and was pushing upwards from a demi-monde rapidly being drawn into the main stream of society. But even they could not hold on to the Victorian code for ever. And the first portent of relaxation was when mother decided after the war to call on Mrs Green.

Now Mrs Green was an attractive soft-spoken south-country lady who had married Mr Green, a Manchester business man, a few years before and come to settle in Alderley Edge. But the Green ménage had a past attached to it. I can no longer recall the exact nature of that past. Either Mr Green had divorced or been divorced by a former wife or Mrs Green had taken a former husband through the divorce court. At any rate, the Greens were satisfactorily married before they settled together in Alderley Edge and, as everyone agreed, appeared to be a very pleasant and quiet couple. But they had this past trailing behind them, and father decreed that although he could meet and like Mr Green at the club, they were not to be invited to mother's home. That was a standard reaction, a part of the old machinery to protect marriage, and in father's case emphasized, no doubt, by his Ruskinian ideology as regards women. Mother, of course, acquiesced, and I think that it was only after his death or at any rate well after the war that she decided on an attitude at once more realistic and more kindly. She had, I think, met Mrs Green on various war jobs and liked her. The result of the exchange of calls was an increase in the richness of mother's Alderley Edge contacts of which she might have had the benefit years before.

The personal morals of Mrs Green herself had never been under aspersion. Mother would not have relaxed so far as to call on a guilty party. Indeed, the hue and cry to chase out the guilty remained in full force long after the war. Some while after I was married I remember being invited to a luncheon in London with two of my aunts and mother. After the preliminaries of general conversation there was a pause and then one of the aunts, I forget which, said:
'Shall we tell her?'
And the other replied: 'Yes, I think we had better.'
And they both looked at mother, conceiving it as her job and waiting, as it were, for her to gather herself for an ordeal.
I wondered what under heaven had happened now.

Then mother explained with a rather painful hesitation that a distant relative of ours had left her husband after some twenty years of marriage and was about to set up afresh with another man, a man of parts and standing with whom apparently she had been in love and who had been in love with her for many years. The aunts chipped in, and from their disjointed comments and information I gathered that Doris had acted with a great deal of self-discipline and restraint since she had held back her lover and maintained her family life until the time when she felt that her children no longer needed the background of a complete home and that she was free of responsibility. She was a middle-aged woman now, she had given up years of happiness to serve her ideal of duty. By the end of the conversation I was regarding her and have ever since regarded her with respect and admiration. And I was in a white heat of indignation at the tone and attitude of complacent righteousness adopted, not so much by mother, who was truly and simply sorry, as by the aunts. The final remark of one of them: 'Well, I hope William doesn't divorce her; she ought to be let stew in her own juice,' horrified me. I felt that I had caught a glimpse, a terrifying glimpse, of the pack in action tearing to pieces the wretched individual who refuses to conform.

If it had not been for that final remark, which was so spontaneous and so vindictive, I might have let it go that the aunts were exaggerating their attitude in order to impress on my youth and inexperience the enormity of Doris's offence. Exaggeration of this kind was a favourite if quite ineffective device for impressing the young. I might even have believed that they were moved, in however misguided and uncharitable a fashion, by a genuine desire to uphold the Christian sanctity of marriage. As it was, I went home convinced that it was all an elaborate and hateful contraption erected to protect the timid and the pharisaically righteous and I was determined never again to take on trust any of their moral judgments.

Their attitude could be expressed in three words: lack of caritas. The old precept 'Hate the sin but love the sinner' had, so it seemed to me, been distorted into 'Hate the sinner because the sinner's action shakes the structure built with so much care and difficulty to shelter the righteous'. But it may be that I am unjust, because even today I cannot recall that conversation and the attitude of my aunts - not of mother - without contempt and indignation.

Have I really separated the different thoughts and emotions out of which the pre-war generation built up the prestige of marriage in particular and its code of sex relations in general? How many of them simply went to the making of that hideous barricade for the protection of the righteous and how many derived from a genuine Christian ideal for which a framework had to be built? How far were their cruelty, their lack of charity, their hypocrisy and their taboos so many clumsy methods for constructing that framework? I cannot say and I am quite sure that they did not know themselves.

It is perhaps only to-day when the barricades have been rased and obliterated that we can begin to think clearly and fearlessly about an ideal of marriage. If that can be done I think that the post-war generation which assaulted and broke the barricades will deserve some thanks. Their motives were mixed, too; the virtues of liberty, sincerity, generosity and self-sacrifice were all involved in their ideal of sex relations, but with a sleight-of-hand twist which gave them applications wildly at odds with traditional practice. To break a marriage because one of the partners might be suffering from a temporary sex wanderlust was the sin of jealousy. But to hold a man or a woman against their will was the sin of egotism. To refuse the pleasures of sex to the unmarried was mutilation, the sin against the body. Not that they referred to any activity as sinful, for sin was an old-fashioned and obsolete conception. They mixed up licence with liberty, self-indulgence with generosity, in fantastic distortions. But primarily they broke the barricades because they so hated self-righteousness and hypocrisy and lack of generosity. In their rough and undisciplined way they did seek for an ideal of caritas. But they wrought a fine confusion in the process and now, paradoxically enough, we are confronted by the Christian ideal of marriage, standing amidst the confusion free and challenging, stripped unwittingly of all the social encrustations with which our parents had obscured it.

In 1913 and 1914 I was too young to feel much circumscribed by father's and mother's view of sex relations, indeed, I doubt whether the girls who had just grown up then felt very much galled by the prevalent view either. Because their society was still so much a going concern; within the terms of it they could have a very good time indeed. And to this good time, as I have said, I looked forward from the watch-tower of the ivory castle of school, looked forward not without some apprehension lest I should fail to hold my own, but none the less with an anticipation filled out as school holidays succeeded each other, bringing the future nearer and giving it shape as more and more I was able to join up with Campbell and his friends, with Olive and Melland, with the boy and girl cousins a little older than myself who appeared when we went away for holidays. From the constricted ivory watch-tower the future looked free and fair enough.

Convalescents at Alderley Edge

A New Year party at an internment camp in Holland. The chauffeur, Richardson, can be seen in the centre of the picture

Chapter Sixteen
VALE

The summer holidays of 1914 bid fair to outdo all others in their plan of enjoyment. Campbell was due for a rare summer leave and had promised to partner me in the bank holiday tennis tournament, my first grown-up tournament it would be. After that I was to go to Belfast to stay with my gay Irish cousins and finally, as the pièce de résistance, father and mother and I were to join my Uncle Albert and his family of boys and girls at Argentières. Not much was said, but I guessed that somehow or another father would get round the ban on Alpine climbing and see to it that I got at least a taste of snow and ice. It was therefore in a mood of exhilarated anticipation that I lay in my bath before dinner on the evening of my return home. The tap spurted hot water plentifully and purposefully, so unlike the miserly tepid trickle at school. There was time to laze; no bath list and no irritated successor calling, 'Your time's up' before you had had a chance even to lie back after soaping. So I sponged and splashed and sang tunelessly and at the top of my voice the comic songs of the day in order to let off my spirits. 'Tony from America', 'Yip-I-Addy', 'Mr Jeremiah Esquire', blared from the bathroom to destroy mother's sensitive ear and fortify her dislike of musical comedy.

At dinner the evening light slid over the mahogany table and was reflected crisply from the facets of the cut-glass water jug and pair of goblets and from the bowl in the centre which was crammed with the salmon-coloured sweet peas which mother particularly liked. The shallow flutings and elaborate scroll work on the belly of the urn gleamed with the gentlemanly extravagance of a Regency buck. I drank suave tomato soup from a thin china plate with a pattern of ivy leaves at its edge, and ate cutlets of fillet steak each with its blob of butter and parsley on top, peas and new potatoes, a dish of raspberries and cream - civilized feeding. Outside the shorn lawns, the trees, the patterned plain, the border brilliant as a herald's blazon prepared lazily for the twilight, and in the greenhouses the last peaches and nectarines, musky carnations and improbable wax or velvet-petalled orchids withdrew from the care of men. Next door, the drawing-room awaited us with the watercolours and the couch in the window and the sofa-table with its band of delicate inlay and the thick Donegal carpet faded to the green of misted grass. It was good to come home on a summer evening to this garden and this frank and gracious house which held no secrets from me.

Campbell on home leave

It was good to wake next morning in my own bedroom, into which the sun streamed across the prickly tops of the hollies outside my window, to lie relaxed in bed, greeting my white-painted furniture, my grey and pink rugs, my pictures and books, and thinking all the time of the long holidays ahead until the gong rang and I hustled up to dress and dash downstairs to the dining-room.

I am not quite sure when I became aware that already a cloud was forming from the chill impact of outside events on my sunny anticipations. But it was very soon. A day or two after I came home the Schills gave a garden-party. It was a heavy afternoon with thunder in the offing, but beyond the croquet players and the parasols and the decorous chatter I had, I can remember it now, an indefinable sense of more than physical oppression, as if a damp hand were slowly passing along the gleaming prospect of the holidays. Was it just the fortune-teller who had sent me out of her tent with some vague ominous warning, was it because I had already been told that I could not go to Ireland because the Round Table Conference had broken down and my Ulster relatives were slipping back the safety catches from their guns, was it that I had been told that Campbell's leave had been cancelled and there would be no tennis tournament? Or was it that the future stepped suddenly backwards a day or two and a thoughtless child felt the darkness as one by one the lights were put out over Europe? I cannot recall the sequence of disappointments during those few days. The crowning one, of course, was when father decided to cancel the Alpine holiday. He and Uncle Albert discussed it over the telephone, I think, and Uncle Albert was for holding on a few days longer, but father knew too much. He knew why Campbell's leave had been stopped, and as that week came gloomily to its close, the Irish troubles receded into the background and The Great Illusion, which lay on the drawing-room table in a sober green binding, seemed to form the letters of its title into a derisive leer. My personal disappointments gave place to a sense of illicit excitement.

At the weekend Richardson, who was a naval reservist, announced that he had received his mobilization papers. He departed for Portsmouth. His elder son was already in the navy and his wife wanted to go south to her own home so as to be nearer her men. On bank holiday mother and I and Auntie May, who was staying with us, went to help her pack up. Richardson lived beyond the tennis club and the short cut to his house led between the courts and the cricket pitch. Tennis and cricket were already in full swing. 'The flannelled fools at the wickets, the muddied oafs at the goal.' Kipling's stinging line suddenly traversed my sixteen-year-old mind like a plane cut stripping away layers of accustomed outlook. How could they bear to be playing cricket and tennis with this sense of terrible excitement surging in? It was incongruous, dense; and we were apart, for Campbell and Richardson had taken us with them into a different world. We found Mrs Richardson sitting amidst a heap of unpacked clothes and household treasures quite literally wringing her hands. As we walked home an hour or two later, mother said in a tone of sad reflection: 'I have often read of people wringing their hands, but never till this morning have I seen somebody actually doing it.'

> *Where are the sons whom we sent to your battlefields?*
> *What has a soldier to do with a wife?*
> *We were all so unprepared for that.*

Tuesday evening my elders sat in the billiard-room, tense and doing nothing, just waiting for midnight when the ultimatum to Germany was due to expire. There was, naturally, no radio to turn on for the news and as the time approached someone rose and went down to the post office to read the telegram stuck up in the window and announcing the German decision.

Snapshots follow in my recollection. Margaret and Gerald Hurst came over to see us. She was soon expecting a baby and rested on the sofa while Gerald sat in an armchair in stiff and uncustomary khaki, for he was a Territorial officer, his candid, clean-shaven, intellectual face looking strange and out of place above the high ochre-yellow collar; To date the soldiers I had known wore clipped moustaches .... Even if I could have foreseen the future it would have been hard to associate Gerald with the beaches on Gallipoli, those beaches whose sudden toll from homes they knew would make father and mother wince with pain when they opened their Guardian on a May morning of 1915 and read the casualty list of Manchester Territorials.

There was a recruiting meeting at Mather & Platt. The workmen, straight from bench and lathe, trooped into an empty shop where a platform had been set up to accommodate the directors and their satellites. I looked down on oil-grimed figures bunched in a drab confusion and starred by sallow thin faces, alert and searching. They gave them patriotic songs to chant, 'Rule Britannia' and the rest, all the conventional set-pieces. No, we were not yet schooled to war; we had even forgotten 'The Girl I Left Behind Me' and 'Soldiers of the Queen'. It was time for the music-halls to get busy on real war songs for us to sing. And the young men were exhorted to join the 'K' battalions of the Manchester Regiment. A year later those same directors would be desperate for hands to fulfil the imperious demands for shells and yet more shells.

Then Campbell's possessions from his barracks sitting-room at

Colchester began to come home in packing-cases, his books and pictures, his blue and scarlet uniform with the gleaming useless sword ....

Besides ours, only two of the neighbouring families had sons in the regulars. There was Denis Chesney, who was a soldier in India, and the eldest son of the doctor whose car I was later on to drive; he was in Campbell's battalion and waiting with him to cross to France. But every day more and more of the young men slipped away from the tennis club, and we heard that this or that friend or cousin had joined the Gunners or the Sappers, the Manchester Regiment, the Loyal North Lancs, or the Duke of Lancaster's Yeomanry. The elder of my Irish boy cousins exchanged his illegal activities with the Ulster Volunteers for His Majesty's commission in the Royal Irish Rifles. He was killed on the Somme in 1916, during that battle when the Ulster division fought side by side with the 16th, the Irish Nationalist division, and stretcher-bearers of an Ulster battalion were proud to carry Willie Redmond to the dressing-station.

Towards the middle of the month father went south alone to say good-bye to Campbell. I have often wondered what were his thoughts as the train carried him through the shires with their deep pastures and pleasant farms which most of the nation had half forgotten, but which were destined so soon to become front page news and the objects of entreaties and blandishments and hectic dangling rewards, carried him to a capital whose newsboys were already calling the ominous headlines of the Belgian communiqués. Did it slide across his mind, even as an uneasy surmise, that he was on his way not only to say goodbye to his son but also inevitably and irrevocably to his era? Could the signs show him that the golden century of the middle classes was about to sink back into history, its ripe strength drained by the armies which for four long years would struggle interlocked across Europe?

Indeed, I think that my own generation has only recently become fully aware that it has lived through a social revolution which began unnoticed in the sweep of more dramatic events on the 4th of August 1914. Like all revolutions it has been partly blind and partly conscious, partly generous and partly mean, partly the result of uncontrollable circumstance and partly directed. And one result of it has been the near collapse of English middle and professional class civilization on its qualitative side. There is a reported saying of Talleyrand's to the effect that douceur de vivre, untranslatable in its succinct French lucidity as the description of a certain sense of touch for life, vanished with the collapse and dispersal of the old aristocracy during the Great Revolution. It has almost vanished from our world, too, but it was understood and practised by the best of the Edwardian Haute Bourgeoisie. For it is certainly not the exclusive art of living of an aristocracy, nor need it depend on luxury, although it is nourished best by the conditions of a certain kind of leisure and a certain amount of money, a sense of security and a prized tradition. And it requires, too, the condition of a certain kind of freedom, the paradoxical liberty of agreed restraint, for it is dependent upon order and discrimination, upon respect for one's own and other people's dignity. Thus, in revolutionary times, it perishes through lack of nourishment because revolutions in their nature negate these conditions. You can live adventurously and bravely and ardently and selflessly during a revolution, but you cannot live securely. You can live with personal dignity but you cannot live in a dignified society. You can fight for freedom and salute the dawn of freedom, but you cannot live freely because the restraints of tact and harmony are not revolutionary virtues.

Even before the 1914-18 war writers like Shaw and Wells and D.H. Lawrence were contributing their art to discredit the values of douceur de vivre, and among the writers of the inter-war years you seldom find its spirit. For between the wars the twentieth-century intelligentsia set out to explode the values of the civilization into which it had been born by ridicule and righteous indignation. We reacted in righteous indignation against our predecessors' stuffy and hypocritical morals, and we raked their conventions and their complacency and their snobbery with the grapeshot of our superior scorn. This was not very difficult because from our personal experience we could all pick on cases of real hypocrisy and slavery to convention, real snobbery and complacency to serve as examples. But we recklessly erected these particulars into universals and used them to arraign a whole society. And then we undermined our predecessors formal code of manners by the subtle method of little rebellions. But as part of that amusing process perhaps we confused the restraints of dignity with our hatred of ossified conventions, the spirit of our predecessors with the letter of their laws. We were so comically anxious in deference to our earnest principles either to remember that we were not gentlefolk or to forget that we were. And so we nearly lost our touch for gentle living which, like the bloom on the grape, gets smeared and rubbed away by rough and careless and promiscuous handling.

If the aftermath of the first world war weakened the setting and scarred the qualities which make for this art of life, the circumstances and aftermath of the second have almost destroyed it. Since first and foremost it requires for its setting a gracious home, and there has been no leisure nor energy and often no physical conditions in which to make gracious homes. Sometimes it is only when you have lost some good that you begin to understand its quality. We are beginning to understand now what douceur de vivre meant and to realize our loss. But when you realize a loss you are at least pointed in the direction whence you may retrieve it. Our problem now is to recapture the spirit of that art of living and hold it in a setting of new social laws whose writ will run more widely and more generously and which will depend less on leisure and outward security, less on the fine and formal appointments to life.

For centuries douceur de vivre has leavened some part of that typically English society which has spread out between the aristocracy on its right hand and the 'people' on its left. You can observe it in the descriptions of St Thomas More's household and family, you can detect it flickering through the pages of George Herbert's poems or Cowper's letters, it is apparent in a rather prim guise in Jane Austen's novels and it underlies, like fine mahogany below a meretricious french polish, the snobbism of Trollope. It was present, too, in homes like Ferns and Firwood and the Schills's, where it was given a sounder and more serious connotation than Talleyrand might have understood or welcomed; honest dealing, public spirit generous in time and money, hard work and play, fair and plentiful living, a warm culture and a certain innate reverence towards the conduct of life. It is true that a number of the homes one knew fell short of this standard, but enough measured up to it to give that small civilization of Manchester 'families' its distinctive form and to link it with a wider and an older tradition.

Hospitalised soldiers at Alderley Edge

APPENDIX

EXTRACT FROM: THE GIANT'S CAUSEWAY TRAMWAY PIONEER HYDRO-ELECTRIC RAILWAY

Sir Wm.Thompson, during examination by the Committee, agreed that he had been engaged in electrical science for many years, and had been consulted at all stages of the electrical experiments on the Tramway. He was closely questioned on the effect which an electric current at 250 volts would have on human beings and animals. He stated that at that pressure, "the maximum current which would pass through a human being would be about 1/10 amp or 1/500 of a strong working current". This quickly brought the question, "If 500 people all touched the conductor rail simultaneously would the tram be stopped?" Sir William refused to be drawn further than to admit that such a contingency "would seriously impair the insulation of the line, and diminish the power of the tram".

Mr W.A.Traill was also examined. Having stated that there was little danger to persons from the live rail, especially as clothing was a fairly good insulator, he was asked would it not be dangerous if a beggar with torn trousers - or a Highlandman - sat on it. Mr.Traill replied that this very same question had been posed during the B.o.T. inspection of the line prior to its opening, by the inspection officers, Maj. General Hutchinson and Major Armstrong. At this time he himself had removed his trousers from the appropriate portion of his anatomy and sat on the live rail, as had Dr. Hopkinson, without any dire result.

Mr Traill stated, furthermore, that far from being dangerous, the shocks received from the live rail were beneficial for rheumatism, and not only himself but other people also, purposely took shocks from the rail with beneficial results. A Portrush doctor sent his patients out to take shocks from the rail and one man who was unable to open his hand at the beginning of the treatment was able to do so after a three week course.

Years later, when relating the live rail sitting incident to his daughter, the latter asked, "And did it really not hurt?" Mr Traill's reply was, "It hurt like blazes, but we weren't going to let the Inspectors know that."

Index

Abbott, Miss, 195 seq.
Acton, Lord, 93
Alderley, 155, 171
Alderley Edge, 15, 43, 107 seq., 155, 171 seq., 185, 237, 251 seq.
Allen, Ronald, 245, 255
Allenby, Lord, 88
Alps, the, 60, 121, 205 seq., 273
Alpine Club, the, 5, 10, 127
Anson, Gertrude (Mrs R. B. Graham), 212, 244, 249
Anson, Mabel (née Hopkinson), 64 seq.
Anson, Mary (Mrs Jackson), 220
Arts and Crafts, 164
Asquith, H. H., 249
Ashtons, the, 157
Austen, Jane, 268

Bankes, Mrs Linnaeus, *The Manchester Man*, 128
Bannister, Mr, 103
Beecham, Sir Thomas, 138
Belfast, 5, 32, 33, 76, 82, 84, 214, 263
Belfast Lough, 62
Belloc, H., *The Path to Rome*, 18
Bles, Mr, 49, 107, 111
Bentley, Phyllis, *Inheritance*, 59
Bernanos, Georges, *Journal d'un curé de campagne*, 87
Birmingham, 135
Blake, William, 72, 125
Bowdon, 49, 62, 64, 134, 138, 166, 252
'Bradshaws', the, 190 seq.
Bright, John, 100, 111, 139
Brodsky, 138
Brontë, Charlotte, *Shirley*, 59
Browning, Robert, 202, 204
Burnham, J., The Managerial Revolution, 120

Cambridge, 4, 20, 60 seq., 91 seq., 100, 119, 164 seq., 178, 197, 217, 240 seq.
Campbell, Augusta, 32
Campbell, Dermot, 77
Campbell, Garrett, 88
Campbell, Gladys, 32
Campbell, Howard, 32, 78, 80, 88
Campbell, John (my grandfather), 75 seq.
Campbell, Mrs John (my grandmother), 75 seq.
Campbell, Michael of Ballyalton, 76
Campbell, Lawford, 76
Campbell, Lloyd, 88
Campbell, General Sir Walter, D.S.O., 32 seq., 86 seq.
Campbell-Bannerman, 82

Capitalism, and the Protestant Ethic, 50, 62; and psychology of the family business and the limited company, 96 seq.,; and socialism,233 seq.
Caragh Lake, Co. Kerry, 208
Catterall, Arthur, 138
Catholicism, 70, 82 seq., 103, 189, 190, 210
Cavendish, Lord Frederick, 86
Chesney, Mr, 112
Chesney, Kathleen, 241
Chesney, Denis, 266
Chloride Electrical Storage Co., 102
Christmas, 32 seq., 61, 66, 88, 136, 172, 192
Church and Chapel, 173 seq.
Church of England and the University Tests, 59 seq.
Clayton Division of Manchester, the, 65, 231, 245
Cobbett, Mr, 108
Cobden, 111
Cole, G. D. H., 233
Collins, Michael, 85
Conservatism, 231, 247, 248
Constantinople, despatch of fleet to, 92
Couchoud, Mlle, 201
Cowper, 268
Crewdson, Mr Alfred, 49, 108, 115, 128, 167

Dangerfield, G., *The Strange Death of Liberal England*, 116
Darwin, Charles, 91, 118
Degas, 137
Dewhursts, the, 4, 59
Dickens, 167
Didsbury, 139, 162, 167, 213, 252
Dinner-parties, 24, 113
Disraeli, Sybil - the two nations, 136 seq.
Duffy, George Gavan, 85
Dunne, Mr D. P., 103
Dupuy, Mlle, 187, 201

Edison's dynamo, 7, 101
Education, 92 seq., 116, 180 seq., 243 seq.
Employers, attitudes of, 45, 59, 95 seq., 116, 120, 134 seq.
Epstein, 140, 211
Ewing, Sir Alfred, 218

Falkland, Lord, 107
Ferns, 9, 17 seq., 55 seq., 62 seq., 81 seq., 97 seq., 117, 160, 169, 171 seq., 213, 214, 253, 254, 268
Firwood, 9, 107, 170, 268
Foggarty, Miss, 198

France, 26, 51 79, 127, 160, 217, 240, 247, 266
Free Trade Hall, the, 138, 229

Gaiety Theatre, the, 136
Games, 32, 49, 162 seq., 179, 197, 205, 213 seq.
Gardens, at Ferns, 43 seq.;
Gaskell, Mrs, 115
Germany, 92, 111, 202, 265
Ghiberti, 100, 114
Gissing, G., *The Ryecroft Papers*, 21 seq.
Gladstone, W. E., 92 seq., 112, 139 seq.
Griffith, Arthur, 85
Great Exhibition, the, 91, 180
Great Illusion, the, 264
'Green', Mrs, 259
Grundy, 22, 35, 43 seq.

Hall, Miss Lucy, 85 seq.
Hallé Concerts, 110, 134, 138 seq.
Hammonds, books of the, 233
Harty Hamilton, 138
Herbert, George, 268
Hopkinson, Dr Albert, 5, 214, 262 seq.
Hopkinson, Sir Alfred, 5, 59 seq., 104, 208 seq., 229 seq,, 246
Hopkinson, Alice (my grandmother), 56, 59 seq.; visits to, 62 seq.
Hopkinson, Austin, 232
Hopkinson, Bertram, 4, 5
Hopkinson, Campbell, 32 seq., 98 seq., 169 seq., 177, 178, 189, 195 seq., 216, 219, 263 seq.
Hopkinson, Charles, 5, 7, 60 135
Hopkinson, Cecil, 5, 217
Hopkinson, Edward (my father), 5, 8, 19 seq., 32 seq., 48 seq., 55 seq., 61 seqw., 76, 78, 81, 83 seq., 91 seq., 100 seq., 107 seq., 111, 113, 118 seq., 126, 134, 160, 165 seq., 171 seq., 185, 186, 190, 197, 199, 205 seq., 218 seq., 229, 230 seq., 234 seq., 239 seq., 252 seq., 259 seq., 263 seq.
Hopkinson, Evelyn (née Oldenburg), 5, 216 seq.
Hopkinson, John (my grandfather) 4, 7 seq., 21, 59 seq.
Hopkinson, John, F.R.S., 5, 59 seq., 101, 216
Hopkinson, Lilian (Mrs Tribe), 64
Hopkinson, Miss Mary, 63 seq., 67 seq., 86 seq., 116, 125, 163, 210
Hopkinson, Minnie, née Campbell (my mother), 4, 5,19 seq., 32 seq., 43 seq., 48 seq., 55 seq., 62 seq.,70 seq., 75 seq., 104 seq., 107 seq., 159 seq., 169 seq., 171 seq., 175 seq., 182, 185 seq., 194 seq., 204 seq., 214 seq., 228, 230, 240, 242 seq., 251 seq., 262 seq.
Home Rule, 83, 93, 230, 245
Horace, 181
Hubbard, Esmé, 254
Hurst, Sir Gerald, 5, 168, 232, 247 seq., 265
Hurst, Margaret, 5, 168, 265
Hutton, Mr, 113
Huskisson, 113

Huxley, Thomas, 91, 114

Industrial Revolution, the, 56, 59, 137, 169, 233
Inglewood, 59 seq.
Institution of Mechanical Engineers, the, 103, 233

Killowen, Lord Russell of, 86
King, Alfred, 230
Kipling, R. 200, 264
Kossuth, 139, 228

Lake District, 8,9, 64, 65, 91, 121, 205, 208, 216, 245
Larne gun-running, the, 83
Lawrence, D. H., 256, 267
Lawrence, T. E., Arabia, 88
Lees, Mr, 107, 112
Liberalism, 94 seq., 111, 230 seq., 245, 248
Liverpool, 86, 110, 113
Lloyd George, 111, 230, 245
Locomotive, the first electrically driven, 8, 97, 100
London, 8, 9, 10, 24, 27, 32, 48, 64, 83 seq., 112, 139, 155, 162, 168, 192, 196, 212, 217, 231, 241, 254, 257, 259
Londonderry, siege of, 75 seq.
Louisa, 22, 25, 33, 43, 191

Macaulay, 20, 178, 229, 244
Manchester, 17 seq., 25, 27, 34, 49 seq., 73 seq., 91, 108 seq, 127 seq, 155 seq., 174 seq., 187 seq, 213, 243, 252, 257, 264
Manchester Art Gallery, 134 seq
Manchester Assemblies, 139, 214, 252, 253
Manchester men, 108, 134, 215
Manchester Royal Infirmary, 5, 135, 215
Manchester University, 5, 7, 25 seq., 60, 91 seq..
Manchester Guardian, 60, 108, 140, 245
Margharetti, Miss, 187
Marriott, J. A. R., 165, 166
Mather, Sir William, 7, 24, 90 seq., 110 seq., 190, 230
Mather & Platt, 8, 90, 96 seq., 119, 165, 265
Masterman, C. F. G., *How England is Governed*, 199
McCarthy, J., *History of Our Own Times*, 244
McCulloch, Alexander, 75
McElfatrick, Eileen, 157
Meme (Miss Morant), 44 seq., 81, 177, 185 seq.
Milton, 20, 59, 178
Moore, George, 256
Morrison, Herbert, 232, 235
Murray, John, 248 seq.
More, St Thomas, 107, 268
Morris, William, *News from Nowhere*, 72
Mossley, Co. Antrim, 76; the mill at, 76 seq.; capitalism at, 76 seq.; 88, 100, 119, 120, 232
Mountaineering, 5, 8, 60, 64, 127, 205, 207, 248

National Gallery, the, 212
Naylor, Mr, 103
Newman, Cardinal, Apologia, 87
Nonconformism, 55 seq.
Norway, 209

Orangemen, 84
Owens College, 178
Oxford, 60, 164, 165, 199, 211, 241 seq.
Oxford Extension Lectures, 164, 199

Parnell, 86
Peel, Sir Robert, 112
Peover, 160
Peterloo, 128
Philanthropy, 115, 163, 185
Philips, Mr Robert, 137
Philips, Miss, 139
Piggott forgeries, 86
Pilkington, Lawrence, 98, 116, 118 seq., 127
Pilkington, Mrs Lawrence, 162 seq., 170
Pilkington, Margaret, 10, 168 seq.
Pilkington, Dorothy, 8, 168
Platt, Mr John, 91, 99
Politics, 8, 25, 35, 51, 70, 83, 92, 97, 111 seq., 124 seq., 135, 200 seq., 229 seq.
Pre-Raphaelites, the, 134, 136

Raphael, 212
Rathfern, 74 seq., 185 seq.
Religion, 35, 66 seq, 81 seq., 86 seq, 94 seq, 124 seq, 174 seq, 194 seq, 201 seq., 214
Revolutions of 1848, 113
Richardson, 101 seq., 191, 231, 264 seq.
Richter, 138
Robey, Traditions of Lancashire, 119
Roby, Mrs, 241 seq.
Rock-climbing, 7 seq., 121 seq., 205 seq., 216 seq.
'Rothstein', Mr, 110 seq., 127
Royal Society, the, 91, 103
Rutherford, Lord, 26
Ruskin, 60, 178, 185, 192 seq., 211, 255, 259 seq.
Russell, The Hon. Mrs (Florence Cumming), 85 seq.
Rylands Library, the, 134

Saints and Social Reformers, 70 seq.
Salford, 49, 60, 70, 92, 93
Salford Royal Hospital, 124, 135
Salisbury, Lord, 93
Sassoon, Siegfried, The Fox-Hunting Man, 167
Schill, Mr Harry, 107, 116 seq.
Schill, Mrs, 66, 86, 155 seq.

Schill, Melland, 216
Schill, Olive, 214, 216, 240 seq., 245
Scott, C. P., 139
'Shaw', Mrs, 160 seq.
Shaw, G. B., John Bull's Other Island, 87; Major Barbara, 94
Sheffield, Lord, 83 seq., 155 seq.
Sims, Miss May (Mrs Galloway), 84
Skipton, 57
Slingsby, Win. Cecil, 4, 205, 207
'Smith', Mrs, 60, 159 seq.
Social conventions, 138 seq., 170 seq., 252 seq., 267 seq.
Soulsby, Miss, 192 seq.
Spring, Howard, Fame is the Spur, 110
Stephen, Leslie, 124
Stephenson, George, 25, 100
Strauss, H., 249
'Swinside', Mr, 111

Talleyrand, 266, 268
Tawney, R. H., 82, 232
Taylor, Mr John, 99
Temple, William, Archbishop of Canterbury, 125
Tennyson, 20, 178, 230
Trojan Epic, the, 183
Trollope, Anthony, 95, 112, 268
Tulloch, Mr, 113

Ulster, 22, 76; and Unionism, 81 seq.; Volunteers, 264, 266
Unionism, 82 seq.
Union Club, the, 127

Vermeer, 79
Villon, 194 seq.

Wales, 48, 208, 230
Walker, the Rev George, 75 seq.
War (1914—18), 55, 65, 88, 99, 104, 120, 136 seq., 207, 212, 220, 267
Water-colours, 21 seq., 101, 114, 118, 124, 134, 137, 164, 169, 204, 214, 262
Weber, 82
Wells, H. G., 256, 267 Ann Veronica, 256
Whitworth Art Gallery, 4, 10, 134 seq.
Wilmslow, 161
Woolley, Hermann, 127
Wordsworth, 59, 63, 178, 203
Workers' Educational Association, 116
Wormald, Sir John, 99 seq., 114, 190
Worthingtons, the, 114 seq.
Young, Geoffrey Winthrop, 7, 124, 205